THE Great Population Spike AND AFTER

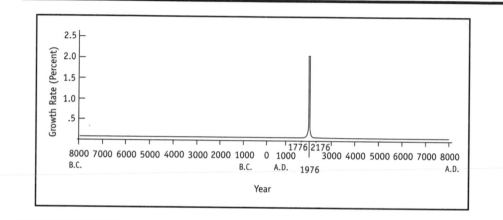

THE
Great Population Spike

AND AFTER

Reflections on the 21st Century

W. W. ROSTOW

New York   Oxford

Oxford University Press

1998

Oxford University Press

Oxford   New York
Athens   Auckland   Bangkok   Bogota   Bombay
Buenos Aires   Calcutta   Cape Town   Dar es Salaam
Delhi   Florence   Hong Kong   Istanbul   Karachi
Kuala Lumpur   Madras   Madrid   Melbourne
Mexico City   Nairobi   Paris   Singapore
Taipei   Tokyo   Toronto   Warsaw

and associated companies in
Berlin   Ibadan

N

Library of Congress Cataloging-in-Publication Data
Rostow, W. W. (Walt Whitman), 1916–
The great population spike and after : reflections on the 21st century /
by Walt W. Rostow.
p.   cm.
Includes index.
ISBN 0-19-511691-7
1. Population forecasting.   2. Economic forecasting.
3. Population—Economic aspects.   4. Twenty-first century—
Forecasts.   I. Title.
HB849.53.R67   1997
304.6—dc21   97-13913

Frontispiece: Population Growth Rate in Long-Term Historical Perspective. *Sources*: Herman
Kahn et al., *The Next 200 Years* (New York: Morrow, 1976), p. 29; Ronald Freeman and Bernard
Berelson, "The Human Population," *Scientific American*, September 1974, pp. 36–37.

9 8 7 6 5 4 3 2 1
Printed in the United States of America
on acid-free paper

To Elspeth Davies Rostow

Preface

This book is an extended essay on the 21st century. It emerged from three converging aspects of my work over the past several years. First, I have been concerned with *the fact that the fall in the birth rate in the developing world, which contains the bulk of the world's population, has been more rapid than had been envisaged by most analyses;* that is, under 2.1 children per family. A number of developing countries have fallen below long-run fertility rates that would assure in time a stagnant or growing population. Others will experience such levels fairly soon, excepting Africa south of the Sahara, where the total fertility rate remains high (5.6 children per family). With this exception, the central problem of industrial societies in the century ahead will be how to maintain full employment and the existing structure of social services with a stagnant or falling population. Taiwan, which is already aware that its gross fertility level is below the long-run replacement rate, is now implementing a pronatalist policy. Such a policy could be widely initiated in the next century. Similar policies and others aimed at increasing the relative size of the workforce will commend themselves as the size of that force diminishes relative to those over 65. Barring corrective action, social policies now in place will be difficult to sustain.

Up to this point, the conventional concern has been the adequacy of resources and the deterioration of the environment as newer industrial countries move forward to technical maturity and beyond. These legitimate concerns will gradually give way in the next century to the quite different agenda of societies with declining or stagnant populations. Affluent urban life has not been the friend of large, cohesive families.

A second concern has been the nature of the post–Cold War world and the proper role of the United States in it. Speculation, of course, about postcontainment doctrine has been a growth industry among scholars and politicians. My view, therefore, about the role of the United States over the next half century has focused on what I call the "critical margin" as opposed to the "sole remaining superpower" (see Chapter 7). Few diplomatic or military enterprises are possible in the contemporary world without the active participation of the United States. On the other hand, the United States does not command the power and influence that the designation of "superpower" implies, and this limitation will grow as the diffusion of power proceeds over the next half century. But it is unlikely that any other national power can play the role of "critical margin" over this interval. Therefore, if chaos is to be avoided—and the contemporary world is clearly capable of a chaotic outcome—the active constructive participation of the United States in global affairs is necessary.

My third concern derives from, for me, a new venture, The Austin Project (TAP). Since finishing *Theorists of Economic Growth* in 1989,[1] I have been engaged with colleagues in the Austin community in mounting a comprehensive urban program built around the familiar but unevenly implemented principle of prevention rather than damage control. The task is not unlike that of working with developing countries over recent decades. But there is an extra dimension in American cities: the abnormally weakened state of the families in disadvantaged neighborhoods. In working on The Austin Project, I have had occasion to learn about and to reflect on the inner cities in general and their significance for the nation's emerging role on the world scene. I have concluded that the ability of the United States to act steadily as the "critical margin" depends not only on our devising with others a political economy for a world moving toward a stagnant or declining population but also on our finding a solution to the acute domestic urban problem explored in Chapter 8.

No such solution now exists. Cities—delightful playgrounds as they are for some—all contain highly combustible materials: racial hostilities; environmental deterioration; violence; AIDS; gangs; drugs; high and persistent unemployment; gravely weakened family structures; disturbing minority dropout rates, and so on. We therefore face the risk that in dealing with these problems, which are still becoming more acute, America might well turn inward, as it has done in the past, devoting its energy, resources, and politics overwhelmingly to these corrosive domestic problems. The result? A world lacking a stabilizing American presence in which chaos might well dominate the course of events.

I am aware, of course, that the combination of demographic, technological, economic, foreign policy, and urban analysis that lies at the heart of this book is not usual. It cuts across disciplines usually kept apart. In particular, Chapters 7 and 8, by convention, do not appear to belong with Chapters 1 through 6. Analysis of and prescription for the inner cities is, in the normal way, cut off from its full domestic and foreign-policy context. But I am convinced that inner-city policy is a central issue for our society, abroad as well as at home.

It is easy enough to write a pessimistic book about the challenges we face in times ahead. But I am inclined to believe that if we devote to the task the energy and enterprise it deserves, the urban problem will prove soluble.

In bringing together these conclusions, I have incurred debts to many colleagues, although they bear no responsibility for the conclusions drawn: Frank Bean, Lester Brown, McGeorge Bundy, William Fisher, James Fishkin, Joseph Fishkin, Wayne Holzman, B. R. Inman, David Kendrick, Charles Kindleberger, George Kozmetsky, Hans Mark, Dudley Poston Jr., Thomas Pullam, Elspeth Rostow, Eugene Rostow, Mickey Russell, Paul Samuelson, Patricia Schaub, Arthur Schlesinger Jr., Anais Spitzer, Robert Sullivan, Charles Warlick, Matt Wayner, Robert Wilson, Molly White, and Barbara Zuckerman. I have also been memorably assisted by the International Division of the Bureau of the Census, Commerce Department.

I owe a special debt to George Kozmetsky and Robert Sullivan of IC² (Innovative Creative Capital). Aside from throwing themselves behind this venture, they offered me both advice and the support of a research assistant.

I am also greatly in debt to William Schwartz, vice president for academic affairs of Yeshiva University in New York, who invited my wife and me to give eight lectures each at the university in the spring term of 1996. In these lectures, I was able to set down a first draft of my thoughts about the 21st century.

As I approached a final draft, Armand Clesse of the Luxembourg Institute for European and International Studies organized a workshop at the Harvard Faculty Club, to consider both this book and, in general, the participants' views of the coming century. The conference was organized by the institute as a part of its long-term multidisciplinary research project on the causes of the rise and fall of countries, begun in 1990, under the general title, "The Vitality of Nations." Some 35 professionals participated. It was a fruitful and enjoyable affair, and I take this occasion to thank Dr. Clesse, his colleagues, and the other participants.

Elspeth Davies Rostow has played an important role in both The Austin Project and in putting these related conclusions about the 21st century in clear historical and contemporary context. As often before, I owe her an incalculable debt.

Austin, Texas   W. W. R.
March 1998

Contents

ONE   The Framework   3

TWO   Population and the Stages of Growth   15

THREE   Technology and Investment   47

FOUR   Relative Prices   79

FIVE   Cycles   97

SIX   The Limits to Growth   119

SEVEN   The Role of the United States in the Post–Cold
War World   139

EIGHT   The Critical Margin and America's Inner Cities   157

NINE   Conclusions   181

Appendix A: A Historical Analogy   187

Appendix B: The Demography of the People's Republic
of China   195

Notes   203

Index   221

THE Great Population Spike AND AFTER

ONE

The Framework

The title of this book, *The Great Population Spike and After: Reflections on the 21st Century*, requires some explanation. The Great Spike is illustrated in the figure that serves as the book's frontispiece.[1] The figure plots the rate of growth of global population from 8000 B.C. to 8000 A.D. In highly stylized form, it exhibits an average growth rate of zero except for the period between 1776 and 2176. In that interval, the spike occurs: the growth rate rises to a bit over 2% per annum in 1976, and then falls to zero again in the next century. Falling growth rates for the global population, the downward part of the spike, are already upon us.

I should emphasize the word "stylized." The world's population growth rate was evidently not static at zero from 8000 B.C. to the middle of the eighteenth century, nor will it remain static for the 8,000 years after the spike. It will fluctuate with the vicissitudes of history. But despite the illustration's oversimplicity, its message is significant.

Figure 1.1 shows, in absolute terms, the leveling off of the global population, which will take place gradually. Global population will attain, according to present estimates, an absolute level of about 10 billion people as opposed to about 790 million in the mid-18th century. This rise, along with the rise in income per capita, is a rough

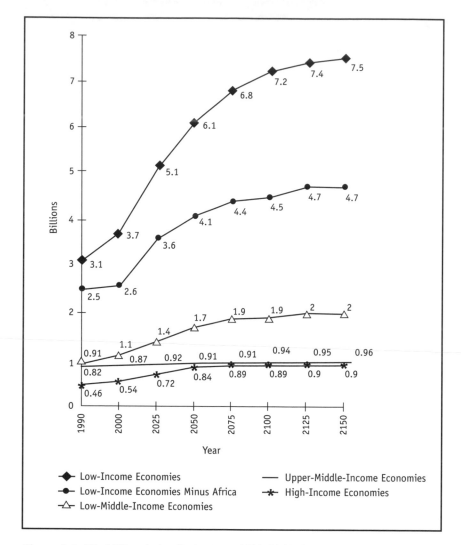

Figure 1.1 World Population Projections, 1990–2150 (Summary Projections for 25-Year Periods). *Source:* From Eduard Bos, My J. Vu, Ernest Massiah, and Rudolfo A. Bultao, *World Bank Population Projections, 1984–1955: Estimates and Projections with Related Demographic Statistics* (Baltimore: Johns Hopkins University Press), pp. 101, 103, 105, 109.

Note: Deceleration and leveling off in Africa come later than in other low-income regions, and consequently a surge in population occurs. By agreement of UN and World Bank demographers, population for all five groups levels off rather than continues declining. After much conversation on this shape of the projections, I have not been able to establish if this is a professional view of demographers or a bow to the sovereignty of nations. Leveling off occurs first in high-income economies; then in upper-middle-income economies; then in low-middle-income economies; then in low-income economies; then in Africa.

measure of what the Industrial Revolution has achieved since the 18th century, but the industrialization of the globe also set in motion forces that will bring about a decline in the rate of increase in population. The demographic transition decrees that after a certain point the birth rate will fall as income per capita rises. These negative forces will come to dominate the 21st century.

Thus, this book concentrates on the period from the 1990s to around 2050, set against the background of the past several centuries. It deals, in effect, with both sides of the Great Spike. It is suffused, however, with the proposition that the 21st century, if it proves relatively peaceful, will soon face a period in which a rising population and effective demand in the presently developing nations will strain technologies and existing resources, followed by a long period in which the Industrial Revolution will have been largely diffused around the world. The central problem will then be that of maintaining full employment and adequate social services with a stagnant or falling population. Science and technology will continue to add to the fund of usable knowledge, although perhaps at a slackened rate. Africa may be a major exception to this general view and the source of much global difficulty, a topic discussed in Chapter 2. Taken as a whole, however, the 21st century will mark a change in the pattern of growth we have taken for granted since, roughly, the second half of the 18th century. Economic growth will no longer be supported by a rising population.

The imprecision about dates that marks this enterprise is intentional. We know a certain amount about the past, although historians have won book awards by arguing about it. But anyone who deals with the future should begin with John Maynard Keynes's warning: "The inevitable never happens. It is the unexpected always." Like so many of Keynes's statements, this is an overstatement with a kernel of truth. In any case, I shall approach the past and the future with a lively sense that any analysis is debatable but also useful, for the least realistic assumption is that tomorrow will be like today. The one thing we know in this terrain is that history is never linear.

Caveats aside, I begin with seven assertions. By 2050 or thereabouts, these points should be clear if present trends persist in a world that avoids major wars.

1. The world's population will level off at about 10 billion people — twice its present level. The bulk of the leveling off will take place by 2050. In fact, deceleration will begin between 2010 and 2020. Population will rise at a decelerating rate for a time, notably in

the presently developing world, where there is a large young population.

2. The central problem of the old industrial countries will be how to cope with aging, stagnant, or falling populations. This problem, which has already begun to develop, will become more obvious with the passage of time. It has many implications, including implications for social services for the elderly and the size of the working force relative to a society's older and younger dependents. As already noted, it might be that the old industrial powers will opt in time for pronatalist policies in order to maintain stagnant population levels, since immigration has its political and social limits.

3. The presently developing countries, with certain exceptions, will feel the effects of a falling birth rate as they also approach a time of stagnant or falling population levels. What is current reality for the older developed countries will have become the expectation of these by-then-developed countries. (A major exception is Africa, south of Sahara, which has not yet achieved industrial takeoff. A falling birth rate is apparent in a few—but only a few—African countries. There are local exceptions, as well, in Asia, the Middle East, and Latin America.)

4. Science and technology will maintain the close linkage gradually and progressively achieved between the 18th and 20th centuries.[2] This will happen despite the leveling off of rates of population increase. However, we simply don't know if stagnant or falling populations will cause a setback in the volume of research and development (R&D) as a percentage of gross national product (GNP). They well might. Some would argue, however, that a shortage of labor might accelerate R&D, as highly productive machines are called on to do the work of men, women, and children.

5. There will probably be a period of rising foodstuff, raw material, and environmental prices and increased expenditures for R&D and other investment requirements for these sectors before 2050. These allocations will be required to cope with the full industrialization of China, India, and other presently developing countries, notably in East Asia and Latin America. Relative prices will in time level off and probably decline under the impact of continuing progress in science and technology, combined with deceleration in population expansion.

6. A way will have been worked out by economists and governments to maintain relatively full employment and inflation control under conditions of a stagnant or falling population. This is a relatively new problem since the 18th century. It was, however, discussed

briefly but intensively during the Great Depression of the 1930s, notably in 1937–1938 when the American economy at the 1937 peak still experienced over 14% unemployment, rising to 19% in 1938. The solution will probably involve increased allocations to improve the quality of life, including support of education, the arts, infrastructure, medical services, and so on. It might involve investment in space travel and other esoteric frontier activities. It might also require a shift from investment to consumption, as Keynesians argued in the 1930s.

7. The continued march of science and technology, even if somewhat slowed, will outstrip any limits on growth from the supply side on a global basis. (This notion of stagnant population at a high income plus continued investment in R&D was first developed by J. S. Mill.) There might be intense regional shortages, however, notably in Africa. Whether shortages will operate elsewhere from the demand side, whether diminishing relative marginal utility will set in for real income itself, and whether people will say enough is enough are still to be determined. But there is no evidence yet that people as a whole have trouble spending more money. And continued progress in science and technology might open up new avenues of consumption.

There is no guarantee, of course, that things will work out peacefully. The greatest danger lies in the use of weapons of mass destruction. There is no guarantee that the rules of engagement and self-discipline that governed the Cold War will hold in a world that will contain many countries technically capable of producing nuclear or biological weapons and headed by persons of uncertain rationality. There is no guarantee against the sort of threats that Thomas Malthus called "positive checks" on population such as the scourge of AIDS, the threat to human reproduction imposed by the use of modern chemicals, or the emergence of strains of bacteria resistant to known antibiotics.

Nor is it guaranteed that the human race will take to a life of peace and affluence. Keynes described in 1930 a projected turnaround in the mid-21st century tersely, dramatically, humorously, and hopefully:

> I draw the conclusion that, assuming no important wars and no important increase in population, the economic problem may be solved, or be at least within sight of solution, within a hundred years. This means that the economic problem is not—if we look into the future—the permanent problem of the human race. . . .
>
> I see us free, therefore, to return to some of the most sure and certain principles of religion and traditional virtue—that avarice is a

vice, that the exaction of usury is a misdemeanor, and the love of money is detestable, that those walk most truly in the paths of virtue and sane wisdom who take least thought for the morrow. We shall once more value ends above means and prefer the good to be useful. We shall honour those who can teach us how to pluck the hour and the day virtuously and well, the delightful people who are capable of taking direct enjoyment in things, the lilies of the field who toil not, neither do they spin.

But beware! The time for all this is not yet. For at least another hundred years we must pretend to ourselves and to everyone that fair is foul and foul is fair; for foul is useful and fair is not. Avarice and usury and precaution must be our gods for a little longer still. For only they can lead us out of the tunnel of economic necessity into the daylight.[3]

About thirty years later, I speculated somewhat less hopefully but along the same lines:

The life of most human beings since the beginning of time has been mainly taken up with gaining food, shelter and clothing for themselves and their families. What will happen when diminishing relative marginal utility sets in, on a mass basis, for real income itself?

Will man fall into secular spiritual stagnation, finding no worthy outlet for the expression of his energies, talents, and instinct to reach for immortality? Will he follow the Americans and re-impose the strenuous life by raising the birth-rate? Will the devil make work for idle hands? Will men learn how to conduct wars with just enough violence to be good sport—and to accelerate capital depreciation—without blowing up the planet? Will the exploration of outer space offer an adequately interesting and expensive outlet for resources and ambitions? Or will man, converted *en masse* into a suburban version of an eighteenth-century country gentleman, find . . . sufficient frontiers to keep for life its savour?[4]

Here we set aside speculation as to whether or not the human race can adjust to being led by "delightful people." I leave such speculation for future history and for future historians. There is much to do in the meanwhile, as Keynes suggests, to assure the survival of the human race in reasonably good order.

The text of the first six chapters of this book, which aim for the latter objective, takes its shape from a dynamic version of the most basic equation in economics. This equation, at its most primitive, asserts that the increase of output is a function of the rate of increase of population and of capital, including in the latter arable land, forests, and so on. In fact, population must be related to the size of the workforce. The technological content of investment must be disaggregated and specified, because technology does not strike the sectors evenly. Moreover, the price of foodstuffs and raw materials relative to manufactures must be specified as well as the timing of the business cycle of nine or ten years. Finally, the limits to growth must be examined, whether they are determined from the supply side by a relative rise in prices of foodstuffs and raw materials or from the demand side by consumers deciding that enough is enough.

These concerns are, in short, a version of the standard production function, elaborated to deal with a changing world. I have used this framework for two reasons. First, it gives, as the subtitle of this book suggests, some historical perspective to the great drama that—if I'm correct—will assert itself in the 21st century. After centuries during which global population fluctuated about a stagnant, falling, or slowly rising trend, population began to expand regularly in the second half of the 18th century. To be precise, global population was about 790 million in 1750; at the moment, it is somewhere between 5 and 6 billion people; and it may reach 10 billion by 2050, when it will be rapidly decelerating or declining in the present industrialized and more advanced developing countries. This means we are reaching a plateau of global population, which will oscillate if all goes well, as it did before the 18th century. It seems proper, therefore, to summarize in each chapter how we came to where we are over the past three centuries and to put the future in a broad historical context. Second, there is a narrower reason for these historical passages. As we climbed over the last two and a half centuries of population growth, we experienced periods—usually in the form of setbacks—in which some of the major issues of the 21st century surfaced briefly and were discussed with some wisdom. They are certainly worth considering as we settle down to devise a political economy for the era of stagnant or falling population. Chapters 2 through 6 perform these two functions.

Chapter 7 turns to the evolution of American foreign policy. We shall see the slow march through history of the United States from colonial status to primacy in the Western Hemisphere; to the defender of the balance of power in the Atlantic and Pacific; to brief superpower status in the wake of the duel with what used to be the Soviet Union; to the role of the critical margin in the contemporary world of rapidly diffusing power. Even in the final chapter on the American urban problem, it is useful to begin by probing the historical roots of the current frustrations in our cities.

In any case, the insights from these and other historical episodes for the 21st century are the reasons I begin with a review of how the world got to where it now stands and some of its anticipatory thoughts along the way.

In confronting the prospect of global population attaining a level of some 10 billion human beings before leveling off, I am in the company of a field of futurologists who in objective terms fall into two categories: the optimists and the pessimists.

The pessimists can and do point to the very large increase in the world's foreseeable population: some 5 or 6 billion additional people before population levels off in the mid-21st century. It took 183 years for the world's population to go from 1 billion to 5 billion. According to the population experts at the United Nations it will take only about 67 years for it to go from 5 billion to 10 billion (see Table 1.1).

Any way one looks at these figures, this is an extraordinary challenge to the planet and its resources. One can see many signs that at present the environment is already under strain: the depletion of the ozone layer; the rise in the earth's temperature; the decline in the number of species of birds, fish, and animals; the pollution of the air and water found in many countries.

Table 1.1. World Population Milestones, 1804–1987 and Projections to 2093

Population	Year
1 billion	1804
2 billion	1927
3 billion	1960
4 billion	1974
5 billion	1987
6 billion	1998
7 billion	2009
8 billion	2021
9 billion	2035
10 billion	2054
11 billion	2093

Source: Population Division, Department for Economic and Social Information and Policy Analysis, *World Population Growth from Year 0 to Stabilization* (New York: United Nations, 1994).

The pessimistic view is well articulated not only by Lester R. Brown and his colleagues at the World Watch Institute in their annual State of the World Series but also at the American Philosophical Society in Philadelphia, whose proceedings for September 1995 included the symposium "Environment and Development."[5] Papers presented at the symposium on food supply, population, and energy might all be described as anxious and pessimistic, but they urged individuals and governments toward promoting "sustainable growth." On the whole, the pessimists are overwhelmed by the scale of the problem and generally advocate constraint of demand.

On the other side, one can find optimists, among them the authors of a 1995 survey in the *Economist*.[6] After detailing the false predictions of disaster in the food supply since Malthus's first edition (1798), this article summarizes the current legitimate grounds for anxiety, lists the reassuring predictions of experts, and speculates on the whole positively about the future, including the possible but not certain role in agriculture of genetic engineering.

Another persuasive optimistic voice is that of William L. Fisher. He deals at length with the case of natural gas. Natural gas is of considerable interest because the additions to reserves are very considerable at a time of falling prices. Fisher, however, looks beyond one energy source and articulates the faith in human creativity and ingenuity that will permit it to solve these constraining problems from the supply side.

> Technology and know-how are not panaceas; they must be assiduously pursued and applied. . . . Will the appreciation of technology be continuously applied to mineral as well as environmental resources? There is nothing about history nor nothing known about the basic human conditions to indicate it will not be, most especially as it becomes a necessity. As Pecora cautioned in the 1968 *Limitations to the Earth*, "Before we sound the note of despair we must be sure we have reached the limit of the main resource, man's intellectual capacity." The reality, I firmly believe, is as Pecora went on to say: ". . . we need to rediscover faith. Faith that man has the capacity to solve his problems with a positive approach, faith that we can extract more information and new resources from the crust of the earth, faith that in the future this increasing consciousness, this increasing intellectual capacity of man, . . . can be directed more toward the fulfillment of basic human purposes. The bridge to that faith will be built by those who believe in it with indomitable spirit."[7] The end is not near, nor has human ingenuity been exhausted.[8]

I have quoted Fisher at length because his argument comes to rest on the decisive issues with which this series of chapters is concerned: faith and works. In the end, we are concerned with the creativity of individuals and governments. Will science and technology find answers to the technical problems thrown up in this climactic passage in the human adventure? Will governments act in time to take advantage of existing scientific and technological findings? These are problems for the whole human race, and here pessimists and optimists are in agreement: They both count on human ingenuity, creativity, and striving to see us through. Both would support Fisher's judgment: "Technology and know-how are not panaceas; they must be assiduously pursued and applied."

The symposium organized by *Daedalus* in its Summer 1996 edition has a similar optimistic cast.[9] It even proposes a new view of the philosophic relation between man and his natural environment in which peace is to be sought by "siting ourselves in the whole of nature."[10] It is argued that mankind should abandon its anthropomorphic view of the world and shift to a view that is nature-centered, including in nature humanity itself.

More concretely, this symposium achieves its "optimistic note on a topic that generally evokes pessimism" by looking at the historical trends in sources of energy; land, water, and agricultural productivity; raw materials used in industrial production; the successes in the fight for the environment; and population as determined by trends in mortality and fertility. In all cases, the trends are such as to give hope that resource and environmental problems will be solved if our population levels off at 10 billion. One wishes, however, that all the authors were as conscious of what it takes to move a wholesome trend forward as Paul Waggoner is: "The logistic curve extending past improvements in yields . . . could mislead humanity into thinking that an unseen hand lifts yields effortlessly. In fact, vigorous research and enterprising farmers do the lifting: 'Technology left on the shelf butters no parsnips.'"[11] Finally, although demographic trends are cited in various parts of this symposium, there is no awareness that a stagnant or falling population calls for a radical revision of our current political economy. At any rate, the *Daedalus* volume takes its place with the optimistic literature, and, in the end, it has the same appeal to human striving and creativity that marks both the optimistic and the pessimistic visions.

Faith and works are more particularly the task of Americans, as Chapters 7 and 8 argue. As the critical margin on the world scene,

America must solve many of its domestic problems, above all the urban problem. This is necessary to the creation of a truly multiracial society consistent with the 18th-century roots of America and its distinctive dream. As Hamish McRae puts it: "Managing a peaceful transition from a US which is dominated by white European culture to one which is truly multi-racial, and very different from Europe, will be the greatest single challenge the US will face in the coming generation. Failure would destroy the American dream, but the transition will test the tolerance and adaptability of the nation more sternly than perhaps any other change in its remarkable history." [12] This is the ultimate challenge to which this book is addressed.

Population and the Stages of Growth

The Origins of Demography

Hamish McRae's *The World in 2020* begins its discussion of population with this blunt sentence: "Of all the forces that will change the world over the next generation, demography is probably the most important."[1] I agree. After all, men, women, and children determine the demand for things; men and women determine the size of the workforce; and if the supply of goods and services they produce and export is not adequate, people go hungry, lack medical services, and all too often perish too young. The rhythm of human life is such that those who are born now will, by and large, live through the middle of the next century. We owe them some things. However, as this chapter argues, the future is complicated by more than simply the rate of increase of the population.

There are those who do not trace the beginning of modern economics to David Hume, Adam Smith, and their colleagues in the Scottish Enlightenment of the 18th century. They prefer the "Political Arithmeticians"—the statisticians—of the late 17th century, the greatest of whom was William Petty. Petty ranged widely over the field of economics including some wise and subtle reflections on the role of minorities in international trade. In 1695, Gregory King estimated the national accounts of England and Wales as of 1688.[2] He used, essentially, a modern balance-sheet method, demonstrating the relationships between output and expenditure for five sectors of the economy. But it was John Gaunt as early as 1662 who cast the longest shadow on the future with his estimates of death rates in London based on the bills of mortality. His work is the beginning of modern demography.

What stirred these late-17th-century inquiries? It was not a precocious academic interest in measuring population and national income; it was a sense that the nations of Europe were emerging from the feudal past and its internal struggles for power into an international arena of hostility and combat. In the following century, Britain and France, for example, were at war for more than 43 years. Dawning was the age of mercantilism, of national rivalries, and of economic precepts based on the assumption of endemic conflict. Nations inevitably began to measure their relative power in terms of population and national income.

Although there were some European and colonial population enumerations in the 17th century, regular censuses began in the 18th century in Sweden, Prussia, and the United States, and then in Great Britain and France by 1801. In 1798, Thomas Malthus, at the age of 32, published the first edition of his work on population. He warned against overoptimism with his insight that population increase would simply result in a demand for more food than could be supplied at existing prices and that, in one way or another, the rise in population had to be checked. By the time Malthus published his second edition in 1803, he was able to amass a considerable body of material, including some statistical data. He softened considerably his initial view. And after 1813, when food prices began to fall, he had moved on to other problems. But to this day, a gloomy perspective on food and population is associated with his views in the 1790s, although when he first wrote he derived his analysis from only an Atlantic world in transitional state, with only the preconditions for economic takeoff. The demographic transition—the fall of the birth rate subsequent to a sustained rise in GNP—was still to be proved.

The development of demographic research appears to have been determined much in the same way as economists as a whole chose to allocate their talent and energies. As Alfred Sauvy put it: "Just as a man is engrossed with the diseased or painful parts of his body, so demographic research was centered primarily around the points where some social malady was indicated. Thus, we see that demography was influenced directly by the very history of population or, more precisely, by anxieties which developed about it."[3]

The 19th-Century Pattern of Demography

For a time, demographic anxieties were pacific, not martial. As centuries go, the 19th was internationally a peaceful lull between the war-torn 18th century and the bloody century now coming to a close. (The 19th century's great conflicts—in China and the United States, for example—tended to be civil wars.)

Continued interest in demography arose instead from increasing concern by government authorities for public health and social welfare.[4] This time also saw the spread of life insurance, stimulating studies of mortality. The late-19th-century wave of immigration from Eastern and Southern Europe generated studies in the United States of the comparative fertility of immigrant and native-born populations. Echoing Benjamin Franklin's 1751 concern that immigrants would, in time, "eat the natives out," economist Francis Walker stirred not only controversy but also a refinement of methods for calculating the net impact of immigration on population. As with fertility and mortality studies, migration studies gathered momentum. So too, as today, did political pressure rise to exclude "undesirable" immigrants.

These and other impulses, derived from specific public-policy problems, stimulated the empirical and theoretical study of population. As the 19th century evolved, this occurred in government departments, international organizations, and universities. There were initially no regular population or demography departments in universities, but men and women were drawn to the study of population from a variety of fields: sociology, mathematics, the physical sciences, public health, and economics, as well as business and government. The term "demography" was invented as early as 1855; beginning in 1882, when the Fourth International Conference on Hygiene convened in Geneva, demographers managed to get together under its tent and kept regularly in touch thereafter. They read each other's work, argued with and learned from each other, and cumulatively built up an increasingly solid statistical base for their analyses.

But something more powerful was at work as the century drew to a close: Both the death rate and the birth rate began to decline in Western Europe in the 1880s. Until then, these rates had been relatively steady and roughly reflected degrees of industrialization and urbanization (see Table 2.1).

Two factors are generally taken as the major causes of this decline in Western European death and birth rates First, the cities, which his-

Table 2.1. Crude Birth and Death Rates of European Countries, 1841–1850 to 1951–1955 (Per Thousand)

Country		1841–1850	1851–1860	1861–1870	1876–1880	1886–1890	1896–1900	1906–1910	1911–1915	1916–1920	1921–1925	1926–1930	1931–1935	1936–1940	1941–1945	1946–1950	1951–1955
Austria[a]	BR	—	—	39.6	41.0	40.0	38.2	34.0	22.1	16.0	21.9	17.7	14.4	14.7	19.1	16.7	15.0
	DR	—	—	31.5	33.2	30.0	26.6	22.5	18.3	21.1	15.6	14.5	13.3	13.9	14.4	15.4	12.2
Belgium	BR	30.5	30.4	32.2	32.0	29.4	29.0	24.7	20.9	14.7	20.5	18.6	16.9	15.5	13.9	17.3	16.7
	DR	24.4	22.6	23.8	21.8	20.3	18.2	15.9	14.6	51.8	13.4	13.7	13.0	13.2	15.1	13.5	12.2
Bulgaria	BR	—	—	—	—	—	41.3	42.1	38.8	26.5	39.0	33.1	29.3	24.2	22.1	24.6[a]	20.7[c]
	DR	—	—	—	—	27.9	24.1	23.8	22.3	23.1	20.8	17.8	15.5	13.9	13.2	14.0[b]	10.1
Czechoslovakia	BR	—	—	—	—	—	—	—	—	24.6	27.1	23.2	19.6	17.1	20.8	22.4	22.0
	DR	—	—	—	—	—	—	—	—	18.6	16.1	15.3	13.3	13.2	14.3	13.4	10.9
Denmark	BR	30.5	32.5	30.8	32.1	31.4	29.9	28.2	25.7	24.0	22.2	19.4	17.8	17.9	20.3	21.6	17.9
	DR	20.5	20.5	19.9	19.4	18.7	16.4	13.7	12.8	13.1	11.2	11.1	10.9	10.6	10.0	9.6	9.0
Finland	BR	35.5	35.9	34.7	36.9	34.8	33.5	30.6	27.3	23.3	23.1	21.1	18.4	20.2	20.1	27.0	22.8
	DR	23.5	28.6	32.6	22.7	20.2	19.5	17.2	16.0	19.5	14.1	13.9	12.6	13.2	17.1	11.7	9.6
France	BR	27.3	26.1	26.1	25.3	23.0	21.9	20.2	17.4	13.2	19.3	18.2	16.5	15.1	14.7	20.7	19.5
	DR	23.2	23.7	23.6	22.5	22.0	20.6	19.1	21.5	22.1	17.2	16.8	15.7	13.2	17.9	13.8	12.8
Germany	BR	36.1	35.3	37.2	39.2	36.5	36.0	31.6	26.3	17.8	22.1	18.4	16.6	19.4	17.4[d]	16.6[ef]	15.8[e]
	DR	26.8	26.4	26.9	26.1	24.4	21.3	17.5	17.7	19.1	13.2	11.8	11.2	11.9	12.2[d]	11.2[ef]	10.5[e]
Greece	BR	—	—	—	—	—	—	—	—	—	21.0	29.9	29.5	26.8	19.6	25.5	19.4
	DR	—	—	—	—	—	—	—	—	—	15.1	16.4	16.5	14.5	17.3	10.8	7.1
Hungary	BR	—	—	—	—	—	—	36.7	32.8	16.0	29.4	26.0	22.5	20.1	19.3[d]	19.9	21.1
	DR	—	—	—	—	—	—	25.0	24.2	22.4	19.9	17.0	15.8	14.3	13.9[d]	14.8	11.4
Italy	BR	—	—	37.9	37.0	37.3	33.9	32.6	31.2	23.0	29.6	26.7	23.9	23.2	20.6	21.2	18.4
	DR	—	—	30.9	29.5	27.0	22.9	21.1	19.6	24.3	17.3	15.9	14.0	13.9	14.6	11.7	9.9
Netherlands	BR	33.0	33.3	35.7	36.4	33.6	32.2	29.6	27.8	26.1	25.6	23.2	21.1	20.3	21.8	25.9	22.2
	DR	26.2	25.6	25.4	22.9	20.5	17.2	14.3	12.8	13.7	10.3	9.9	8.9	8.7	10.2	9.5	7.5
Norway	BR	30.7	33.0	30.8	31.8	30.8	30.3	26.0	24.9	24.5	22.1	17.9	15.2	15.0	17.7	20.8	18.7
	DR	18.2	17.1	18.0	16.6	17.0	15.6	13.7	13.2	14.1	11.5	11.0	10.4	10.2	10.7	9.3	8.7
Poland	BR	—	—	—	—	—	—	39.8	—	—	34.7	32.3	27.6	25.4[g]	—	27.9[f]	30.1
	DR	—	—	—	—	—	—	22.8	—	—	18.5	16.7	14.6	14.0	—	11.4[f]	11.1
Portugal	BR	—	—	—	33.3	32.6	31.6	30.9	33.7	30.6	33.3	30.9	29.0	27.1	24.5	25.6	23.9

Country																	
Rumania	DR	—	—	—	23.2	22.4	22.2	20.0	20.4	26.6	20.7	18.4	16.9	15.9	15.8	13.8	11.7
	BR	—	—	41.8	40.9	39.9	39.3	40.3	42.0	—	37.9	35.2	32.9	30.2	23.2	—	23.7[h]
	DR	—	—	26.6	28.7	30.2	26.8	26.0	24.5	—	23.0	21.2	20.6	19.6	19.1	—	11.5[h]
Spain	BR	—	—	37.8	—	36.1	34.5	33.2	30.8	28.8	29.8	28.5	27.0	22.0	22.0	22.3	20.3
	DR	—	—	30.6	—	31.1	29.0	24.0	22.1	24.6	20.2	17.9	16.3	17.9	15.3	11.9	10.2
Sweden	BR	31.1	32.8	31.4	30.3	28.8	26.9	25.4	23.1	21.2	19.1	15.9	14.1	14.5	17.7	19.0	15.5
	DR	20.6	21.7	20.2	18.3	16.4	16.1	14.3	14.1	14.5	12.1	11.8	11.6	11.7	10.8	10.4	9.8
Switzerland	BR	29.8	27.8	30.2	31.3	27.4	28.4	26.0	22.7	19.2	19.5	17.5	16.4	15.4	17.9	19.4	17.3
	DR	22.8	22.4	23.0	23.1	20.3	18.1	16.0	14.3	15.0	12.5	12.1	11.8	11.6	11.4	11.2	10.1
United Kingdom (England and Wales)	BR	32.6	34.1	35.2	35.3	31.4	29.3	26.3	23.6	20.1	19.9	16.7	15.0	14.7	15.9	18.0	15.2
Scotland	DR	22.4	22.2	22.5	20.8	18.9	17.7	14.7	14.3	14.4	12.1	12.1	12.0	12.5	12.8	11.8	11.7
	BR	—	24.1[l]	(35.0)	34.8	31.4	30.0	27.6	25.4	22.8	23.0	20.0	18.2	17.6	17.8	19.8	17.8
	DR	—	20.8[l]	(22.1)	20.6	18.8	17.9	15.1	15.7	15.0	13.9	13.6	13.2	13.5	13.8	—	12.1
Yugoslavia	BR	—	—	—	—	—	—	39.0	—	—	34.9	34.2	31.9	27.9	—	28.3	28.8
	DR	—	—	—	—	—	—	24.7	—	—	20.1	20.0	18.0	15.9	—	13.3[i]	12.5

Sources: Reprinted by permission from W. W. Rostow, *The World Economy: History and Prospect* (Austin: University of Texas Press, 1978), p. 717; P. V. Glass and E. Grebenik, "World Population, 1800–1950," in M. M. Postan and H. J. Habakkuk, eds., *The Cambridge Economic History of Europe,* vol. 6, pt. 1, *The Industrial Revolution and After* (Cambridge: Cambridge University Press, 1966), pp. 68–69.

[a] Austria-Hungary before 1906.

[b] 1945–1947.

[c] 1951–1954.

[d] 1940–1943.

[e] West Germany.

[f] 1946–1949.

[g] 1935–1938.

[h] 1953.

[i] 1948–1950.

[j] 1947–1949.

[k] Birth rates before 1876 not corrected for underregistration.

[l] 1855–1860.

torically had higher death rates than the farming areas, improved in diet, sanitation, and education. Second, the medical revolution brought about in time by the discovery of the causes of infections began in this period. The birth rate decreased with the rise in urban income and the spread of education. Moreover, the cities lacked the incentive for large families that has generally been typical of agricultural life.

There were two notable pre-1914 exceptions: the United States and Russia. The American population had a birth rate of about 40 per thousand in the post–Civil War years, falling to 30 by 1910. The death rate had fallen from a post–Civil War figure of about 20 to 16 in 1910, though it ranged from 14 for whites to 22 for African Americans. The American population increased at 3% per annum before the Civil War. From 1870 to 1910, it fell from 2.4% to 2.0%. Birth rates for prerevolutionary Russia suggest a rise from 40 per thousand between 1811 and 1820 to over 50 as late as the 1880s. But with the Russian takeoff in the 1890s and rapid urbanization, the figure began to fall, reaching 47 per thousand for 1901–1910, with death rates at that time about 30 per thousand.

In short, the American and Russian figures exhibit the high birthrate figures expected of nations filling out their frontiers; but the higher Russian death rate is more typical of relative latecomers to industrialization. On balance, the U.S. population was in the range of 2–3% rate of increase; czarist Russia, about 1.5%. The normal figure for Europe was in the range of 0.4–0.8%.

The Interwar Years

Meanwhile, academics who interested themselves in demography formulated three concepts that crystallized in the interwar years: the *demographic transition*; the *optimum rate of population increase*; and, more professionally, the *net reproduction rate*. I shall first define these concepts and then apply them to the three periods into which the interwar years fall: the 1920s, the Great Depression (1929–1933), and the incomplete recovery through 1939. These concepts are all relevant to the course of population from 1996 to 2050 and beyond.

The *demographic transition* is the link between the rate of increase of population and the degree or stage of development, usually defined in terms of income per capita. As one would expect, the average deviation of birth rates is higher than that for death rates. Evidently cultural and religious values play a larger role in birth rates than in death rates. Nevertheless, the broad inverse correlation between income per capita and both birth and death rates is clear from Figure 2.1. The most advanced countries—which had their takeoffs early—are clustered low and to the right in that figure.

The *optimum rate of population increase* was an issue debated during the Great Depression as the rate of population increase sagged sharply and fell well below the long-run replacement rate in the United States and almost all of Western Europe (see Table 2.1). The classical optimum-population level was defined statistically as the point when real income per capita was at a maximum—that is, after the benefits of increasing returns were exploited but before they began to be overwhelmed by decreasing returns. This view was challenged by Gunnar Myrdal, the Swedish economist and sociologist. He specified the economic and social forces accounting for a falling population in Sweden, analyzed in detail the dynamic degenerative effects of a falling population on savings and investment, unemployment, and poverty, and concluded that a set of positive economic and social policies redistributing income in favor of those with large families would "take away the obstacle preventing an ordinary person from following their natural urge to marry and to have children."[5] Since the objective was to both improve the quality of and sustain the size of the population, Myrdal proposed a wide range of social legislation to achieve the required redistribution of income. Clearly, the anxiety about population trends was used by Myrdal to heighten the case for the welfare state.

The third concept developed to assess interwar problems was the *net reproduction rate*. This rate measures the number of daughters born to a birth cohort of girl babies by the end of their childbearing period, assuming that current rates and patterns of fertility and mortality remain fixed. A net reproduction rate of 1.00 implies that in the long term population will remain stable. During the depression of the 1930s a number of advanced countries fell below this level, thus forecasting a future decline in population unless patterns of fertility and mortality changed, as, indeed, they did. (See Table 2.2.) A related concept is the total fertility rate, which measures the number of children a female will bear during her childbearing years. A figure of 2.1 also foreshadows a static population.

These three concepts were used in the interwar years to illuminate the experiences through which various nations passed. The United States, for example, enjoyed in the 1920s a period of prosperity. This

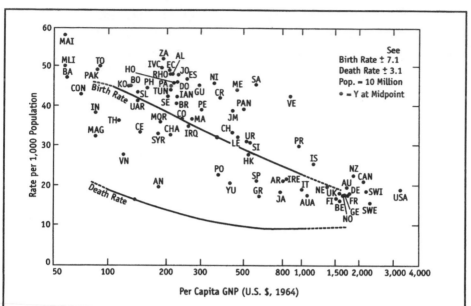

Key to Country Codes

1. Afghanistan	AF	35. Haiti	HA	69. Papua	PNG
2. Algeria	AL	36. Honduras	HO	70. Paraguay	PA
3. Angola	AN	37. Hong Kong	HK	71. Peru	PE
4. Argentina	AR	38. India	IN	72. Philippines	PH
5. Australia	AU	39. Indonesia	IND	73. Portugal	PO
6. Austria	AUA	40. Iran	IRN	74. Puerto Rico	PR
7. Belgium	BE	41. Iraq	IRQ	75. Rhodesia	RHO
8. Bolivia	BO	42. Ireland	IRE	76. Saudi Arabia	SAU
9. Brazil	BR	43. Israel	IS	77. Senegal	SE
10. Burma	BA	44. Italy	IT	78. Sierra Leone	SL
11. Cambodia (Khmer)	CB	45. Ivory Coast	IVC	79. Singapore	SI
12. Cameroon	CM	46. Jamaica	JM	80. Somalia	SO
13. Canada	CAN	47. Japan	JA	81. South Africa	SA
14. Central African Republic	CA	48. Jordan	JO	82. Spain	SP
15. Ceylon (Sri Lanka)	CE	49. Kenya	KE	83. Sudan	SU
16. Chad	CD	50. Korea (South)	KO	84. Sweden	SWE
17. Chile	CH	51. Lebanon	LE	85. Switzerland	SWI
18. China (Taiwan)	CHA	52. Liberia	LBR	86. Syria	SYR
19. Colombia	CO	53. Libya	LBY	87. Tanzania	TA
20. Congo (Zaire)	CON	54. Malagasy	MAG	88. Thailand	TH
21. Costa Rica	CR	55. Malawi	MAI	89. Togo	TO
22. Dahomey	DA	56. Malaysia	MA	90. Tunisia	TUN
23. Denmark	DE	57. Mali	MLI	91. Turkey	TU
24. Dominican Republic	DO	58. Mexico	ME	92. Uganda	UG
25. Ecuador	EC	59. Morocco	MOR	93. U.A.R. (Egypt)	UAR
26. El Salvador	ES	60. Mozambique	MOZ	94. United Kingdom	UK
27. Ethiopia	ET	61. Netherlands	NE	95. U.S.A.	USA
28. Finland	FI	62. New Zealand	NZ	96. Upper Volta	UV
29. France	FR	63. Nicaragua	NI	97. Uruguay	UR
30. Germany (West)	GE	64. Niger	NIR	98. Venezuela	VE
31. Ghana	GH	65. Nigeria	NGA	99. Vietnam (South)	VN
32. Greece	GR	66. Norway	NO	100. Yugoslavia	YU
33. Guatemala	GU	67. Pakistan	PAK	101. Zambia	ZA
34. Guinea	GUI	68. Panama	PAN		

Table 2.2. Net Reproduction Rates. Selected Advanced Industrial
Countries, 1935–1939, 1955–1959, and 1975–1979

Country	1935–1939	1955–1959	1975–1979
Austria	—	1.12	0.80 (1975–1979)
Belgium	0.96 (1939)	1.14	0.80 (1978)
Bulgaria	—	1.03	1.05 (1976)
Canada	1.16	1.82	0.84 (1978)
Czechoslovakia	—	1.23	1.16 (1975)
Denmark	0.94	1.19	0.82 (1975–1979)
Finland	0.99 (1936–1939)	1.31	0.79 (1978)
France	0.86 (1936–1937)	1.27 (1956–1960)	0.88 (1978)
Germany			
(Federal Republic)	—	1.04	0.65 (1978)
Germany (GDR)	—	1.11 (1959)	0.90 (1978)
Hungary	1.04 (1930–1931)	1.07	0.97 (1978)
Italy	1.18 (1936–1939)	1.08 (1959)	0.91 (1977)
Japan	1.49	0.96	0.86 (1977)
Luxembourg	—	0.98	0.70 (1978)
Netherlands	1.15	1.46	0.76 (1978)
Norway	0.81	1.32	0.88 (1975–1979)
Poland	1.15 (1932–1934)	1.52	1.05 (1977)
Sweden	0.78 (1936–1939)	1.06	0.81 (1975–1979)
United Kingdom			
(England and			
Wales)	0.79	1.13	0.83 (1978)
United States	0.96	1.73	0.86 (1978)
USSR	1.53 (1938–1939)	1.29 (1958–1959)	1.07 (1978–1979)
Yugoslavia	—	1.55 (1950–1954)	1.00 (1977)

Sources: Reprinted by permission from W. W. Rostow, *Theorists of Economic Growth from David Hume to the Present: With a Perspective on the Next Century* (New York: Oxford University Press, 1990), p. 200; *Population Index.* April 1973, April 1974, April 1975, April 1976, and Summer 1981.

Note: the population of European Russia declined sharply in recent years, although it now may have risen somewhat.

happened although Congress, responding to widespread antiforeign political pressures, passed the Immigration Act in 1924. This in turn contributed to the decline in housing investment before 1929. The population increase continued at a slower rate than before 1914 as the birth rate fell more than the death rate did, despite low unemployment. On the other hand, Western Europe experienced chronic

◄ **Figure 2.1** Demographic Transition: Scatter for Birth Rate in 76 Countries, 1965. *Source:* Reprinted by permission from Hollis B. Chenery and Moises Sryquin, *Patterns of Development*, 1950–1970 (London: Oxford University Press, 1975), p. 57.

double-digit unemployment. There was more uneasiness as the severe losses of World War I did not give way to a complete rebound in the rate of increase of population. In the depression years (1929–1933), however, birth rates fell in North America as well as in Europe, and economists turned to the whole population question.

The Great Depression slowdown in population growth entered into the then-new Keynesian analysis and came to be regarded as one of the major causes of the depression. The subsequent slow revival during the latter part of the 1930s was also attributed to the deceleration in population increase and a consequent decline in house building, automobile purchases, and other forms of investment related to population growth and family formation.

The cave-in of the American expansion in 1938 was significant. As noted earlier, unemployment rose from 14% in 1937 to 19% in 1938. This led not only to a gloomy prognosis for the American economy but also to a consensus among most economists that after the war, the whole Western world of advanced industrial societies would return to a regime of chronic unemployment.

Postwar Demography, 1945–1995

The economists' prognosis proved inaccurate. Until about 1960, the birth rates and rate of population increase brought the Western European and North American net reproduction rates for a time above 1.00. The prewar trend was not continued. But the extension of the normal postwar birth rates to 1960 came as a surprise to social scientists in general and to demographers in particular. As Table 2.2 shows, the baby boom subsequently reversed.

More profound was the medical revolution that followed World War II. Antibiotics saved lives on a large scale, as did the killing of mosquitoes by DDT and the subsequent attenuation of malaria in the underdeveloped world. The inverse link between death rates and degree of development was substantially broken, yielding a surge in population growth in the developing world.

Suddenly, the medical revolution produced rates of increase in underdeveloped countries of 2 percent per annum or more as estimated for 1950–2000 (Table 2.3). This more than any single factor accounts for the rather frightening Great Spike. Specifically, the medical revolution after World War II lifted the global rate of popu-

Table 2.3. "Medium" Estimates of Population of the World and Major Areas, 1750–1950 and Projections to 2000 (Millions)

Areas	1750	1800	1850	1900	1950	2000
World total	791	978	1,262	1,650	2,515	6,130
Asia (exc. USSR)	498	630	801	925	1,381	3,458
China (mainland)	200	323	430	436	560	1,034
India and Pakistan	190	195	233	285	434	1,269
Japan	30	30	31	44	83	122
Indonesia	12	13	23	42	77	250
Remainder of Asia	67	69	87	118	227	783
Africa	106	107	111	133	222	768
North Africa	10	11	15	27	53	192
Remainder of Africa	96	96	96	106	169	576
Europe (exc. USSR)	125	152	208	296	392	527
USSR	42	56	76	134	180	353
America	18	31	64	156	328	992
Northern America	2	7	26	82	166	354
Middle and South America	16	24	38	74	162	638
Oceania	2	2	2	6	13	32

Sources: Adapted from John D. Durand. "The Modern Expansion of World Population." *Proceedings of the American Philosophical Society* 111, no. 3 (June 22, 1967):137. It should be noted that the 1973 "medium" UN estimate of world population in the year 2000 was 6.4 billion.

Note: Figures have been rounded; totals do not in all cases equal the sums of component figures.

lation increase to just over 2%; the demographic transition will eventually bring down the rate of population increase to something just above zero. Total global population will rise accordingly from under 1 billion to a ceiling of 10 billion.

In the course of this ongoing drama, the more industrialized countries have pretty much kept to older rates of population increase. On the other hand, death rates in developing as well as the industrial world averaged about 10 per thousand by 1987. This represented, roughly, a minimum figure at this stage of history, given the average length of life, as determined mainly by the role of the circulatory diseases and cancer.

The post–World War II medical revolution, thus, had two major consequences in the developing areas. First, it violated the historical curve of the demographic transition. Specifically, it lowered death rates quite suddenly and permitted a population expansion that was not geared sensitively, as in the past, to the level of income per capita in the various countries. Second, the demographic transition continued to operate in the other direction, bringing down birth rates; this natural tendency was heightened as countries making progress in the stages of growth tended to mount national policies to reduce population increase by reducing birth rates. The net result of these two forces produced the pattern exhibited in Table 2.4.

Table 2.4 shows clearly that by 1987 death rates were, compared to the past, uniformly low; birth rates were highest in the poorest countries but dropped as income per capita rose and modern medical techniques worked their wonders. This was the situation in the late 1990s as experts and statesmen peered ahead to the next century.

Global Prospects for Population to 2050 and Beyond

The first broad question to ask about the future is: Assuming that the demographic transition maintains its form of recent decades, how close has the human race come to a more or less stationary global population? The demographers' answer is that after 2025 the rate of population increase will slow down rapidly and stabilize at about 10 billion.[6] (See Figure 1.1.) The demographers may be right, but history generally produces irregular outcomes.

There will continue to be an extraordinary divergence in population prospects between presently less developed and more developed

Table 2.4. Crude Birth and Death Rates and Population Increase, by Income, 1956 and 1987 (Per Thousand)

Countries by Income	Births		Deaths		% Population Increase	
	1965	1987	1965	1987	1965	1987
Low income	42	31	16	10	2.6	2.1
Lower middle income	41	32	14	8	2.7	2.1
Middle income	38	30	13	8	2.5	2.2
Upper middle income	33	27	11	8	2.2	1.9
High income	19	14	10	9[a]	0.9	0.5

Source: Reprinted by permission from *World Development Report 1989*, (New York: Oxford University Press, 1989), p. 216, table 27.

[a]The rise in the death rate in high income countries reflects the relative aging of their populations.

nations. Population in the more developed nations will approximate constancy after 2025. In the presently less developed nations, constancy will be achieved around 2100, after a prolonged period of deceleration. The proportion of the total population in presently more developed countries will decline between 1980 and 2100 from 21% to 12%. This will be a revolutionary shift. Since 1650, that proportion is estimated to have fluctuated between 34% and 26%. The greatest percentage increase among the presently developing regions is calculated for East, West, and South Africa: from 8% to 22%, with Nigeria exceeding 500 million people when stability is reached. Expert opinion holds that this relative increase will occur despite the powerful impact of AIDS, civil war, and Malthus's other "positive checks."

The years when the net reproduction rate equals 1.00 (or the gross fertility rate equals 2.1) come, of course, much earlier than the date of a constant population. The interval between that date and a stationary population is determined by prior population-growth rates and the consequent age structure of the population.

Prospects for Development

What of the prospects of GNP per capita? Table 2.5 provides rough estimates of the length of time required to achieve U.S. levels of GNP per capita (as of 1985) for four groups of countries. The upper-middle-income countries achieve 1985 levels of U.S. affluence around 2050. The lower-middle-income countries achieve this level in the fourth quarter of the next century. India and China take longer, starting as they do from low income levels; but if they find it politically possible to release the potentialities of their private sectors and use their pools of scientific and engineering manpower efficiently, as both countries now appear to be doing, they might achieve higher growth rates than in the past. In any case, they are likely by the middle of the next century to have achieved command over all the then-current technologies. This calculation sets aside the question of whether or not their efforts to achieve full industrialization will be frustrated by food and other shortages—a subject considered in Chapter 3. On the basis of the experience of others, all of the present middle-income countries will have achieved by 2050 the maximum proportion of manufacturing in GNP of about 25%.

Only the broadest conclusions can be drawn from these precarious exercises in projective arithmetic, but they are not trivial.

Table 2.5. Projected Real per Capita Income: Poor, Middling, and Rich Countries

Type of Economy	Population mid-1985 (Millions)	GNP Per Capita, 1985 U.S. $	% of U.S. GNP	Average Annual Per Capita Growth Rate, 1960–1980	Average Annual Per Capita Growth Rate, 1965–1985	Number of Years to Attain U.S. 1985 Per Capita Using 1965–1985 Rates
Low income ($110–$390)	2,439.4	270	.016	1.2	2.9	146
China	1,040.3	310	.019	NA	4.8	87
India	765.1	270	.016	1.4	3.1[a]	137
Low midddle income ($420–$1,570)	1,242.1	820	.049	3.8	2.6	103
Upper middle income ($1,640–$7,420)	567.4	1,850	.111	3.8	3.3	69
Industrial market ($4,290–$16,690)	737.3	11,810	.708	3.6	2.4	16
United States	239.3	16,690	1.000	2.3	1.7	—

Source: Reprinted by permission from *World Development Report* (New York: Oxford University Press, 1982), pp. 110–111, and ibid. (1987), pp. 202–203.

[a]As reported by the Indian Embassy (U.S.), August 10, 1987.

- Barring major catastrophes, the global population is likely to more than double by 2050, with marked deceleration through the end of the 21st century, as indicated by Table 1.1.
- The proportion of total world population in the presently developed countries will decline drastically from roughly 21% to 12%.
- If present growth patterns persist, the presently more advanced developing regions will achieve or surpass present U.S. levels of GNP per capita by the mid-21st century; the lower-middle-income countries will do so somewhat later in the century. The proportions of GNP derived from industry and manufacturing will be at or beyond the present conventional maximum of 25%, giving way to the relative rise in services that appears to characterize affluence as we now know it.
- The period from the present to the mid-21st century is likely to be the time of the maximum strain on resources and the environment and the interval of maximum readjustment in the locus of popula-

tion, economic potential, and political influence in the international community.

By way of summary and disaggregation, Table 2.6 exhibits the expected population growth of the presently developing regions between 1990 and 2050. There are, for our purposes, three significant features of this table aside from the much higher overall rate of population growth of the presently underdeveloped countries. First, Latin America, India, and the rest of Asia will at least double in population in this period. Second, China has succeeded, especially in the cities, in a policy that controls family size and is expected to increase in population only modestly. The conventional forces that reduce population growth with a rise in income (the demographic transition) have also operated in China. Accelerated urbanization brought with it a decline in family size since the late 1970s. In contrast, India failed to impose a strict family-size policy except during Indira Gandhi's brief emergency period of rule (1975–1977). India is, therefore, relying on the rise in per capita income plus more conventional policies of birth control to bring down birth rates. The upshot is that by present estimates the Indian population will exceed that of China between 2025 and 2050. The Chinese population will level out in this interval and then decline; the Indian population will continue a relative slow increase for about another century. Third, the greatest increase in population is estimated for Africa. Nevertheless, the demographic transition is already operational to a degree in Africa, though more powerful elsewhere.

Table 2.6. Expected Population Growth of the Presently Developing Regions, 1990–2050

Region	1990	2050	Absolute Increase (millions)	% Increase
Total world population	5,292	10,019	4,727	89
Total population of presently underdeveloped countries	4,203	8,786	4,583	109
Latin America	448	922	474	106
China	1,139	1,521	382	34
India	853	1,699	846	99
Other Asia	1,121	2,379	1,258	112
Africa	642	2,265	1,623	253

Source: Long-Range World Population Projections, 1950–2050 (New York: United Nations, 1992), pp. 28–31.

So much for the broad implications of these arbitrary projections for the developing countries and their relative positions in terms of the world totals. Perhaps the most remarkable account for a single country is the article by Jessie Cheng in the December 1995 edition of *Free China Review*. (Population prospects in the People's Republic of China are reviewed in Appendix B.) According to Cheng,

Between 1953 and 1993, the annual birthrate [in Taiwan] declined from about forty-five births per thousand persons to less than sixteen. During the same period, the average number of children per Taiwan couple declined by more than two-thirds, from about 7 to 1.7. The current average is below that of the United States (2 children per couple), mainland China (1.9), and Britain or France (both 1.8). The Taiwan figure also means that since 1984 the birthrate has dropped below the "replacement level."

Another trend is also changing the face of Taiwan's population: the average life span is steadily rising, leading to a growing proportion of elderly people. In 1951, local men lived an average of 53 years, and women lived 56 years. Today, men average 72 years and women 77. Because the trend toward fewer children and more senior citizens is expected to continue, sociologists predict that the elderly proportion of the population will increase steadily. While persons aged over 65 made up just over 7 percent of the population in 1994, they are expected to account for 22 percent by the year 2036—a figure that could mean more than five million senior citizens.

The result is an overall "graying" of society and a new set of social welfare needs that must be met—nursing homes rather than nursery schools, day care programs for the elderly rather than for preschoolers. Social scientists predict that these demands will be hard to fulfill. "In the future, there won't be enough young people to support the older people," says Chen [Chen Kuan-jeng, a research fellow in the Institute of Sociology at Academia Sinica]. Sociologists are particularly concerned that expanding health care costs for senior citizens will mean a large financial burden for taxpayers. Another concern is that a dwindling population of working-age adults will slow economic growth. . . .

The government launched its latest family planning campaign in May 1995, this one urging people to marry earlier and to have at least two children. "Based on medical and social considerations, and ROC law [which sets the minimum marrying age at 20], we think twenty-two to thirty is the optimal age range for marriage," Chien [Chien Tai-lang, director of the Department of Population, Ministry of the Interior] says. The new policy is being promoted by TV, radio, and

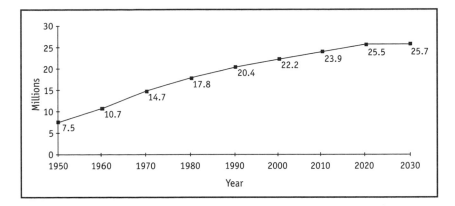

Figure 2.2 Taiwan's Population Growth, 1950–2030. *Source:* Reprinted by permission from Jessie Cheng, "More Senior Citizens, Fewer Kids," *Free China Review* 45, no. 12 (1995): 42–45.

the print media. Regulations on marriage and birth subsidies have also been revised. In the past, among civil servants, men under the age of twenty-five and women under twenty-two were not allowed to apply for the marriage and birth bonuses, each equivalent to one month's salary. In 1993, the government reduced the minimum age to twenty for both men and women.[7]

The demographic transition in outlook and policy through which Taiwan is now passing (see Figures 2.2 and 2.3) is likely to be representative of that which both the industrial societies and the more advanced developing societies will soon experience.

Sub-Saharan Africa

In this effort to identify and speculate about the principal problems and opportunities of the 21st century, I have systematically made an exception of Sub-Saharan Africa. Egypt, Algeria, Morocco, Tunisia, and Libya are excluded as is South Africa. I cannot pretend to have a detailed operational program to present for Africa thus defined, but it would be inappropriate to identify this region as an exception to the trends of the next century and go on with the analysis as though one can deal with the world without Africa. This is particularly true because the largest increase in population, as nearly as can be predicted, will be in Africa

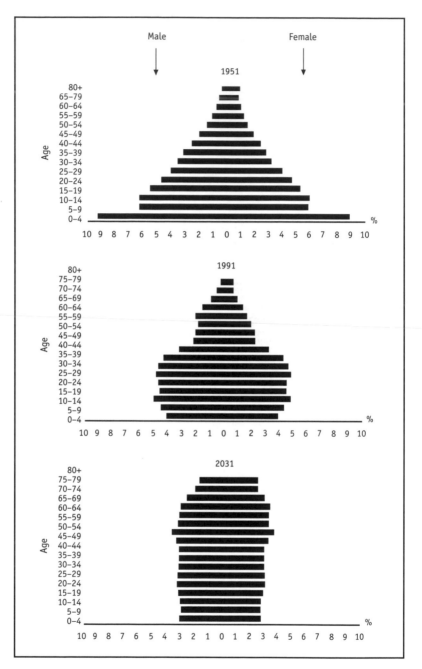

Figure 2.3 Structural Change of Taiwan's Population. *Source:* Reprinted by permission from Jessie Cheng, "More Senior Citizens, Fewer Kids," *Free China Review* 45, no. 12 (1995): 42–45.

(Table 2.6): an increase of 1.6 billion or 253% between 1990 and 2050. This is 34% of the estimated global increase over that time.

The high fertility rate reflected in these figures is accompanied, as one would expect, by an appalling recent record in development.[8]

- Africa's share of global GNP dropped from 1.9% to 1.2% between 1960 and 1989.
- Its share of global trade fell from 3.8% to 1% in this interval.
- Its share of developing-world private investment fell from 25% to 15%.
- The decline in commodity prices of exports cost Africa some $50 billion between 1986 and 1990, and price prospects remain dim.
- Africa's external debt tripled since 1980 and is now as large as its total GNP. Debt service is about 19% of total exports of goods and services.
- Per capita income has declined 1.7% per year between 1980 and 1989, and wages in the modern sector dropped 30% on average between 1980 and 1986.
- Perhaps most tragic, by 1987 nearly one-third of Africa's skilled people had moved to Europe.

In a striking reversal, the 1972–1982 annual average of the transfers to developing countries by the World Bank and the IMF combined was $21 billion; the 1983–1990 annual average was $21.5 billion. Between 1985 and 1989, the net contribution to Sub-Saharan Africa was a *negative* $700 million per year.

In the words of the *Human Development Report 1992*, "One thing Africa is not short of, however, is external advice. In fact, Africa has perhaps received more advice per capita than any other continent."[9] This advice has touched on macroeconomic adjustment policy as well as sectoral policy.

Africa, however, is not uniform in its economic and social pathology. Using the Human Development Index (HDI) developed by the United Nations, the countries of Africa can be divided as shown in Table 2.7. The HDI combines a good many social as well as economic development variables. Advanced industrial societies are rated as 1.00. For comparison, South Korea has an HDI index of .871. The most difficult cases evidently fall below .300, although certain countries rated between .300 and .400 are extremely troubling. The brute fact is that none of these countries, a few endowed with valuable raw materials, has yet entered takeoff or gone far down the road in the demographic transition.

Table 2.7. African Rate of Human Development Index

.050–.300	.300–.400	.400–.500	.500–
Angola	Ghana	Cameroon	Burkina Faso
Benin	Liberia	Kenya	Gabon
Burundi	Madagascar	Lesotho	Mauritius
Central African Rep.	Nigeria		
Chad	Tanzania		
Ethiopia	Zaire		
Guinea	Zambia		
Mauritania	Zimbabwe		
Mozambique			
Niger			
Rwanda			
Senegal			
Sierra Leone			
Somalia			
Sudan			
Togo			
Uganda			

Source: Reprinted by permission from *Human Development Report* 1992 (New York: Oxford University Press, 1992), p. 20.

Moreover, the inherent political difficulties of postcolonial Africa cannot be judged as direct causes of this troubling lag, although they have obviously played a part. For example, Nigeria not only is a large country but is well endowed with natural resources, not limited to oil and gas. Under the strain of an exploitative government and the relative decline of oil and gas prices, it may experience a break in its unity as the fourteen or so tribes it contains assert themselves. Liberia and Ethiopia have had long periods of independence. A number of these countries cut across traditional tribal boundaries, and in some cases the conflict across these barriers has led to much difficulty. But this is by no means universally true. African laggards are not all small, close to the break from colonialism, lacking in resources, or troubled by the clash of tribal and national boundaries. Jeffrey Sachs and Andrew Warner have recently added to the large prescriptive literature a useful essay, "Sources of Slow Growth in the African Economies."[10] They ask why Africa has not achieved regular rates of growth greater than the advanced industrial countries. Why did Africa not exploit the very large technological backlog bequeathed to it?

The authors first introduce in answer to those questions the three economic considerations that bear on them:

1. the extent of overall market orientation, including openness to trade, domestic-market liberalization, private rather than state ownership, protection of private-property rights, and low marginal-tax rates;

2. the national saving rate, which in turn is strongly affected by the government's own saving rate; and

3. the geographic and resource structure of the economy, with land-locked and resource-abundant economies tending to lag behind coastal and resource-scarce ones.[11]

Moving beyond the economists' answers, Sachs attributes the frustration of these hopes to the policies of "self-sufficiency" and "state leadership" popular in developing countries of the 1960s. It is essential to recall that these policies had, at the time, an enormous political appeal. For politicians, fresh from victories over their colonial masters, they defined a sharp line between the Cold War contenders and the "neutralists." For the politicians, they also simplified the national political arena and permitted a struggle for power with a limited number of contenders. They also made monetary corruption easier. For civil servants, these policies multiplied the areas they could control and manage and the power they could accumulate. For the public at large, "self-sufficiency" and "state leadership" gave substance to a sense of nationhood and national destiny that was frail at best. It is here, in the political underpinnings of development policy, that Sachs's and Warner's arguments are weakest: Politics has always had primacy.[12]

In proposing a solution, Sachs must prove that the end of the Cold War has reduced Africa's leverage on the major contestants; the success of the more or less free marketeers of Asia and Latin America is understood, and the coming to responsibility of a new generation of bureaucrats has set the stage for a new start for Africa, some 35 years after independence. I wholly support their contingent joint aid proposal for a "New Compact for Africa" in which the United States, Western Europe, and Japan would join, assuming the time is right and the ground is well prepared. The proposal might be launched with the most promising of the African countries.

It is important, in a larger setting, not to lose hope and to remember that other countries exhibited little net progress and underwent a long period of preconditions before they began to experience sustained growth. For example, Mexico and most of the other countries of Latin America, China, India, and the countries of Northeast and Southeast

Asia (excepting Japan) all took a century or more of preconditioning before they found the political basis for sustained growth.

In addition to the tragic conflicts selected for display on CNN, there are some hopeful signs out of Sub-Saharan Africa in the 1990s. The global elevation of democratic, multiparty politics and the growing vitality in the private sectors have not wholly overlooked Africa, and such changes have improved the competence of some governments. Human development has, moreover, proceeded. Life expectancy has increased; the literacy rate and the proportion of young people enrolled in primary and secondary schools have doubled in the last quarter century; the population per house and the number of non-immunized infants have been halved in the past generation. No one seeing pictures of the seemingly endless lines of potential voters in South Africa's first free election can be wholly pessimistic.

In short, Africa remains an extremely difficult development problem, but there is some reason for long-range optimism. And it contains and will contain too many people to be ignored.

The Older Industrial Countries

What are the prospects for the presently developed countries? In general, the average age is rising in the older industrial countries, population increase is slowing down, and, in a few important cases, population change has already turned negative. Among the major economies, negative population growth has already appeared in European Russia and Germany.

Despite the broad trend in the older industrial countries, there are a number of anomalies and surprises, as Figures 2.4 and 2.5 reveal.

- In 1960, Britain and France had a relatively high average age among the industrial countries; in 2020, along with the United States, Britain will be the youngest.
- Japan[13] and Italy, whose high population growth was a source of anxiety after World War II, will age rapidly, the former a bit faster than the latter.
- The European populations of most of the old Soviet Union and its Eastern European empire have declined, except for Poland and Moldova; the Asian successor states have increased their populations.
- Canada will move from being a society younger than the United States to one that is older.

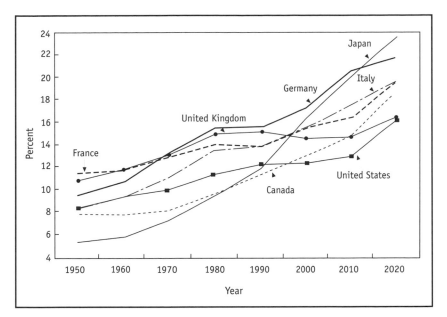

Figure 2.4 International Comparison of Aging Population (Share of Population Aged 65 and Over). *Source:* Reprinted by permission from OECD, "Ageing Populations" (1989), and British Ministry of Welfare, "White Paper on Welfare" (1988), in OECD, *Long-Term Prospects for the World Economy* (1992).

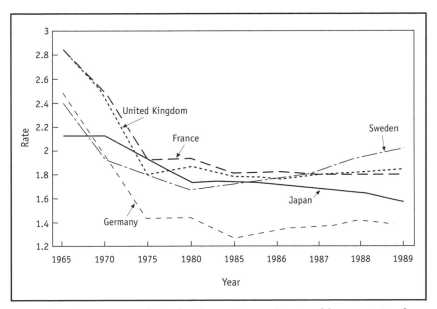

Figure 2.5 Comparison of Fertility Rates. *Source:* Reprinted by permission from United Nations, "Demographic Yearbook," and Council of Europe, "Recent Demographic Developments in the Member States," in OECD, *Long-Term Prospects for the World Economy* (1992).

The relative youth of the American population flows from an expected high rate of immigration. This rate will gradually change the racial composition of American society as it is now doing—a central fact for the future taken up in Chapter 8.

As for fertility rates (Figure 2.5), after 1969 there was a general rapid decline from a rate over the replacement level (2.1) to a rate below it (1.4–1.8), where rates have stayed since the mid-1970s. Sweden is an intriguing exception. According to a fact sheet provided by the Swedish embassy in Washington, the rise in the fertility rate is due to the rise in net immigration between 1982 and 1984.

It is certainly not to be ruled out that there will be a general revival of birth rates in the advanced industrial world similar to the protracted baby boom after World War II. The fact, however, is that, as McRae says: "We have no experience of the effects of a slow, steady decline in a complex industrial society."[14] Unless there is a rather remarkable rise in birth rates, we shall see installed various measures to enlarge the workforce by changing inherited, essentially social rules. Indeed, these changes are already under way, and they will become more urgent as the older industrial societies increasingly find the whole fabric of their social outlays will crumble if they fail to enlarge the effective workforce.

Some of the measures that can be anticipated include the following:

- Retirement ages will rise.
- Female participation rates in the workforce will climb.
- Part-time working (including working at home) will continue to increase.
- University students will be expected to work part-time while studying, a process already begun.
- Greater efforts will be made to reduce unemployment.
- Retraining for different jobs several times in a career will become more normal.
- Volunteer labor will be used to a greater extent.
- There will be more pressure on children to learn marketable skills.

All of these measures are designed to increase the labor supply. As an *Economist* article on the "Economics of Ageing" says: "Perhaps the most effective way of boosting the labour supply would be to raise the retirement age, which elegantly combines an increase in revenue from taxes and social-security contributions with a reduction in pension spending. But would-be pensioners would have to wait for their benefits, and labour markets remain hostile to older workers, particularly at times of high unemployment."[15]

Immigration is economically simple but socially exceedingly complex. If there is a decline in the indigenous population, the shortfall can, in theory, easily be made up by men and women from another country. Indeed, immigration is increasing in virtually all of the advanced industrial countries in Western Europe and Japan, as well as in the United States. There are two contrary forces that, however, come into play: political resistance within the host country to a real or believed change of the demographic content of the society and the unskilled character of many immigrants, resulting in long-term unemployment and a consequent rise in welfare expenditures. The balancing of these considerations against the additions to population could limit the role of immigration in making up the shortfall in the workforce.

Behind recommendations to enlarge the workforce at this stage is a powerful fiscal reality. As Figure 2.6 roughly demonstrates, the contributions to pension funds will be exceeded by present commitments to expenditures after about 2005.[16] The consequent, foreseeable fiscal crisis in pension funds reflects a radical change in the dependency burden carried by members of the Organization for Economic and Cooperative Development (OECD) working force: "The current ratio in most developed countries is around four or five people of working age for every person over 65. But by 2025 that ratio will be down to about three to one in America and around two-and-a-half to one in

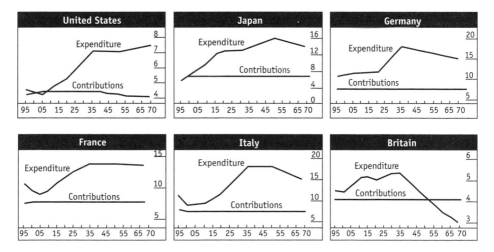

Figure 2.6 Pension Payments and Contributions as Percentage of GDP. *Source: Economist,* January 27, 1996, p. 9, derived from OECD data.

most European countries. Add in dependent children and young people, and workers look seriously overstretched."[17]

Examining the pension and health costs of the aging of populations and the noneconomic consequences of population decline, one is inclined to feel that citizens of democracies will opt at first for measures to enlarge the working force, then for a pronatalist policy to maintain a more or less static population. This could happen despite the likelihood that such a policy would confront the transitional generation with the risk of supporting an enlarged cadre of the young as well as the enlarging cadre of the old. It also will raise a deeper social question. There has been in the 20th century a notable change in the role of women in the workforce. This has been more than a quantitative increase in the proportion of women who have jobs: Women now have a higher proportion of jobs requiring intellectual and administrative skills. Although a margin of women now work because a family's real wages have been under downward pressure in recent decades, the rise in the proportions and stature of women in the workforce has been a powerful long-term trend.

If this demographic analysis of the future is correct, the advanced industrial countries will move toward pronatalist policies to avoid living under a regime of declining population. The pressure on men to share more fully in the raising of children as well as the pressure on women to have more children will also grow.

Obviously, the shortage and aging of the population and working force in the older industrial countries contrasted with the continued rapid growth of the presently developing countries in the short run will raise important questions. Will the developed countries, following the example of Sweden, be willing to accept immigration from the regions with a higher rate of population increase? What social and demographic changes will accompany such immigration? Will there be a tendency for the advanced industrial countries to tighten their bonds and face together the demographic and resource problems that seem slated for the next century? Or will the ties among them — as well as their present domestic cohesion — crumble?

The Importance of Stages of Growth

It should be underlined that the relative rise in population of the presently underdeveloped countries has been accompanied by a relative rise in production and technological sophistication. As emphasized earlier, the shift in the locus of population growth alone would not have as profound an effect on the world economy. After all, as of 1990, the advanced industrial countries constituted only about 20% of the world population, and by 2050 the figure will be about 12%.

Since World War II, however, one developing country after another found the political, institutional, and human setting to mount a take-off. Since that time, we have seen in the developing world a systematic catching up, as those nations swiftly absorbed technological backlog. This was much like the spread of industrialization from Britain to Western Europe, the United States, and Japan after 1815. For evidence, consider the takeoff sequence over the past two centuries as set out in Figure 2.7.

Recalling Hamish McRae's dictum at the beginning of this chapter, it is the coming to technological maturity of what I have designated as the fourth graduating class, rather than demography alone, that will reshape the world in the next half century.

The American Case

The immigration dilemma of the United States is an important component of the population problem as a whole; and it is a heightened version of the problem confronted in Western Europe, Canada, and Japan. A part of the problem comes to rest on the swiftness of the transitions in the racial composition of American society. This is not the first time that the pace of immigration detonated a xenophobic reaction. There was, for example, such a reaction to the arrival in Boston of the wave of Irish immigration in the late 1840s and early 1850s. The reaction to the pre-1914 wave of immigration from Southern and Eastern Europe, climaxed by the legislation of 1924, was designed explicitly to maintain the existing racial balance. (See Figure 2.8.)

This old theme was heightened in the 1990s by the feeling that immigrants from Latin America and Asia were taking jobs from Americans as well as raising public-welfare expenditures at a time when the stability of employment, the scale of welfare outlays, and the protracted stagnation of real wages were major national political themes.

Three propositions about immigration into the United States at the close of the 20th century are fairly certain. First, immigration from

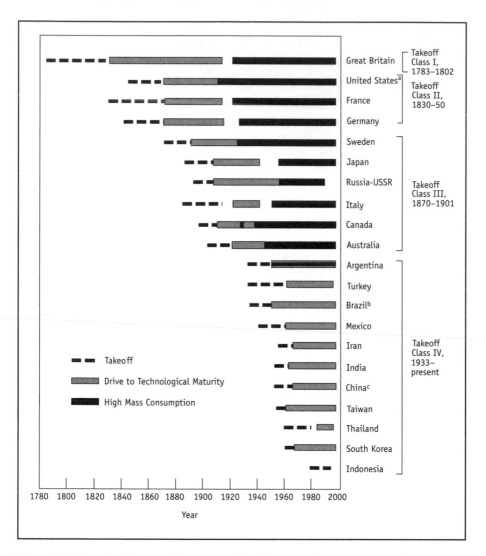

Figure 2.7 Four Graduating Classes into Takeoff: Stages of Economic Growth, 21 Countries. *Source:* Reprinted by permission from W. W. Rostow, *The World Economy: History and Prospect* (Austin: University of Texas Press, 1978), p. 51 and pt. 5.

[a]New England regional takeoff, 1815–1850.

[b]São Paulo regional takeoff, 1900–1920.

[c]Manchuria regional takeoff, 1930–1941.

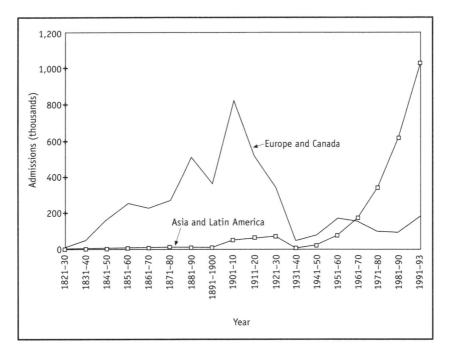

Figure 2.8 Average Annual Number of Immigrants Admitted to the United States by National Origin, 1821–1993. *Source*: Frank D. Bean, Robert G. Cushing, and Charles W. Hayes, "The Changing Demography of U.S. Immigration Flows: Patterns, Projections, and Contexts," in Klaus J. Bade and Myron Weiner, eds., *Migration Past, Migration Future: Germany and the United States* (Oxford: Berghahn Books, 1997).

Latin America and Asia has surged in the 1970s and 1980s.[18] Second, this surge, which continues, is likely to produce a substantial decline by 2040 in the proportion of "whites" in the American population.[19] As shown in Table 2.8, the proportion is estimated to fall by 22 points, from 75.2% in 1990 to 52.8% in 2050. The third proposition is that people in the Hispanic population, and to a lesser extent in the Asian population, tend to marry persons of different race/ethnic groups, and younger persons are more inclined to marry out of their group than are their elders. Most of these mixed marriages are with "whites." Therefore, with the passage of time, the change in racial composition of the population will be mitigated. For example, the proportion of Hispanics in mixed marriages constitute 34% of the total; the proportion of Asians, 22% of the total. This subject will be further pursued in Chapter 8.

Table 2.8. U.S. Population by Race/Ancestry, 1900–1990 and Projections to 2060 (Thousands)

Year	Total	Non-Hispanic White	Black	Hispanic	Asian	Native American
Population						
1900	76,195	66,225	8,834	656	243	237
1910	93,879	82,049	10,255	999	299	277
1920	110,747	96,969	11,512	1,632	389	244
1930	127,585	111,543	12,736	2,435	527	343
1940	136,928	119,425	13,767	2,814	577	345
1950	155,156	134,351	15,668	4,039	739	357
1960	182,055	154,969	19,071	6,346	1,146	524
1970	205,567	170,371	23,005	9,616	1,782	793
1980	226,625	180,392	26,482	14,604	3,726	1,420
1990	248,712	187,139	29,986	22,354	7,274	1,959
Percent						
1900	100	86.9	11.6	0.9	0.3	0.3
1910	100	87.4	10.9	1.1	0.3	0.3
1920	100	87.6	10.4	1.5	0.4	0.2
1930	100	87.4	10.0	1.9	0.4	0.3
1940	100	87.2	10.1	2.1	0.4	0.3
1950	100	86.6	10.1	2.6	0.5	0.2
1960	100	85.1	10.5	3.5	0.6	0.3
1970	100	82.9	11.2	4.7	0.9	0.4
1980	100	79.6	11.7	6.4	1.6	0.6
1990	100	75.2	12.1	9.0	2.9	0.8
1995		73.6	12.0	10.2	3.3	
2030		68.5	13.1	18.9	6.6	
2050		52.8	13.6	24.5	8.2	
2060		59.2	12.4	18.1	9.7	

Source: Adapted from J. S. Passel and Barry Edmonston, *Immigration and Ethnicity: The Integration of America's Newest Arrivals* (Washington, D.C.: Urban Institute Press, 1994), p. 81. *New York Times*, March 14, 1996.

Note: Populations include 50 states and District of Columbia for 1900–1990.

A fourth less certain proposition is that the number of Hispanics, particularly Mexicans, who will seek to migrate to the United States might well decline by 2050. By World Bank reckoning, a net reproduction rate of 1.0 will be reached in Mexico by 2005. By the middle of the 21st century, if not before, Mexico will probably achieve the hypothetical size of a stationary population (170 million). With this easement in the pressure of Mexican population growth and in relative Mexican poverty, it is not irrational to assume a sharp decline in the pressure to migrate north.

Conclusion

The conclusions of this chapter can be summarized in nonstatistical terms to dramatize two things: First, the numbers in any projective exercise of this kind are approximate, despite their apparent firmness; second, this chapter contains some critically important conclusions that the availability of numbers may conceal.

What is clear is that the combination of population growth and the spread of industrialization once takeoff begins will change the shape of the world. If the earth can carry a doubling of population in the next half century without a general catastrophe, we shall have two countries, with populations of about 1.5 billion each, that are essentially industrialized: India and China. This is, for each country, about five times the estimated peak population level of the United States. They should each command by the middle of the next century all the then-available industrial and agricultural techniques. Much the same can be said of the other major countries of Asia and Latin America.

Historically, it is such up-and-coming countries that have been gripped by "dreams of glory": Germany (twice), Japan, and Russia. As W. Arthur Lewis wrote:

> If there is any connection between dreams of glory and the stage of economic development, it is found in the "middle" stages of economic growth. The richest countries tend to be peaceful, enjoying what they have and envying none; and the poorest countries are too lethargic and disorganized for war. It is the up and coming country, which has risen a cut above its neighbours, which often develops aggressive aspirations, wishing to make for itself a place in the sun. Growing competition with the older and richer countries for markets and for raw materials may urge in the same direction. The countries which are dangerous to world peace are more often those which think they have a great future ahead of them than those which are able to glorify their great past.[20]

Thus, the period from now until 2050 will be a period not only of maximum strain on resources but also one in which new industrial powers will enter the world arena. This is the reason why the United States has potentially such an important role to play as "the critical margin," a role considered in Chapter 7. That role will not be to confront the new powers but to seek their cooperation in building a world at peace, under law. With modern weapons of mass destruction available to many nations, that is the best option available to all of the human race. That result cannot be achieved, however, by an America that oscillates between isolationism and a late attempt to salvage its direct interests by convulsive military action as in 1917, 1941, and, indeed, 1947.

The second grand conclusion to be drawn from this exercise relates to the deceleration of population growth. This is best shown, again, by turning back to Figure 1.1, which exhibits the growth rate of population by degrees of development. The conclusions to be drawn from that figure and the questions it raises are clear and central to this book: To what extent will the political and social restraints on immigration limit the reestablishment of population equilibrium? When will Europe, the United States, and Japan decide that they, like Taiwan, will have to launch pronatalist policies to have a chance at a stagnant instead of a falling population? When will the less-developed regions become conscious of the implications of their falling birth rates? Or more generally, when will the human race become conscious that it is on the downward part of the spike in rate of population growth brought about by the demographic transition and the virtuousity of modern medicine that have accompanied the spread of the Industrial Revolution?

THREE

Technology and Investment

Introduction

Technology has been at the heart of economic growth, from the swift Dutch commercial boats of the 17th century—called "fly boats" in English—to the latest computer or product of genetic engineering at the end of the 20th century. Since the middle of the 18th century, economists have recognized two categories of technologies. Adam Smith, for example, drew a line between the inventions of those whom he called "philosophers" (and we call scientists) that involved "new powers not formerly applied" and incremental improvement in ways of doing things that more or less automatically accompanied the widening of the market and consequent specialization. Since there were limits to the widening of the market and Smith assumed his scientific inventions were sporadic, it followed that, in the end, decreasing returns would set in. The process ended as stagnation or decline when nations had acquired their "full complement of riches." However, that is not the way it happened in the last two centuries, when innovation became a flow rather than an occasional event.

A preliminary word about technology and investment. Private, domestic investment is conventionally divided into nonresidential,

47

residential, and inventories. Nonresidential investment is the sum of business structures plus producers' equipment. Residential is primarily nonfarm structures, although relatively small items for farm structures and producers' durable equipment go with these structures. Inventories fluctuate rather stably in a 3.2 to 3.5 relation to final sales. The most volatile items in this statistical array are the linked figures for business structures and equipment and residential nonfarm structures.

The hypothesis at which I have arrived is that the macroeconomic convention of viewing investment as dependent on the rate of growth of consumption (or in a fixed proportion to consumption) is too aggregated a view of the investment process. Net business investment (excluding obsolescence requirements) is primarily a function of the size of the technological backlog a country has available. The bulk of business investment that takes place is a consequence of the plowback of profits. The profits, in turn, are mainly earned in the new innovational industries with high rates of growth and those linked to them. And each cycle is led by investment in the innovation sector or sectors.[1]

Investment in nonfarm residential structures is the other form of investment on a large scale. In the long run, such investment accommodates itself to the rate of family formation but is postponable at times of cyclical depression. Housing fluctuates with fair sensitivity to interest rates, but overall it rises and falls with the major cycles. These, in turn, link well to innovational investment. Thus, there is a tendency for both major forms of investment to be linked by a complex set of relations to innovational investment.

This raises another important question. The expansion in production that has been spreading through the world since the 18th century has been, in macro terms, tolerably linear when presented as five-year moving averages. When I plotted on a semilog (i.e., geometric) basis per capita GNP and industrial production after takeoff, they took the form, generally, of fairly straight lines.[2] On the other hand, this relatively steady aggregate growth was arrived at only by absorbing successively a sequence of technological leading sectors, each of which followed a quite different, decelerating path of, at first, rapid growth and, in time, progressively slower growth and even decline. For illustrative purposes, Figures 3.1 and 3.2 give the aggregate and sectoral data on Great Britain from 1700 to the 1970s. (In the countries that followed Britain into the Industrial Revolution, the absorption of technologies after takeoff was generally more compressed in time and the aggregate growth rate higher.)

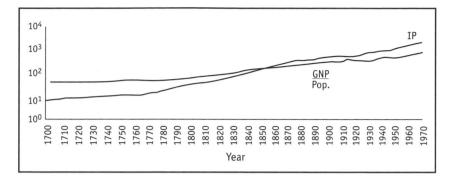

Figure 3.1 Great Britain, 1700–1970: Aggregate Data (Smoothed). *Source:* Reprinted by permission from W. W. Rostow, *The World Economy: History and Prospect* (Austin: University of Texas Press, 1978), p. 375.

Note: GNP/Pop. = GNP per capita; IP = industrial production index.

How were the macro and sectoral figures related? When a society failed to absorb a sectoral technological revolution, its overall, macro performance declined. The Soviet Union, for example, failed to absorb fully two successive technological revolutions (or "leading sectors") in the civilian economy, and, as a result, the rate of increase of GNP gradually declined from the 1960s to the Brezhnev stagnation of the early 1980s.[3] The two technological revolutions missed were the automobile–durable consumer goods revolution and the computer–

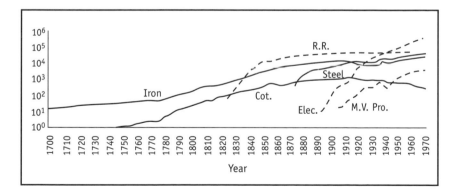

Figure 3.2 Great Britain, 1700–1970: Sectoral Data (Smoothed). *Source:* Reprinted by permission from W. W. Rostow, *The World Economy: History and Prospect* (Austin: University of Texas Press, 1978), p. 375.

Note: The six major sectors are railroads (in miles) (R.R.); raw cotton consumption (Cot.); iron; steel; electricity (Elec.); and motor vehicles (M.V. Pro.).

genetic engineering–laser-industrial materials revolution that took shape in Japan and the West in the 1970s. At the time of its breakup, the Soviet Union's civilian economy had the look of Europe's in the early 1950s. In the long run, however, after whatever vicissitudes history has in store, Russia will create the political and social setting for rapid growth, like that of Japan after 1955, for there is a large technological backlog in Russia to apply to the civilian economy.

These technological revolutions came along every 60 years or so since the 1780s. If the rhythm persists, there should be at least one more breakthrough by 2050. Will we have economical fusion power? Will there be a breakthrough in one of the other possible sources of electric power? Will genetic engineering and the computer combine to produce a better approximation of the human brain? Will we find and establish contact with inhabitants of other planets? Will genetic engineering produce an agricultural revolution, especially in the production of grain, equivalent to the Mexican wheat strains and the IR-8 rice created at Los Baños in the Philippines? Will nanotechnology (extreme miniaturization of motors and other components) constitute a true breakthrough or a refinement of existing techniques? These are among the possibilities for what Adam Smith meant by the contribution of scientists in providing technologies incorporating "new powers not formerly applied" and what I mean by "leading sectors."

This book looks forward to technological prospects from a base rooted in history as it in fact unfolded. I shall, in particular, briefly review the four major technological revolutions that have marked the period since the first Industrial Revolution began toward the end of the 18th century. These have been based on a more or less regular flow of "new powers not formerly applied," demand for each new innovation of this heroic character promptly succeeding its predecessor. From this approach will emerge a map of the past two centuries that might guide us usefully but roughly over the half century ahead.

The First Industrial Revolution

The first Industrial Revolution occurred in the last two decades of the 18th century. It started with the British takeoff in that period, and its leading sectors were machinery-manufactured cotton textiles, with coke-manufactured iron a secondary leading sector that would not have assumed the shape it did but for the simultaneous invention by James Watt of the steam engine with a separate condenser and other refinements. Each of these innovations had, of course, a long prior period of experiment and trial. The first takeoff, then, had three leading sectors related to each other: cotton textiles led the way, but coke-made iron in large foundries and Watt's steam engine were critical as well.

What did the cotton sector look like in quantitative terms? (See Figure 3.3.) In the period 1695–1704, Britain imported 1.14 million pounds of raw cotton; in 1770–1779, 4.80 million pounds; in 1795–1804, 42.95 million pounds. In 1625–1635, British pig-iron output was about 26,000 tons per year; in 1775, it was 44,000 tons; in 1818, 325,000 tons. (See Figure 3.4.) The preconditions for this takeoff were evident throughout Western Europe in France, Belgium, Switzerland, Germany, in parts of Italy and Spain, and even in the colonies that were to become the United States. But, without question, Britain was first out of the gate, although certain economic historians argue this was a matter of luck as compared to France. Others view British innovational precocity as such that it was most likely to be the first out of the gate. (I belong to the latter school.)

This demonstration by the British was a transcendent historical event, whether a matter of chance or the logical outcome of a long historical sequence. And it was irreversible. From that time forward, people knew that self-sustained growth was possible. Cotton manufacture spread, but the British had pretty well captured the export markets. To put the matter into a framework of a technological theory of growth, invention rapidly increased in number and regularity. In

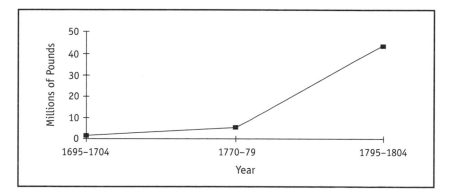

Figure 3.3 Great Britain Raw Cotton Imports, 1695–1804. *Source:* Reprinted by permission from B. R. Mitchell and Phyllis Deane, *Abstract of British Historical Statistics* (Cambridge: Cambridge University Press, 1971), pp. 177–178.

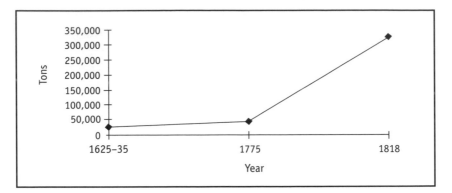

Figure 3.4 Great Britain Pig Iron Output, 1625–1818. *Source:* W. W. Rostow, *How It All Began* (New York: McGraw-Hill, 1975), p. 165.

the decade 1630–1639, 75 English patents were granted; in 1750–1759, the figure was 89; in 1800–1809, the figure was 924. (See Figure 3.5.)

In short, something quite remarkable happened in Britain in the latter years of the 18th and the early years of the 19th century. The first graduating class into takeoff consisted of Britain alone. As we saw in Chapter 2, a second graduating class (Western Europe and the United States) came along in the second quarter of the nineteenth century; a third graduating class, of which Japan and Russia were the leading members, took off in the 1880s and 1890s; a fourth graduating class began in the 1930s, and, after World War II, it was joined in the 1950s

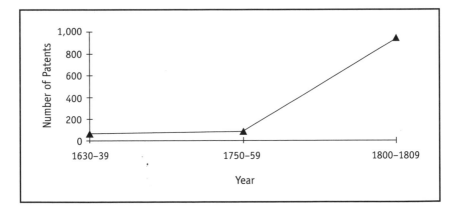

Figure 3.5 Great Britain Patents Granted, 1630–1809. *Source:* Reprinted by permission from B. R. Mitchell and Phyllis Deane, *Abstract of British Historical Statistics* (Cambridge: Cambridge University Press, 1971), p. 268.

by India, China, and a good many others. (See Figure 2.7.) But it was the British who proved that a high sustained rate of growth as compared with the long past was possible.[4] The event was so important and so related to the Great Spike that it is worth tersely summarizing one economic historian's view of how it came about.

Three forces converged in Europe starting toward the end of the 15th century. These set in motion the preconditions for takeoff. They were the emergence of the nation-state, of which Henry VII's accession to the British throne is a useful symbol; the commercial revolution, which can roughly be taken to begin with Columbus's discovery of America in 1492, profiting from the earlier and more systematic work in Portugal of Henry the Navigator; and the scientific revolution, which can be dated from the posthumous publication in 1543 of Copernicus's explosive conclusions that put the sun rather than the earth at the center of the solar system.

But one should pull the camera back and take an even wider view. Granted forty years of unbroken peace in the second half of the fifteenth century, the Italian Renaissance, rooted in an earlier humanism, produced its remarkable contributions to civilization. Also, at that time, the three inventions Francis Bacon recognized as fundamental to an emerging modern way of life—printing, the compass, and gunpowder (in all of which Sung China anticipated Europe)—were vigorously put to work in the West. In the fifteenth century, the Germans not only built a good many of their great cathedrals and set up their academies, they also gave to the West printing by metal type—an invention that diffused with remarkable speed. It was in that century that the fall of Constantinople to the Turks helped move the Portuguese and others out onto the high seas, where they began the voyages of discovery that brought the Western Hemisphere and the Far East into the daily life and consciousness of Europe, and brought too a number of popular imported commodities. In the middle of the century, the cannon came into its own, making cheap the destruction of the feudal castle and opening the way to the more economical consolidation of larger political units, despite a subsequent improvement in fortification against artillery attack. By the end of the fifteenth century, Spain had overwhelmed the last enclave of Moslem rule and had achieved a reasonable degree of unity. The English were out of a France where Louis XI had consolidated a national state. And, with the coming of Henry VII in 1485, England had reestablished the power of the crown after the bloody, exhausting duel between the Yorkists

and Lancastrians. In Russia, Ivan III had refused to pay annual trib-
ute to the divided Golden Horde, consolidated the position of Moscow, and emerged, in effect, as the first national sovereign of Russia.

No one can tell the story of the preconditions to the first Industrial
Revolution without evoking the emergence of the contentious nation-
states that, guided by mercantilist doctrine, were soon at war with one
another and in acute competition when they were not fighting. No
one can tell that story without evoking the commercial revolution that
not only widened the horizons of Europeans and brought to Europe
sugar and spices but also brought Indian cottons that, under market
pressure from European women, drew creative talent to the machinery for doing what Indian hands could do but European hands could
not. No one can tell that story without evoking the century and a half
between the death of Copernicus and the publication of Newton's
Principia, a period when Galileo, Brahe, Kepler, Gilbert, Huygens,
and Descartes made their measurements and in time spread the doctrine that people had the power to manipulate nature if they knew its
rules, which were knowable.

It is my conclusion, looking closely at the traditional societies —
East and West, North and South — that this essentially psychological
dimension of the period in Europe from the 15th to the 18th centuries
alone was unique. Put another way, there had been in the past the
equivalent of nation-states and mercantilism and the equivalent of the
commercial revolution, but there was no equivalent in the past to
the line from Copernicus to Newton. The key to the Industrial Revolution was thus essentially psychological, and it was captured by
Edmond Halley in his prefatory ode to Newton's *Principia*:

> Here ponder too the laws which God
>   framing the universe, set not aside
> But made the fixed foundations of His work.[5]

All of previous history had been governed by the rule that R. V. Jones,
the Scottish physicist, tersely put: "They (the rulers) could ably gov-
ern . . . any situation that their minds could contemplate; but they
could not legislate for anything they could not imagine."[6]

From this new way of looking at things arose the Industrial Revolution by three routes: by insisting that God (or Nature) operated the
universe by laws that could be discovered by people; by setting people
off not only to discover those laws but also to discuss the scientific
adventure with inventors and businesspeople who translated their

insights into commercially profitable innovations; and by thus creating a market for toolmakers who made possible empirical search for both scientific knowledge and profitable applications. Never before had people regarded the physical world this way.

The Second Industrial Revolution: Railroads and Cheap Steel

Although he had some predecessors, Michael Mulhall, a 19th-century Irish statistician, was the authentic innovator in the collection and organization of statistics on the British Industrial Revolution and its spread. Moreover, his *Dictionary of Statistics* includes imaginative calculations of energy per capita and national wealth itself in the various countries. On the whole, his data and manipulations of them stand up rather well and are respected by modern statisticians.

Table 3.1 presents Mulhall's data on the spread of the railway revolution from 1840 to 1888. Excepting the continental United States, Britain maintained its primacy until 1880; France lagged behind Germany by a little; precocious, small Belgium outstripped Holland for the first time in the modern era; continental Russia began building railroads seriously after the Crimean War; Northern and Southern Europe came along after 1870, in that order; Japan began in earnest with its takeoff in the 1880s. The bottom half of Table 3.1 indicates how universally this macroinnovation had spread by 1888.

The cotton industry in Britain and New England pioneered the railways as a commercial innovation. The industry needed a form of transport to bring raw cotton cheaply from the ports to the factories, which were confined at first to locations by waterfalls, and then to take the finished textiles back to the ports. Thus, the Manchester-Liverpool and the Boston-Lowell railroad lines were both completed in 1830. The steam engine had already been applied to boats on the rivers and in the coastal trade, and manufacturers were able to switch briskly from textile to railroad machinery.

Meanwhile, at the other end of the process, a similar dynamic was soon at work. The size and momentum of the railroad industry exerted great pressure to learn how to produce cheap steel in place of the iron rails, which had a high rate of obsolescence. A breakthrough occurred in the late 1860s when several ways of producing cheap steel were invented. The industry expanded wherever coking coal could

Table 3.1. Expansion of World Railroad Mileage, 1840–1888

Country	1840	1850	1860	1870	1880	1888
United Kingdom	838	6,620	10,430	15,540	17,930	19,810
France	360	1,890	5,880	9,770	14,500	20,900
Germany	341	3,640	6,980	11,730	20,690	24,270
Russia	16	310	990	7,100	14,020	17,700
Austria	90	960	2,810	5,950	11,500	15,610
Italy	13	270	1,120	3,830	5,340	7,830
Spain	—	80	1,190	3,200	4,550	5,930
Portugal	—	—	40	440	710	1,190
Sweden	—	—	375	1,090	3,650	4,670
Norway	—	—	40	170	690	970
Denmark	—	20	70	470	830	1,220
Holland	11	110	200	780	1,440	1,700
Belgium	210	550	1,070	1,800	2,400	2,760
Switzerland	—	15	650	890	1,600	1,870
Romania	—	—	—	150	860	1,530
Serbia	—	—	—	—	100	340
Bulgaria	—	—	—	—	200	430
Greece	—	—	—	—	10	370
Turkey	—	—	40	390	700	900
Europe total	1,879	14,465	31,885	63,300	101,720	130,000
United States	2,820	9,020	30,630	53,400	93,670	156,080
Canada	16	70	2,090	2,500	6,890	12,700
Mexico	—	—	—	220	660	5,010
Peru	—	—	50	250	1,180	1,630
Chile	—	—	120	450	1,100	1,750
Brazil	—	—	135	505	2,175	5,580
Argentina	—	—	15	640	1,540	5,550
Uruguay	—	—	—	60	270	450
Japan	—	—	—	—	75	910
India	—	—	840	4,830	9,310	15,250
Australia	—	—	250	1,230	5,390	10,140
South Africa	—	—	—	—	1,010	2,010
Algeria	—	—	—	—	780	1,840
Egypt	—	—	275	550	1,120	1,260
West Indies	—	—	—	100	650	1,280
Various	—	—	—	200	900	2,870
World total	4,715	23,555	66,290	128,235	228,400	354,310
Annual average rate of increase (%)		18.0	10.9	6.8	5.9	5.6

Source: Adapted from Michael Mulhall, *The Dictionary of Statistics* (London: Routledge, 1892), p. 495.

be produced or shipped economically. The steel industry was, at first, an adjunct of the railroad industry. But as the expansion of the railways waned, steel was successively a major input in the construction of machine tools, skyscrapers, long-distance ships, and, after a while, automobiles.

The full revolutionary impact of railroadization is difficult to measure. It had powerful, multiple effects: it lowered transport costs; brought new areas and supplies into national and international markets; in some cases helped generate new export earnings that permitted the whole process of development to move ahead at a higher rate; stimulated expansion in output and the accelerated adoption of new technologies in the coal, iron, and engineering industries; set up pressure (via the need for more durable rails) that helped give birth to the modern steel industry; altered and modernized the institutions of capital formation; and accelerated the pace of urbanization, with all of its dynamic playback effects on economic as well as social and political development.

The Third Industrial Revolution:
The Internal Combustion Engine, Electricity,
and Modern Chemicals

There is a paradox concerning science and the Industrial Revolution. On the one hand, the psychological dimension of the Scientific Revolution was critical to the development of the preconditions for takeoff in Western Europe and for the British takeoff itself. But invention and innovation were only obliquely linked to the scientific revolution.

Take, for example, the intriguing case of Nicolas Leblanc's method of manufacturing soda. This method evolved late in the 18th century under the supervision of scientists of the French Academy. Charles Gillispie, the historian of this period of French science and innovation, writes:

> Leblanc seems to have found his process, not through some flashing theoretical insight, but by means of a fallacious analogy with the smelting of iron ore. Not only so, but after he had worked it out, neither he nor any of the other artisans interested in alkali production made any attempt to investigate or explain the nature of the reactions involved. They concentrated their efforts—though for a long time with no success—on trying to make money by one method or another—in Leblanc's case by first persuading the Government to subsidize him.[7]

Perhaps James Watt had it right. He was a toolmaker for the professors at Glasgow University, including Joseph Black. He was asked if Black's theory of latent heat had suggested his separate condenser for the steam engine: "Although Dr. Black's theory of latent heat did not suggest my improvements on the steam-engine, yet the knowledge upon various subjects which he was pleased to communicate to me, and the correct modes of reasoning, and of making experiments of which he set me the example, certainly conduced very much to facilitate the progress of my inventions."[8]

That is the way it was with the major inventions of the first and second Industrial Revolutions, including cheap steel. People learned to make cheap steel before the chemistry of steel was established; and, of course, the problems of the railroads were solved by human ingenuity, not by the direct application of scientific principles.

It was a bit different in the third Industrial Revolution. Whereas Ford's moving assembly line and, indeed, the Model-T were, again, the products of an engineer's ingenuity, the work on chemicals and electricity was influenced by the concurrent scientific work in those fields. It is no accident that Pierre Du Pont's contribution to chemicals (including pharmaceuticals), Charles Kettering's work on the self-starter and the diesel engine, the contribution of the National Advisory Committee for Aeronautics (later NASA) to aerospace, and, above all, the creation of the Bell Laboratories foreshadowed the vital sectors of the post-1950s American economy. These sectors absorbed some 80% of the nation's research and development.

Thus, the third Industrial Revolution was somewhat closer than its predecessors to the unfolding work in science, notably with respect to electricity, chemicals, and aerospace. The tie between General Motors and Kettering, however, did not extend to the post–World War II years. It took the shock of high energy prices and Japanese competition in the 1970s and 1980s to reestablish the link between high technology and the American automobile industry.

Tables 3.2 and 3.3 and Figure 3.6 show the typical momentum of the leading sectors of the third Industrial Revolution. They capture the following:

1. The pre-1914 American lead in the production of private automobiles; the leap in 1914–1915 when the moving assembly line for the Model-T came in; the continued momentum in the 1920s compared to the countries of Europe; the relative catching up of Europe during the depression of the 1930s; the resumption of momentum

Table 3.2. Number of Private Automobiles in Use Per Million Population in Certain Countries, 1900–1958

Year	United States	Canada	France	Great Britain	Germany	Italy	Japan	Russia
1900	100	—	80	—	—	—	—	—
1901	190	—	—	—	—	—	—	—
1902	290	—	—	—	—	—	—	—
1903	410	—	—	—	—	—	—	—
1904	670	86	—	220	—	—	—	—
1905	920	100	560	410	—	—	—	—
1906	1,240	230	—	600	—	—	—	—
1907	1,610	330	—	830	—	—	—	—
1908	2,190	470	—	1,030	—	—	—	—
1909	3,380	710	—	1,200	—	—	—	—
1910	4,960	1,320	1,370	1,310	—	—	—	—
1911	6,590	3,020	—	1,760	—	400	—	—
1912	9,460	4,930	—	2,150	—	480	—	—
1913	12,200	7,130	2,290	2,560	740	580	20	52
1914	16,800	9,420	2,710	3,160	—	610	—	—
1915	23,200	—	—	—	—	—	—	—
1916	33,000	—	—	—	—	—	—	—
1917	45,800	—	—	—	—	—	—	—
1918	53,800	—	—	—	—	—	—	—
1919	63,900	41,200	—	—	—	670	70	—
1920	76,400	47,800	3,460	4,440	—	870	100	—
1921	84,900	48,100[b]	4,410	5,660[a]	970	900	140	—
1922	97,300	51,800	5,500	7,320[a]	1,340	1,070	170	—
1923	118,000	57,200	6,670	8,870	1,610	1,390	210	—
1924	135,000	62,800	8,730	10,900	2,110	1,460	250	47
1925	151,000	68,800	11,200	13,300	2,770	2,160	350	53
1926	161,000	77,900	13,200	15,400	3,250	2,650	460[a]	54
1927	169,000	85,200	15,700	17,600	4,180	2,980	580	56
1928	177,000	93,700	18,500	19,800	5,460	3,570	760	57
1929	189,000	101,000	22,600	21,800	6,690	4,170	820	69[a]
1930	186,000	103,000	26,700	23,300	7,700	4,460	880[a]	61
1931	180,000	98,700[a]	29,900	24,000	7,990	4,490	980	68[a]
1932	167,000	90,000	30,600	24,800	7,570	4,510	1,010	92
1933	164,000	86,200	33,300	26,400	7,910	5,200	1,020	157[a]
1934	170,000	90,900	34,100	28,600	10,200	5,560	1,120[a]	201
1935	177,000	91,300	—	32,400[a]	12,100	5,700	1,200	260
1936	188,000	95,100	40,300	35,900	14,300	5,160	—	270
1937	197,000	99,900	41,900	39,100	16,600	6,250	850[b]	380[a]
1938	194,000	104,000	44,100	42,100	19,000	6,610	830	500
1939	200,000	106,000	49,000	43,600[a]	17,800[b]	6,710	—	—
1940	207,000	—	—	—	—	—	—	—
1941	222,000	—	—	—	—	—	—	930
1942	—	—	—	—	—	—	—	—
1943	—	—	—	—	—	—	—	—
1944	—	—	—	—	—	—	—	—

(*continued*)

Table 3.2. (*continued*)

Year	United States	Canada	France	Great Britain	Germany	Italy	Japan	Russia
1945	—	—	—	—	—	—	—	—
1946	201,000	100,000	38,300	37,300[a]	—	3,240	—	1,100[b]
1947	214,000	109,000	—	40,600	4,160	4,020	360	—
1948	227,000	117,000	36,700	40,500	4,650[a]	4,730	380	—
1949	244,000	124,000[a]	36,500	43,800	7,480	5,750	390	—
1950	266,000	139,000	—	46,100	10,700	7,310	520	—
1951	277,000	150,000	37,900[a]	48,600	14,100	9,010	680	1,000
1952	280,000	159,000	41,300	51,100	18,500[a]	10,800	1,020	—
1953	292,000	169,000	47,200	56,100	23,000	12,900	1,320	1,200
1954	300,000	175,000	62,100[a]	62,800	28,000[a]	15,500	1,560	—
1955	316,000	186,000	69,300	71,100	33,100	18,200	1,710	1,800
1956	323,000	197,000	79,300	78,100	40,000	21,700	2,000	2,000
1957	327,000	203,000	89,700	83,600	47,300	25,500	2,410	2,000
1958	327,000	—	—	90,300	56,300	—	—	—

Source: Reprinted by permission from W. W. Rostow, *Stages of Economic Growth*, 3d ed. (Cambridge: Cambridge University Press, 1991), p. 171.

[a]Change in series.

[b]Major change in series.

in the post–World War II years but the larger percentage of European gains through 1957.

2. In electricity consumption, the similar figures of the United States and Europe for the period 1920–1929, the relative sag of the United States during the 1930s, and the resumed American relative strength in the postwar period, when both resume growth at a somewhat faster pace than earlier in the century.

But looking past the details, we can see that the 20th century was dominated up to the mid-1970s by the diffusion of the automobile. It had profound social consequences. Not only did this product of the age make possible the suburbs, but it changed everything from courting habits to getaway methods of bank robbers. From our narrow point of view, it represented a combining of the internal-combustion engine, cheap steel from the second technological revolution, the new chemicals from the third—notably, the cracking of petroleum and vulcanizing of rubber—and electricity derived from batteries in the ignition system. In chemicals the United States was behind Europe until after World War II except for products connected with the automobile.

After World War II, the internal-combustion engine, much refined, permitted the aeronautic and space industry to develop second stage

Table 3.3. Production of Chemicals in Europe, United States, and Rest of World, 1913–1951 (% of World Production)

Product or Product Group	Europe				United States				Rest of World			
	1913	1929	1938	1951	1913	1929	1938	1951	1913	1929	1938	1951
Sulphuric acid	70	52	46	35[a]	27	37	28	42[a]	3	11	26	23[a]
Superphosphates	63	55[b]	45	33[a]	28	28[b]	21	32[a]	9	17[b]	34	35[a]
Nitrogen products	36	59	56	48	5	12	12	27	59	29	32	25
Soda ash	—	46	48	40	—	47	40	42	—	7	12	18
Sodium hydroxide	—	—	50	40	—	—	25	45	—	—	25	15
Chlorine	—	—	60	30	—	—	30	58	—	—	10	12
Calcium carbide	87	(80)	65[c]	60	13	8	9[c]	17	—	(12)	26[c]	23
Benzene	—	—	(75)	(50)	—	—	(20)	(45)	—	—	(5)	(5)
Petroleum products	—	3	5	8[a]	—	78	67	64[a]	—	19	28	28[a]
Natural gas	—	—	3	1	—	—	88	88	—	—	9	11
Chemical products derived from petroleum and natural gas	—	—	—	—	—	—	—	(95)	—	—	—	—
Synthetic dyestuffs	96	95	50	40[a]	2	23	17	33[a]	2	12	33	27[a]
Plastic materials	—	—	60	30	—	—	30	65	—	—	10	5
Synthetic rubber[d]	—	—	85	—	—	—	15	95	—	—	—	5
Total chemical products	58	47[e]	50	33	34	42[e]	30	43	8	11[e]	20	24

Source: Ingvar Svennilson. *Growth and Stagnation in the European Economy* (Geneva: UN Economic Commission for Europe, 1954), p. 165.

Note: Except where noted below, years are given in column headings.

[a]1950.

[b]1928.

[c]1936.

[d]Excluding USSR.

[e]1927.

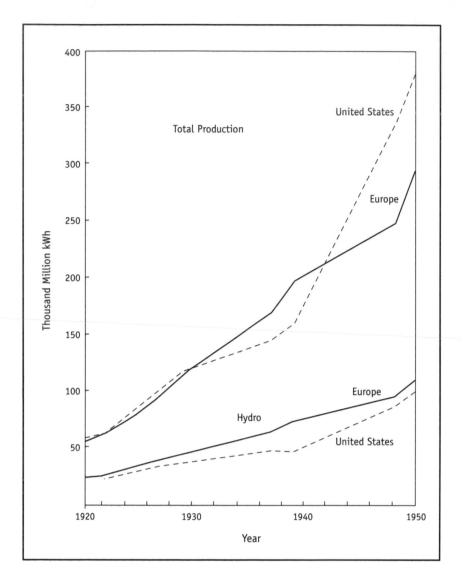

Figure 3.6 Electricity Production in Europe and the United States, 1920–1950.
Source: Ingvar Svennilson, *Growth and Stagnation in the European Economy* (Geneva: UN Economic Commission for Europe, 1954), p. 114.

boosters in the form of jet aircraft and spacecraft, which had undergone a forced development during the war.

The Fourth Industrial Revolution:
Computers, Genetic Engineering, the Laser,
and Still Newer Industrial Materials

The 1970s were notable as a decade that began with a grain shortage at the end of 1972 soon followed by a quadrupling of the oil price. No sooner had the world economy settled down in the mid-1970s than a second oil shock occurred, centered on the 1979 Iranian Revolution. It briefly doubled the oil price and again threw the world economy into disarray. The American economy, which averaged 4.3% unemployment in the 1950s and 1960s, averaged 6.1% unemployment in the 1970s.

In the midst of this disarray and its succession of crises, a sober debate was going on about future productivity. There were, again, pessimists and optimists.[9] One of the pessimists, Edward Renshaw, presented a useful, eclectic summary to a committee of Congress. His central theme was that "the United States and the more industrialized nations of the world cannot avoid a fairly rapid and inevitable decline in the future rate of productivity advance."[10] He argued that labor productivity and other measures of technical progress have increased historically at a fairly regular compound rate; but this does not mean such rates will continue in the future. His most basic hypothesis was that science itself—that is, creativity—was subject to diminishing returns. He argued that an S-shaped curve of returns was likely—that is, a path of acceleration followed by deceleration. He believed the human race might have just passed the halfway mark in the golden age of technological change and therefore would confront a slippery, decelerating slope in the time ahead.

As one would expect, the whole of Renshaw's argument was set against a background of expected diminishing returns and higher relative prices for energy, food, and raw materials. Among Renshaw and those who shared his perspective, we are back to a version of the arguments of *The Limits to Growth*. Somewhat in the spirit of that book, Renshaw argued that, while accepting the inevitability of a progressive retardation in productivity, we should act vigorously in various directions to improve the quality of life and to reduce the boredom of repetitive tasks.

Renshaw could mobilize in 1976 much evidence, including the pessimistic February 16 issue of *Business Week* and a dour report on November 25 from the President's Committee on Science and Technology.

In these transitional years between the third and fourth Industrial Revolutions, there were also optimists. I probed into the basis for optimism. I raised the issue systematically with a group of practicing scientists and those who had a duty, by the nature of their professions, to form an opinion about the prospects for science, asking them if diminishing returns were setting in for science and invention.

The long and short of it was that I ended up concluding that J. M. Clark's dictum was still correct: "The only factor of production not subject to diminishing returns is human creativity." And a good thing, too, for I was writing at the beginning of the fourth Industrial Revolution, which might turn out over the next half century to be the most powerful of them all.

I cite this story, however, to illustrate a major point about the sectoral basis of steady growth. Growth is carried forward by a succession of leading sectors, each subject to retardation, as Figure 3.7A indicates. Only computers and peripherals indicate growth. It is natural that, looking backward, Renshaw, testifying in the mid-1970s before the computer revolution had gained momentum, was impressed by the evident retardation of the key sectors of the third Industrial Revolution and the sluggishness of R&D in those sectors. It was equally natural for someone looking ahead to concentrate on the new sectors beginning to form, of which computers and peripherals were symbolic. In all conscience, the new leading sectors were not difficult to find.

The fourth Industrial Revolution also brought to fruition the explicit linking of science and technology, which suffused only a few sectors in the third Industrial Revolution. This linkage accounts for the pace of obsolescence in computers, which turn over every three years or so. What effect this will have on the timing of sectoral growth is still not known. Will it shorten the time in which a given sector dominates by bringing on the decelerating portion of the sector's curve

---

Figure 3.7 U.S. Sectoral Data, 1970–1994, and U.S. GNP Per Capita and ➤ Industrial Production, 1970–1995 (Moving Five-Year Averages). *Source:* U.S. figures brought up-to-date from W. W. Rostow, *The World Economy: History and Prospect* (Austin: University of Texas Press, 1978), pp. 679–680.

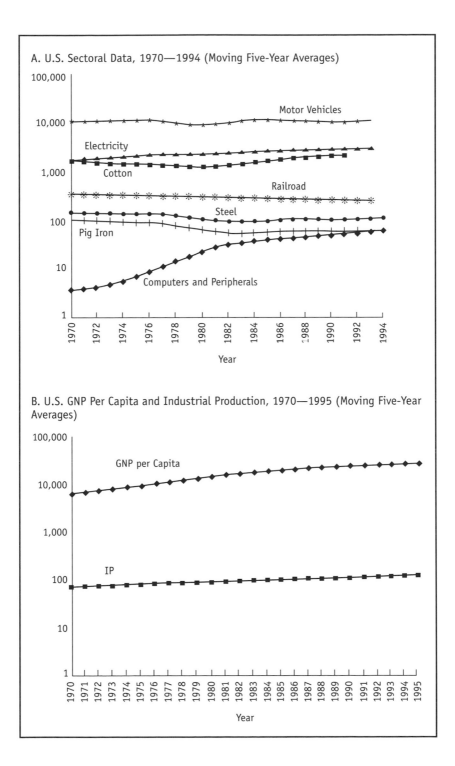

A. U.S. Sectoral Data, 1970—1994 (Moving Five-Year Averages)

Motor Vehicles

Electricity

Cotton

Railroad

Steel

Pig Iron

Computers and Peripherals

Year

B. U.S. GNP Per Capita and Industrial Production, 1970—1995 (Moving Five-Year Averages)

GNP per Capita

IP

Year

sooner? Or will it virtually wipe out the timing of sectoral deceleration by producing a series of scientific boosters to the curves of invention and innovation?

What we do know in the late 1990s that could not be so clearly
discerned 20 years ago is that the current Industrial Revolution has
four major components: computers, genetic engineering, the laser,
and new industrial materials. But surely physicist John Wheeler was
prescient in the mid-1970s when he said about his field: "We would
call today the golden age of astrophysics if all the signs of the time did
not tell us that ten years from now would be closer to the golden age
of astrophysics."[11] And this was true of many fields that now are part
of the fourth Industrial Revolution.

Reflections on Technology and Futurology

When I turned to the future against the background of the four technological revolutions that have taken place over the past two centuries, I found a notable lack of speculation about what may lie ahead
in the fifth Industrial Revolution. We ought to discern now its begin-
nings, at least, if history is any guide. After all, the fourth Industrial
Revolution was clearly, if roughly, evident in the mid-1970s as the third
Industrial Revolution leveled off. There was no lack of speculation
among futurologists as the computer revolution unfolded, along with
the related communication revolution, the revolution in genetic engineering, and the industrial revolution in ceramics, optical fibers, and
other new materials. Perhaps the way to explain the missing speculation about the fifth Industrial Revolution is provided by Ken Coleman,
head of SRI International Technology Management Group, in Barry
Minkin's *Future in Sight* (1995): "Do we need major discontinuity all
the time? . . . Coleman envisions a world where there are fewer and
less important major technological breakthroughs but there is a slow
steady improvement in the conditions of the masses."[12] Minkin's book
looks into the early part of the 21st century, which will still be dominated by the evolution of the fourth Industrial Revolution.

The same can be said of Hamish McRae's *The World in 2020* (1995).
He discusses technology within the bounds of the presently known
breakthroughs. He is considering a time within the fourth Industrial
Revolution. But the same can be said of Herman Kahn's *The Next
200 Years* (1976). He and his team devoted some 140 pages of a 225-

page book to energy, raw materials, food, and the environment but little to new technologies.

Now it is perfectly legitimate to assume that, harking back to Adam Smith's distinction, there will be no more innovations by philosophers involving "new powers." After all, we have only four cases, dominated respectively (but symbolically) by factory-manufactured textiles, railroads and cheap steel, the automobile and the airplane, and the computer. Perhaps the closing of the gap between science and technology will also eliminate the major discontinuities no longer perceived by Ken Coleman. We can speculate about the fifth Industrial Revolution, if it is to happen, and we do. But here we shall address the unfolding of the fourth Industrial Revolution through 2050.

Computers

The chapter on computers in Robert J. Gordon's austere but revolutionary book *The Measurement of Durable Goods Prices* begins with the following quotation: "If the auto industry had done what the computer has done in the last 30 years, a Rolls Royce would cost $2.50 and would get 2,000,000 miles to the gallon."[13] This analogy is meant, of course, to dramatize the extraordinary growth and refinement of the computer market in the past 40 years. The figures are given by units and value of sales in Table 3.4 for 1955, 1965, 1975, 1984,[14] and the totals of units sold and their values are plotted annually in Figures 3.8 and 3.9.

Table 3.4. Growth of the Computer Market, 1955–1984 (Millions of Dollars)

	Mainframes		Minis		Micros		Total	
Year	Units	Value	Units	Value	Units	Value	Units	Value
1955	150	63	—	—	—	—	150	63
1965	5,350	1,770	250	29	—	—	5,600	1,670
1975	6,700	5,410	11,670	642	5,100	77	23,470	6,128
1984	10,700	10,360	72,130	4,185	2,100,000	7,750	2,182,005	22,295

Sources: Reprinted by permission from Robert J. Gordon, *The Measurement of Durable Goods Prices* (Chicago: University of Chicago Press, 1990), p. 193; Marcus E. Einstein and James C. Franklin, "Computer Manufacturing Enters a New Era of Growth," *Monthly Labor Review* 109 (Sept. 1986): 9–16; Montgomery Phister, *Data Processing Technology and Economics*, 2d ed. (Santa Monica, Calif.: DEC, 1979), table II.1.21.

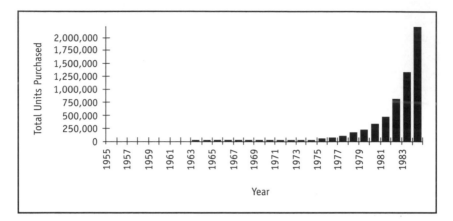

Figure 3.8 U.S. Domestic Purchase of Electronic Computers, 1955–1984: Number of Units. *Sources:* Reprinted by permission from Robert J. Gordon, *The Measurement of Durable Goods Prices* (Chicago: University of Chicago Press, 1990), p. 193.

The history of the computer is relatively straightforward. It is proper to bow respectfully to Charles Babbage. He was a 19th-century successor to Isaac Newton in the Lucasian Chair of Mathematics at Trinity College, Cambridge. He conceived of the computer clearly but was frustrated in finding an industrial source of power. This led him to tour the Western European industrial world, out of which came his best-seller, *On the Economy of Machinery and Manufactures*. He

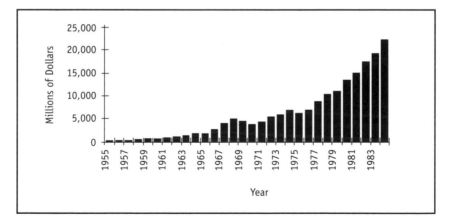

Figure 3.9 U.S. Domestic Purchase of Electronic Computers, 1955–1984: Value of Units. *Sources:* Reprinted by permission from Robert J. Gordon, *The Measurement of Durable Goods Prices* (Chicago: University of Chicago Press, 1990), p. 193.

had a distinct influence on both John Stuart Mill and Karl Marx. The British government, however, despaired of his efforts to construct a calculating machine and ceased their subsidy to him. A model of Babbage's proposed machine has been recently constructed in Britain; with modern power sources, it works.

It was not until World War II that on both sides of the Atlantic computers were constructed to help break German and Japanese codes. The first electronic computer, ENIAC, is described by Gordon:

> The ENIAC had a trifling computational capacity in comparison with today's PCs, yet was gigantic in size, measuring 100 feet long, ten feet high, and three feet wide, and containing about 18,000 vacuum tubes. This machine was programmed by setting thousands of switches, all of which had to be reset by hand in order to run a different program. It is reported to have broken down "only" about once per day.[15]

UNIVAC followed, purchased by the U.S. government to help with the census of 1950 but in fact first used to prove by calculation that Edward Teller's hydrogen bomb would work. The first commercial purchase was in 1955, when the mainframe series in Table 3.5 begins. As background, Gordon lays out the computer generations as follows:

> Early first-generation machines through the late 1950s operated with vacuum tubes, followed by the second-generation machines based on transistors, starting with IBM 7000 series introduced in 1959. The first IBM third-generation machines with integrated circuits were the series 360 models, first installed in 1965. Since the introduction of semiconductor chips, continuous improvements have been achieved by packaging increased numbers of circuits closer together, both lowering the marginal cost of additional memory and reducing instruction execution time.

Computers can handle, store, and make available a steadily increasing volume of information and can perform with increasing speed a steadily increasing number of calculations on that information. Because of these characteristics, the computer has changed virtually every field of science and engineering, the social sciences, the organization of private and public bureaucracies, education, and the shape of the working force. This transformation is impressive but still limited. A computer's impact ranges from the trivial (if not negative) substitution for human telephone operators to pragmatic solution by fast computation of theoretical problems that had been unsolved for centuries; such as the problem in astrophysics of three bodies.[16] The computer has, in

Table 3.5. U.S. Domestic Purchase of Electronic Computers, 1955–1984 (Millions of Dollars)

	Mainframes		Minis		Micros		Total	
Year	Units	Value	Units	Value	Units	Value	Units	Value
1955	150	63	—	—	—	—	150	63
1956	500	152	—	—	—	—	500	152
1957	660	235	—	—	—	—	660	235
1958	970	381	—	—	—	—	970	381
1959	1,150	475	—	—	—	—	1,150	475
1960	1,790	590	—	—	—	—	1,790	590
1961	2,700	180	—	—	—	—	2,700	880
1962	3,470	1,090	—	—	—	—	3,470	1,090
1963	4,200	1,300	—	—	—	—	4,200	1,300
1964	5,600	1,670	—	—	—	—	5,600	1,670
1965	5,350	1,770	250	29	—	—	5,610	1,799
1966	7,250	2,640	385	40	—	—	7,635	2,680
1967	11,200	3,900	720	69	—	—	11,920	3,968
1968	9,100	4,800	1,080	100	—	—	10,180	4,900
1969	6,000	4,150	1,770	152	—	—	7,770	4,302
1970	5,700	3,600	2,620	210	—	—	8,320	3,810
1971	7,600	3,900	2,800	218	—	—	10,400	4,118
1972	10,700	5,000	3,610	271	—	—	14,310	5,271
1973	14,000	5,400	5,270	369	—	—	19,270	5,769
1974	8,600	6,200	8,880	577	—	—	17,480	6,777
1975	6,700	5,410	11,670	642	5,100	77	23,470	6,128
1976	6,750	5,580	17,000	816	25,800	374	49,550	6,770
1977	8,900	6,600	24,550	1,203	58,500	761	91,950	8,563
1978	7,500	7,590	29,550	1,596	115,600	1,098	152,650	10,284
1979	7,200	7,330	35,130	2,038	160,000	1,488	202,330	10,856
1980	9,900	8,840	41,450	2,487	250,500	2,104	301,850	13,431
1981	10,700	9,540	44,100	2,699	385,100	2,503	439,900	14,842
1982	10,600	10,300	47,820	2,821	735,000	4,190	793,420	17,311
1983	9,985	10,480	45,420	3,330	1,260,000	5,300	1,315,405	19,110
1984	10,700	10,360	72,130	4,185	2,100,000	7,750	2,182,005	22,295

Sources: Reprinted by permission from Robert J. Gordon, The Measurement of Durable Goods Prices (Chicago: University of Chicago Press, 1990), p. 193; Marcus E. Einstein and James C. Franklin, "Computer Manufacturing Enters a New Era of Growth," Monthly Labor Review 109 (Sept. 1986): 9–16; Montgomery Phister, Data Processing Technology and Economics, 2d ed. (Santa Monica, Calif.: DEC, 1979), table II.1.21.

addition, become a mammoth leading sector, outstripping the automobile industry in working force, value of output, and proportion of GNP. Moreover, it is evolving rapidly, having gone through three generations—mainframes, minicomputers, and microcomputers—without exhibiting the typical deceleration of a leading sector.

On the other hand, computers up to this point produce more information than people can absorb. Thus, we say, "I am drowning in information" and wonder how to get less but more relevant information. Hamish McRae notes that specialists are needed to render the flow of information "relevant."[17] This, incidentally, is an old problem, familiar to historians and those who have worked in intelligence-gathering operations. Relevance is, of course, a tricky concept both philosophically and in practice.

Nevertheless, there are enthusiasts about the Internet and its future as well as those who deride what it does and is likely to do. On one side is Nicholas Negroponte, author of *Being Digital*.[18] Negroponte is head of a multimedia laboratory at M.I.T. and an enthusiast. His striking dictum is: "Computing is not about computers any more. It is about living."[19] And no doubt he is correct about the quantitative rise, ubiquity, growing power, and diminishing size of the computer. He sees clearly a time when, "as we interconnect ourselves, many of the values of a nation-state will give way to those of both larger and smaller electronic communities."[20] He believes this is the world the young will create. The book, although shot through with almost mystical visions of the world being created by the new media, is mainly about the next steps that might be taken in the hyperactive technical and financial world he inhabits. He switches, for example, from the superiority of E-mail over the fax to Seymour Papert's insights into the proper use of computers in education.

In the end, though, his vision is simple and coherent:

> The forces of nationalism make it too easy to be cynical and dismiss any broad-stroke attempt at world unification. But in the digital world, previously impossible solutions become viable.
>
> While the politicians struggle with the baggage of history, a new generation is emerging from the digital landscape free of many of the old prejudices. These kids are released from the limitation of geographic proximity as the sole basis of friendship, collaboration, play, and neighborhood. Digital technology can be a natural force drawing people into greater world harmony.
>
> But more than anything, my optimism comes from the empowering nature of being digital. The access, the mobility and the ability to effect change are what will make the future so different from the present. The information superhighway may be mostly hype today, but it is an understatement about tomorrow. It will exist beyond people's wildest predictions.[21]

Clifford Stoll's book *Silicon Snake Oil* is the work of an astronomer knowledgeable about computers and is the polar opposite of

Negroponte's. Stoll believes, using Negroponte's phrase, that the information highway will continue to be "mostly hype." His book is a lively tour through the arguments for getting on the Internet and staying the course. For each argument he applies a lucid if garrulous counterargument. His conclusion and theme are stated thus:

> The popular mythos tells us that networks are powerful, global, fast, and inexpensive. It's the place to meet friends and carry on business. There, you'll find entertainment, expertise, and education. In short, it's important to be on line.
>
> It ain't necessarily so.
>
> Our networks can be frustrating, expensive, unreliable connections that get in the way of useful work. It is an overpromoted, hollow world, devoid of warmth and human kindness.
>
> The heavily promoted information infrastructure addresses few social needs or business concerns. At the same time, it directly threatens precious parts of our society, including schools, libraries, and social institutions.
>
> No birds sing.
>
> For all the promises of virtual communities, it's more important to live a real life in a real neighborhood.[22]

Against this controversial background, I am not inclined to pontificate about what a computerized world might be like in 2050. Therefore, I am inclined at this stage to present three scenarios:

1. Perhaps there will be a breakthrough in computers that will allow them to approximate the skill of the human brain in reacting and adjusting to changing circumstances. At the moment, the smaller switches in the human brain have an advantage over the computer of some nine orders of magnitude. It is conceivable that linking the computer revolution to the revolution in biology will solve this problem. Work to bring these two revolutions together is now under way. This, indeed, will be a major breakthrough and a discontinuity that cannot now be described, nor can its unfolding be specified.

2. Perhaps a phase of technical deceleration will come. The world will be transformed—as it was by the factory, the railway, the telephone, and the automobile—but it will still be recognizable. The limits of computers will be recognized as well as their virtues.

3. Perhaps the computer will be recognized as a powerful tool that will work only if it is in harness with and directed by good, able human beings. For example, in education, computers are powerful when combined with good teachers but not very effective by themselves in the laboratories to which they are often confined.

This agnostic conclusion (which makes me lean toward scenario 3) is based on convergence of Plato, David Hume, and Sigmund Freud, who all saw human beings as governed by three variables: the "spirited" side of mankind, "action," and the "id"; the voracious side of mankind, "appetite," "pleasure," and "ego"; and the civilizing side of mankind, "reason," sympathy," and the "superego." These men were not merely philosophers. They were poets. Their three similar categories were evocative. Human beings are even more complex than they made out. Hume once wrote, "These principles of human nature, you'll say, are contradictory; but what is man but a heap of contradictions?" I believe we will only achieve the world we want by heightening reason, sympathy, and superego; expressing in moderation appetite, pleasure, and ego; and channeling spirit, action, and id in benign directions. At the moment, the computer can't do this by itself, and it might never be able to do it. It follows, among other things, that I find the computer highway unlikely to produce a sea change in human and international relations; but, as Keynes said, the unexpected might happen.

Genetic Engineering

Like most innovations, genetic engineering has a long, pre-commercial history (see Table 3.6). The scientific turning point was the work of James Watson and Francis Crick in discovering the double-helix structure of DNA (1953). The commercial breakthrough was the founding of Genentech in 1976.

There is a curious tentative, if not negative, quality to the relevance of genetic engineering to agriculture. An evaluation by the *Economist*, says, almost as an afterthought: "Biotechnology may yet revolutionize farming worldwide."[23] Hamish McRae concludes: "It is not clear that another green revolution is imminent—without one, it may be impossible to increase yields by the amounts needed."[24] The evaluation of Lester R. Brown and John E. Young includes as its heading "Biotechnology: A Limited Contribution."[25] And the authoritative World Bank technical paper on the subject is entitled *Agricultural Biotechnology: The Next "Green Revolution"?*[26]

This equivocation stems from three factors. First, it stems from the difference between the agricultural priorities of the presently developed countries and those of presently developing countries. The

Table 3.6. Evolution of the Science of Genetics, Leading to Modern Biotechnology, 1866–1988

Year	Event
1866	Mendel postulates a set of rules to explain the inheritance of biological characteristics in living organisms.
1900	Mendelian law rediscovered after independent experimental evidence confirms Mendel's basic principles.
1903	Sutton postulates that genes are located on chromosomes.
1910	Morgan's experiments prove genes are located on chromosomes.
1911	Johannsen devises the term *gene* and distinguishes genotypes (determined by genetic composition) and phenotypes (influenced by environment).
1922	Morgan and colleagues develop gene-mapping techniques and prepare gene map of fruit fly chromosomes, ultimately containing over 2,000 genes.
1944	Avery, McLeod, and McCarty demonstrate that genes are composed of deoxyribonucleic acid (DNA) rather than protein.
1952	Hershey and Chase confirm role of DNA as the basic genetic material.
1953	Watson and Crick discover the double-helix structure of DNA.
1960	Genetic code deciphered.
1971	Cohen and Boyer develop initial techniques for recombinant DNA technology to allow transfer of genetic material from one organism to another.
1973	First gene (for insulin production) cloned, using recombinant DNA technology.
1974	First expression in bacteria of a gene cloned from a different species.
1976	First new biotechnology firm established to exploit recombinant DNA technology (Genentech in United States).
1980	U.S. Supreme Court rules that micro-organisms can be patented under existing law (*Diamond v. Chakrabarty*). Cohen/Boyer patent issued on the technique for the construction of recombinant DNA.
1982	First recombinant DNA animal vaccine approved for sale in Europe (colibaciliosis). First recombinant DNA pharmaceutical (insulin) approved for sale in the United States and United Kingdom. First successful transfer of a gene from one animal species to another (a transgenic mouse carrying the gene for rat growth hormone). First transgenic plant produced, using an Agrobacterium transformation system.
1983	First successful transfer of a plant gene from one species to another.
1985	U.S. Patent Office extends patent protection to genetically engineered plants.
1986	Transgenic pigs produced carrying the gene for human growth hormone.
1987	First field trials in United States of transgenic plants (tomatoes with a gene for insect resistance).
	First field trials in United States of genetically engineered micro-organisms.
1988	U.S. Patent Office extends patent protection to genetically engineered animals. First genetically modified micro-organism approved for commercial sale as biocontrol agent of a plant disease (crown-gall of fruit trees in Australia).

Source: *Agricultural Biotechnology: The Next "Green Revolution"?*, World Bank Technical Paper no. 133 (Washington, D.C., 1991), p. 3.

former are mainly concerned with expanding the availability and cutting the price of proteins, whereas the major concern of presently developing countries, given the scale of undernourishment, is the availability and price of basic grains. The Green Revolution, after all, had its major impact in the evolution of highly productive strains of wheat and rice in, respectively, Mexico (Chapingo) and the Philippines (Los Baños).

Second, this difference in interest is heightened by characteristics of the R&D process in the world of modern genetic engineering: R&D is heavily concentrated in the developed countries, and it is largely in the hands of private firms. Profits in agriculture are made in the areas of proteins, vegetables, and fruit rather than basic grains, which are in surplus in both the United States and Western Europe. These areas, with populations leveling off, are likely to be more concerned with increasing the quality of diet than with making a gross quantitative leap forward in basic grains. The Green Revolution in wheat and rice was watched over, after all, by nonprofit international laboratories.

Third, the most exciting R&D enterprise in the field of genetic engineering is the mapping of the human genes in the Genome Project. This massive effort is likely to yield, at first, mainly medical results.

On the whole, then, the early results of genetic engineering are likely for multiple reasons to be focused around the mitigation or cure of human diseases and the other commercial interests of the advanced industrial countries (see Figure 3.10). It is not to be ruled out that, over a longer period, genetic engineering will yield major agricultural results of interest to developing countries—even another Green Revolution. But we should not count on a major breakthrough.

Other Possibilities

The United Nations study of *Global Outlook 2000* (1990) states in summary: "Information technology, new materials technology, biotechnology, space, and nuclear technology are widely recognized to be the five most important new technologies."[27] These technologies are ranked with respect to their impact on employment by the year 2000. Here, the criterion is somewhat different: It is whether by 2050

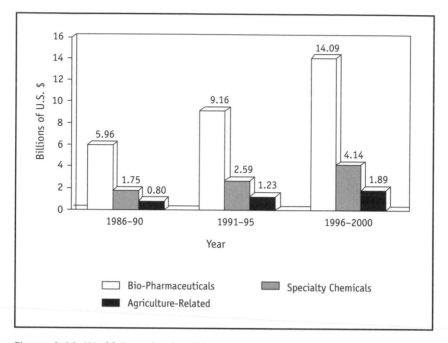

Figure 3.10 World Biotechnology Market (Annual Average). *Source: Global Outlook, 2000* (New York: United Nations Publications, 1990), p. 157.

they are likely to yield a fundamental breakthrough in the production process. That is the rationale for going into such detail on the computer and genetic engineering.

Against this criterion, the other innovations of our time have had wide diffusion and widespread consequences. The laser, for example, has useful applications that stretch from the supermarket to eye surgery to industrial processes. But the literature about them, in general, does not suggest that they will produce a breakthrough that will alter the main themes of this exposition. The new industrial materials (notably ceramics, polymers, and composites) will play an important part in cutting the weight of both automobiles and aircraft, as they already have.[28] The brute fact is that the per unit consumption of raw materials in industrial production has declined rapidly in recent years. This has had important effects that will continue but do not constitute a breakthrough. Yet a half century is quite a long time. Lasers, for example, might yet play an important part in making fusion power commercially viable.

Military R&D

This chapter would be incomplete without a word on the broad impact of military R&D. After all, World War II yielded the computer, nuclear power plants, jet engines, radar, rockets, and space satellites as by-products of military innovation. At the moment, military R&D expenditures in the United States are $45 billion as opposed to only $75 billion in the whole private civilian sector. Three areas under R&D development in the military may have, in time, important civil applications: the improvement of lasers for purposes of precision bombing; electric magnet guns; and space-based weapons systems for missile defense.

Conclusion

This chapter concerns the technical and investment pattern to be expected in the period ahead. It is to be read in conjunction with the previous chapter on the probable course of population and the stages of growth on the world scene. Taken together they set out many of the problems that must be solved to create the new political economy that the 21st century will require.

Let us assume that the rise in population and industrial growth in the developing world does not produce unmanageable global crisis in the first quarter of the 21st century. Then the common political economy problem of the now developed and the newly developed nations will become the management of societies of constant population framed by continuing allocations to R&D. As already noted, this vision dates back to J. S. Mill (1806–1873). In his *Principles*, Mill sets out five cases employing the three variables that determined the outcome: population, capital, and the arts of production. If population was fixed by birth control, J. R. Hicks thus phrased Mill's outcome: "Instead of land being the main fixed factor, so that (as in the Ricardian stationary state) surplus production is swallowed up in rent, it is labour that becomes the main fixed factor, so that surplus production can be made to go, at least in large measure, to wages. This is an altogether different, and much more agreeable, picture. The Stationary State is no longer a horror. It becomes an objective at which to aim."[29]

Mill explicitly assumed that an increase in "the arts of production" was possible. Thus, this stationary state might include a rise of real wages for labor. Another passage from Mill makes this connection between new technology, real wages, and a static population even more explicit: "There is hardly any creation of fixed capital which, when it proves successful, does not cheapen the articles on which wages are habitually expended. . . . All these improvements make the labourers better off with the same money wages, better off if they do not increase their rate of multiplication."[30]

That is the prospect envisaged here. But three challenges must be met before this outcome is possible. First, as the portion of investment now devoted to meeting the needs of an expanding population declines, there must be a switch to infrastructure and other investment that will increase the quality of life of a static population. Second, there must be an increase in the working force plus possibly a transfer of income to meet the needs of an enlarged aging population. And third, there must be an increase of public R&D to balance the possible decline in private R&D as population levels off.

FOUR

Relative Prices

Do Regular, Long Relative-Price Cycles Exist?

In viewing the time ahead, especially the next quarter century, I have been inclined to conclude that the industrial progress of India, China, Southeast Asia, and the major countries of Latin America are likely to produce a phase of rising prices in foodstuffs and raw materials and increased outlays to deal with the forces of environmental degradation. It is my hypothesis that for a time, in the early part of the 21st century, these developments will outstrip the deceleration of population. The more or less regular occurrence of such phases of demand pressure has marked the story of the world economy since the end of the 18th century.

At least since about 1789, there have been successive periods when foodstuffs and raw materials were expensive and then cheap, relative to manufactured goods. From 1789 to 1920, these periods lasted about 25 years. After 1920, the cycles were much less regular and were significantly affected by wars, by the successive rise in the importance of oil, by outlays to preserve the environment, and finally by the involvement more directly of politics in the setting of basic prices.

But economic historians are likely to agree that the period 1789–1914 was marked by two-and-a-half long relative-price cycles in raw material versus manufactured goods (see Figure 4.1). Although he had several predecessors, N. D. Kondratieff, a Russian economist who was immortalized by Joseph Schumpeter as the discoverer of the Kondratieff cycle or long wave, identified, dated, and discussed analytically this long cycle in the interwar years. He died in one of Joseph Stalin's labor camps in Siberia.

The approximate dates and length of these long cycles through 1920 are shown in Table 4.1. The successive phases of falling and rising relative prices continued to follow one another despite two world wars, a pathological interwar period, and an unexpected postwar recovery, illustrated in Table 4.2. The peak of the early 1980s came in the second quarter of 1982 (or, on an annual basis, in 1981). More fundamental to the rhythm of the Kondratieff cycles, however, are these two characteristics of the 1970s:

1. The long cycles from 1790 to the early 1970s were focused around wheat and other mainly agricultural materials. As befitted the automobile age that emerged after World War II, the raw materials around which the price fluctuations of the 1970s and the 1980s took

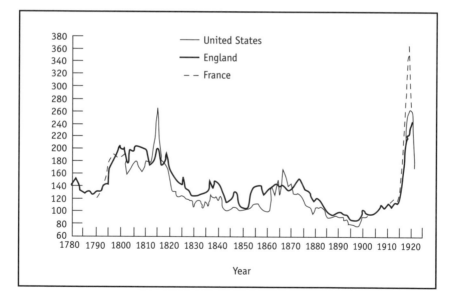

Figure 4.1 Index Numbers of Commodity Prices, 1780–1922: England, United States, France (1901–1910 = 100). *Source:* Reprinted by permission from N. D. Kondratieff, "The Long Waves of Economic Life," *Review of Economic Statistics* 17, no. 6 (1935): 106.

Table 4.1. Relative Price Cycles, 1789–1920

Cycle	Length
Trough about 1789	
Peak about 1814	25 years
Trough about 1849	35 years
Peak about 1873	24 years
Trough about 1896	23 years
Peak about 1920	24 years

place were in good part the relative movements in energy prices: oil, gas, coal, and so on.

2. The policies of governments toward basic commodities played a modest part in the movement through 1914. Thereafter they were a major element in the story, notably through agricultural subsidies and tariffs, plus stockpiling schemes as well as the devastation caused by two world wars. In the 1970s, two oil shocks related to the role of governments: The Organization of Petroleum Exporting Countries (OPEC) quadrupled the oil price in the early years of the decade, and the political crisis in Iran toward the decade's end caused a further doubling of oil prices. These not only produced abnormally large speculative price increases but also set in motion abnormally large and prompt reactions in the form of oil production from new sources and energy-saving measures.

The general answer to the question posed at the beginning of this section, then, is yes, there have been and there are likely to be long waves or cycles in the relative prices of raw materials versus manufactures. This answer has to be given, however, with a historian's acceptance that many forces are now simultaneously at work in the world economy, some of them economic, some noneconomic. These long cycles are woven together with other economic factors, for example,

Table 4.2. Relative Price Cycles, 1920–1982

Cycle	Length
Peak about 1920	24 years
Trough about 1933	13 years
Peak about 1951	18 years
Trough about 1972	21 years
Peak about 1981–1982	9–10 years

conventional business cycles (see Chapter 5). They are also affected by noneconomic events such as wars, and, in the past quarter century, they are affected by the policies of governments. Above all, they are not immune to changes in the relative importance of grain, oil, and environmental investment. To give some notion of how these economic and noneconomic forces have woven together, I will briefly summarize the history of these long cycles.

Kondratieff Cycles through 1914

The latter part of the 18th century was a period when population growth accelerated and pressed against the domestic food supply. Early in the 18th century, Britain was a food exporter, but food imports were rising as a proportion of consumption when war broke out in 1793. The war disrupted the flow of grain from the continent. This loss was made good in part by the increase in exports of flour from the United States but mainly by an increase in British agricultural production made profitable by an average higher range of prices. This generalized view covers the whole period from the outbreak of war in 1793 to the 1802 Peace of Amiens and, after war resumed in 1803, to its end in 1815.

The wheat price peaked, however, as early as 1812 and fell rapidly. Toward the end of 1813, Napoleon, hard-pressed by his retreat, opened the French ports for exports of wheat to Britain with a memorable phrase in a memo of December 22, 1812, to his minister of commerce: "Undoubtedly it is necessary to harm our foes, but above all we must live."[1]

The Kondratieff downswing to the late 1840s is less erratic than the upswing that proceded it, less influenced by the impact of the success or failure of blockades or the course of military events on both sides of the Atlantic. Major business cycles peaked in 1825, 1836, and 1845 (1847 in the United States), but the decline in prices continued as a matter of trend from 1815 to 1848 — a rather classic Kondratieff downswing. It was broken only in the 1830s by the rise in cotton prices and investment in additional American cotton land.

The long upswing to 1872 was affected by the Crimean War, the Indian Mutiny, Bismarck's three wars of the 1860s, and, of course, the Civil War in the United States. Still, the major cycles continue their roughly regular rhythm, peaking in 1858, 1866, and 1873.

The course of food prices was much affected, with a lag, by the opening of the American Middle West with railways in 1850s and the post–Civil War drive to the West Coast. An enormous volume of wheat acreage was thus made available, laying the basis for the decline in the wheat price from 1873 to the mid-1890s. This decline brought about the first protracted rise in the real wages of the urban workforce throughout the industrial world. This decline was driven forward not only by new suppliers of a key raw material but also by a technological breakthrough: long-distance steel ships and a consequent dramatic decline in freight rates (see Figure 4.2).

A clear-cut break in prices occurred in the mid-1890s a few years after the end of the American Frontier was announced. The movement of world prices is captured in Table 4.3. It is impossible here to

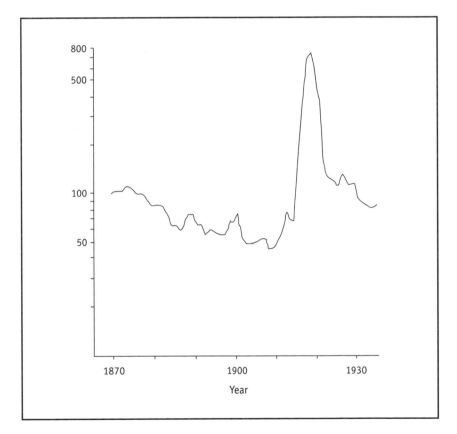

Figure 4.2 Index of Tramp Shipping Freights, 1869–1935. *Source:* Reprinted by permission from L. Isseriis, "Tramp Shipping Cargoes and Freights," in B. R. Mitchell and Phyllis Deane, *Abstract of British Historical Statistics* (Cambridge: Cambridge University Press, 1971), p. 224.

Table 4.3. Index of Raw-Material Prices, United Kingdom, 1870–1913 (1900 = 100)

Year	Coal	Copper: Ore and Regulus	Crude Zinc	Block Tin	Lead	Cotton	Imported Wool	Wood and Timber	Imported Wheat
Peak, Early 1870s	124 (1873)	103 (1872)	113 (1873)	105 (1872)	144 (1873)	163 (1872)	161 (1875)	180 (1874)	191 (1873)
Trough, 1890s	53 (1896)	56 (1894)	72 (1895)	45 (1896)	55 (1894)	69 (1898)	84 (1897)	88 (1895)	79 (1894)
1913	84	92	115	154	107	140	108	96	122

Source: William Page, ed., *Commerce and Industry: Statistical Tables* (London: Constable, 1919), pp. 218, 222.

trace out in the detail devoted to wheat the course of events between the 1870s and 1914 for all of the major commodities. But as Table 4.3 makes clear, the irregular downward sweep from the early 1870s to a trough in the 1890s and the lift to a higher range in the pre-1914 years suffused a good many raw material prices.

World War I produced typical food and raw-material shortages that continued in the still-impoverished postwar years to 1920. The upward trend that began in the second half of the 1890s gave way, then, to a war-distorted version of a Kondratieff downswing.

Interwar Cycles

Except in the United States and Japan, the period 1920–1929 was a time of troubles in the major countries of the world economy (Table 4.4). In Britain, Scandinavia, and Germany (1923–1929) there was an average double-digit unemployment. France did a bit better, especially from 1925 to 1931, when French devaluation made Paris an attractive place to visit and live. But the demand for food and industrial materials was weak, and various stockpiling and protective schemes were put into effect among producers around the world. The prices of these commodities were low compared to manufactured goods, and this benefited those who had regular jobs in the cities.

The 1920s were prosperous, however, compared to the Great Depression of 1929–1933, when the whole fabric of the world economy fell apart. Unemployment rose as high as 22% in Britain, over 30% in Scandinavia and Germany, and 27% in the United States. It was even

Table 4.4. Unemployment in Six European Countries and the United States, 1921–1938 (Unemployed as % of Labor Force)

	United Kingdom	Germany	Sweden	Denmark	Norway	Austria	United States
1921	17.0	2.9	26.1	19.7	17.7	—	11.7
1922	14.3	1.5	22.7	19.2	17.1	—	6.7
1923	11.7	9.7	12.5	12.6	10.6	—	2.4
1924	10.3	14.2	10.1	10.7	8.5	—	5.0
1925	11.3	6.9	11.1	14.8	13.1	—	3.2
1926	12.5	18.1	12.2	20.6	24.3	—	1.9
1927	9.7	8.8	12.0	22.5	25.4	13.6	3.3
1928	10.8	8.4	10.6	18.5	19.2	12.1	4.2
1929	10.4	13.1	10.7	15.5	15.4	12.3	3.2
1930	16.1	22.2	12.2	13.7	16.6	15.0	8.7
1931	21.3	33.7	17.2	17.9	22.3	20.3	15.9
1932	22.1	43.7 (30.1)	22.8	31.7	30.8	26.1	23.6
1933	19.9	(26.3)	23.7	28.8	33.4	29.0	24.9
1934	16.7	(14.9)	18.9	22.1	30.7	26.3	21.7
1935	15.5	(11.6)	16.1	19.7	25.3	23.4	20.1
1936	13.1	(8.3)	13.6	19.3	18.8	22.9	16.9
1937	10.8	(4.6)	11.6	21.9	20.0	20.4	14.3
1938	12.9	(2.1)	11.8	21.3	22.0	—	19.0

Sources: Ingvar Svennilson, *Growth and Stagnation in the European Economy* (Geneva: UN Economic Commission for Europe, 1954), p. 31; U.S. Department of Commerce, Bureau of Census, *Historical Statistics of the United States* (Washington, D.C.: Government Printing Office, 1975), p. 135; figures in parentheses are from B. R. Mitchell, *European Historical Statistics* (London: Macmillan, 1975), p. 170.

extremely serious in France and Japan, which generally did not experience severe unemployment in depressions.

Cooperation failed in 1933 as each country undertook more or less independent recovery measures. When the smoke had begun to clear, the Japanese military was installed in Tokyo, Adolph Hitler was in power in Berlin, and Benito Mussolini, who had taken over Italy in 1922, was preparing to join Japan and Germany in their global adventures. Recovery proceeded rapidly in Germany and Japan, aided by the armaments expansion in Germany after 1936 and in Japan after 1931.[2] Elsewhere recovery was partial. At the peak in 1937, there was still double-digit unemployment in Britain, Scandinavia, and the United States.

Relative prices bottomed out in 1933 and rose more rapidly than industrial prices before, during, and after World War II. They broke downward in 1951 as world agricultural production expanded, beginning just over 20 years of relative decline.

The Postwar Boom, 1951–1972

The period 1951–1972 will be much studied in economic history. The advanced industrial countries grew at about three times their historic average, with low levels of unemployment. Foodstuffs and raw-material prices fell off sharply in the 1950s, gradually decelerating in their decline; but overall this was a rather shapely Kondratieff downswing like those of 1815–1848 and 1873–1896. Japan and Western Europe went forward faster than the United States, their advance focused on automobiles and consumer durables. These industrialized countries gained much ground in the fields the United States had earlier pioneered. Then, at the end of 1972, the roof fell in, with the crises in grain prices followed in 1973 by the quadrupling of oil prices by OPEC.

Although his analysis only covers through 1965, Miyosei Shinohara's disaggregated view of the postwar Japanese economy reveals clearly the role of the automobile sector in the great Japanese boom.[3] Shinohara notes that postwar Japan successfully made the structural adjustment that Britain made so imperfectly in the 1920s and 1930s. In one grandiose sweep (with minor retardations along the way), Japan moved from a state of technological maturity at a low level of income per capita to high mass consumption at a Western European level. Meanwhile, Western Europe, its interwar problems overcome, was also moving through this stage at a rapid but more decorous pace, with Spain and Italy (like Japan) catching up with the industrial nations whose takeoffs had come earlier.

The boom in Western Europe and Japan after 1951 had a special character. It involved a convergence of favorable terms of trade, a catching up with U.S. patterns of durable consumer-goods consumption, including motor cars, and enlarged social expenditures by governments. This boom was almost totally unexpected by conventional economists, who expected a return to the chronic depression of the 1930s. This error stemmed from two supply factors that were largely ignored by the Keynesian (and monetarist) analysts of the time: the favorable terms of trade for the industrial countries and the large technological gap between the United States on the one hand and Western Europe and Japan on the other.

The underdeveloped areas, which at that time relied heavily on the prices of foodstuffs and raw-material exports, were depressed, notably in the 1950s. Their protests and palpable hard times, combined with Cold War competition and simple equity, led to a substantial increase in foreign aid. This came in the 1960s, after the worst of the fall in the international terms of trade had taken place. Relative prices leveled out at a low rate, rising somewhat in the late 1960s as stocks were drawn down in food and energy.

The world economy that emerged and moved forward in this rather remarkable way during the quarter century after World War II generated four major vulnerabilities. First, the rate of population increase in the less-developed parts of the world began in the 1970s to outstrip the rate of increase in world agricultural production. This process was exacerbated by faulty doctrines of economic growth in the less-developed parts of the world, illusions about American agricultural surpluses, and, as a consequence, inadequate allocation of resources to agricultural sectors. World stocks of grain fell, and idled grain lands were put back into production in the United States.

Second, the rate of industrial expansion in the more-developed parts of the world, pulled forward by energy-intensive leading sectors, began in the 1960s to draw down ready energy reserves in the Western Hemisphere, which left the world vulnerable to monopolistic price setting by OPEC.

Third, endemic inflation existed in the more-developed nations, as relatively high levels of employment, the expectation that such levels would be sustained, and the relative exhaustion of supplies of rural and migrant labor caused the gap between wage increases and productivity increases to widen progressively, notably after 1965.

Fourth, the post–World War II currency system set up at Bretton Woods had depended on the U.S. dollar being convertible into gold at fixed rate. This system eroded as (1) the increased virtuosity of Western Europe and Japan in the technologies of high mass consumption reduced the U.S. trade surplus; (2) large net U.S. overseas security outlays exerted continuing strain on the dollar; (3) the American economy drifted from the leading manufacturing sectors of high mass consumption to the rapid expansion of certain services, the latter generating in the short run virtually no new technologies capable of sustaining U.S. exports; and (4) the wage-price guideposts, which had successfully protected the dollar over the previous five years, were gravely weakened beginning around the summer of 1966, to be abandoned in January 1969. Taken together, these forces destroyed the Bretton Woods monetary system in 1971, yielding uneasy and unstable transitional arrangements that, like other expedients, could persist for a long time.

The Distorted Kondratieff Upswing of the 1980s, 1972–1982

The price revolution of 1972–1976 broke the back of the great postwar boom by undercutting its leading sectors, and it exacerbated gravely the population-food balance, the problem of inflation, and the disarray of the international monetary system.

Figure 4.3 shows on a monthly basis how certain categories of wholesale prices moved in the United States during the period of January 1972–December 1975. The impact of the price revolution was peculiarly acute for two reasons. First, the industrialized world was enjoying a strong and virtually universal boom in 1972–1973. Effective demand for food, fuel, and raw materials was high, stocks were falling, and prices were vulnerable both to the bad harvests of 1972–1973 and to the action of OPEC in October 1973. Second, the crisis occurred against a background of accelerating wage-push inflation — that is, a rise of prices caused by wage increases larger than the increase in productivity. Phillips curves (measuring the change in prices associated with a change in the level of unemployment) were moving to the right, indicating that a given decline in unemployment yielded progressively higher rates of inflation; or, put the other way, a given rate of inflation was associated with lower levels of employment. In this setting, the rise of international prices for basic materials in 1973–1974 yielded an especially prompt and sharp initial increase in inflation rates and accelerated increases in money wages. Its effects on real income, not fully compensated for by increases in energy-related investment, brought unemployment to a level of 14.5 million men and women within the OECD nations by the close of 1975.

Taken altogether, the price revolution of 1972–1975 was the most traumatic economic event in the world economy since 1945. It struck directly at the energy-intensive leading sectors of the postwar expansions in Western Europe and Japan and caused declines in output and increases in unemployment on a scale that had not been experienced since the interwar years.

Then came the second oil-price jump in 1978–1979, which was triggered by the Iranian Revolution and the cutback of Iranian oil production and exports. The 1974–1975 convulsive rise in the inflation rate was repeated in 1979–1980. Although the rise in the oil price might well have been overdone, the decline in productivity was markedly more severe, reflecting the now-protracted prior period of low investment.

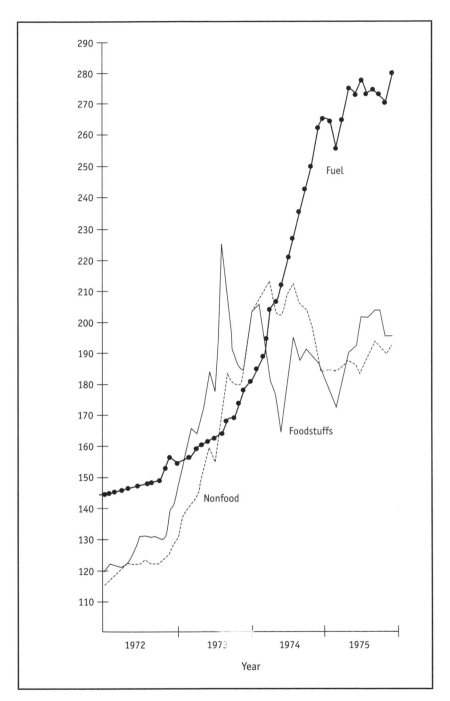

Figure 4.3 Price Revolution of 1972–1975: U.S. Wholesale Prices Monthly (1967 = 100). *Source: The Economic Report of the President to Congress*, February 1975, pp. 301–302; January 1976, pp. 227–228.

The economy began to revive slowly after August 1980, as real oil prices again declined and monetary restraint was eased after the Congressional elections of 1982, perhaps with an eye on the upcoming presidential elections. The inflation rate, however, continued at double-digit levels, and interest rates remained high. Unemployment stood at 7.6% in October 1980.

Perhaps the most striking and unforeseen result of the two oil shocks of the 1970s was the decline in the pattern of oil and gas consumption in the United States. The relation between American GNP and oil and gas consumption was for a long period about 1:1. After the two oil shocks, it fell to roughly, 1:0.25. Most of the decline had occurred by the mid-1980s. Since then, this ratio has fallen slowly and then risen slightly with the increasing popularity of vans, which have a larger gas consumption per mile than the average consumption of cars. In addition, the reaction to the eight-fold increase in energy prices was not merely an extraordinary decline in American oil and gas use but an increase in oil production in many places. This reduced the leverage OPEC had on the energy market, a leverage not recovered by the 1990s.

A Kondratieff downswing occurred for most of the 1980s in the sense that the prices of manufactures rose more than those of raw materials. Taking each at 100 at the trough of 1982, in 1994 finished-goods prices were 125, but crude materials were only 102. These sectoral index numbers, however, conceal a much sharper rise in medical services—from 100 in 1982 to 211 in 1994—and a virtual stagnation in energy prices, which were 105 in 1994. Moreover, this was the period during which the old USSR was undergoing a complex transition; the new technologies of the fourth Industrial Revolution were first commercialized; and the world became conscious that it faced an expensive task in protecting the environment if not in managing regional and global crises. In short, the relative-price problem did not dominate the 1980s and 1990s in the way it did during the 1970s.

If there were central themes in the 1980s and 1990s, they were the momentum of Asia, notably the breaking away from Mao Tse-tung's policy in China from the late 1970s accomplished by Deng Xiaoping, and the entering onstage of the fourth Industrial Revolution in the United States, Western Europe, and Japan.

In a sense, however, each story of the individual countries of the OECD in the 1990s is unique. The United States seemed to be pulling out of the lethargy of the late 1980s. It resumed fairly rapid growth in 1993–1997. The average level of unemployment fell from 7.4% in

1992 to just under 5% in 1997, half the average level in Western Europe. The United Kingdom, after a long passage of double-digit unemployment, did better after 1987 but lacked the élan of the post-war generation. The Japanese entered into a crisis in the 1990s that seemed to touch its political and social life as well as its economic dispositions—a true generational crisis marked by a distinct loss of confidence. Germany was taken up for some time with the recovery of East Germany and a stubbornly high level of unemployment. Three of the former Soviet satellites, however, made their way fairly successfully through the transition to a market economy: Poland, Hungary, and the Czech Republic. After initial declines, they bottomed out and went forward at a decent pace.

A generalization of this period of uneven and uneasy development in the OECD world would be that the economies were borne down by the aging of the automobile–durable consumers' goods sectors and by the shift away from Cold War military expenditures at a time when the new technologies did not come on fast enough to compensate for these losses in effective demand. At the same time, the new technologies called for increasingly skilled manufacturing labor. This led to an accentuated split in the workforce on both sides of the Atlantic, which we shall examine in Chapter 8.

The central theme of the 1990s in the advanced industrial countries was, as noted earlier, not related to relative prices, except negatively. After the stormy 1970s, basic commodity prices remained low, and this was taken for granted. The central theme was paradoxical: a painful cutting back of the commitments to social expenditures made in the 1950s, 1960s, and early 1970s as populations aged and the average level of unemployment rose in the period 1973–1996. At just this time, there was adjustment to the ongoing skill-intensive technological revolution through which the advanced industrial societies were passing.

Relative Prices, 1996–2050

What, then, is the prospect for relative prices in the time ahead? Here, the most important point to note, as compared to the longer past, is that there is likely to be a difference in the first quarter of the 21st century between the strains experienced in the less-developed countries and those in the more-developed countries.[4] (See Appendix A.)

Food and Water

Hamish McRae opens his discussion of water with a bald assertion: "A shortage of fresh water is probably going to be the most serious resource problem the world will face in 2020."[5] McRae adduces four reasons for this view:

- Further increases in irrigated land are vital for the world's food production.
- The growth in the urban population of the developing world will require a large increase in water supplies.
- The normal method of increasing available supplies, building more dams, has grave environmental consequences which are only recently coming to be fully appreciated. In any case, most of the world's best dam sites have already been taken.
- When rivers cross national borders, countries may grab what they can at their neighbours' expense.[6]

In fact, McRae lists four candidates for diplomatic conflict or war:

- The diversion of water from the Sea of Galilee into Israel's national Water Carrier.
- The Gabcikovo Dam on the Danube in Slovakia.
- Threats to dam the upper Blue and White Nile.
- The damming of the upper reaches of the Tigris and Euphrates by Turkey, and the Euphrates by Syria.

I have presented McRae's view because I respect his judgment, and his analysis of the water problem addresses both its impact on agriculture and the rise of the cities in the developing world. But there is something more to be said.

The use of water in the United States and around the world is now grossly inefficient. With existing technology, it is estimated that current irrigating systems are approximately 37% efficient.[7] This means that there is considerable scope for economy. In the United States, the following techniques are available:

- "Ground leveling" permits water to be distributed more evenly; horses, tractors, or methods guided by the use of computers can be used for leveling.
- "Surge" irrigation is possible by timing the release of water to seal the soil, reduce percolation losses, and distribute water more evenly.
- "Low-energy precision application" (LEPA) delivers water directly to crops; this is used in connection with ground leveling and surge techniques.

- "Drip methods,"[8] pioneered in Israel, have been found applicable in California for the production of cantaloupes, tomatoes, sweet corn, cotton, and other high-value crops. (Drip irrigation delivers water via underground pipes with very small holes).[9]

In less-developed countries, a wide array of water-saving methods are also available:

- small-scale dams
- shallow wells
- low-cost pumps
- rainwater-harvesting methods (terracing)

These methods have been listed because the shortfall in agricultural production is likely to bear on certain developing countries in the period before time and the demographic transition bring down the birth rate. In a number of countries, water is likely to be the bottleneck in agriculture. These simple methods, if applied soon enough, will buy time, which might be the scarcest commodity of all in determining both these regions' capacity to feed themselves and the American, European, and other advanced countries' export capacity. These methods of water conservation are not, therefore, to be underestimated any more than the methods by which the United States, faced by the rise of energy prices in the 1970s, brought down the amount of energy necessary to produce a unit of GNP.

In the long run, the water bottleneck might depend upon the cost of desalting seawater. Here, the capacity to maintain a population of 10 billion people might depend upon the emergence to commercial status of fusion power or some other form of energy that is vastly cheaper than current ones.

Food, Energy, and the Environment

I have dealt with water at some length because, as of 1996, it is the most flagrant of the bottlenecks to food supply. The out-of-control surpluses of the United States and Europe give to the whole world (and to this analysis) an optimistic cast when the food prospect is viewed in global terms. The present and foreseeable import needs of Japan, South and Southeast Asia, Latin America, and the Middle East seem manageable. Yet there is a book by Lester R. Brown entitled *Who Will Feed China?*,[10] and none of the futurologists has a plan for feeding Africa.

As for China, the pessimistic argument is as follows. China is following the pattern of Japan, South Korea, and Taiwan. It is experiencing a rise in food imports as it industrializes rapidly, with real wages rising and the population tilting toward the cities. The key relationship that Brown points to is the increased consumption of proteins as people grow richer. The production of proteins is extremely expensive in basic grains. Although it is not put this way in the public rationale of the Chinese Communist Party, the extreme limitation of family size, successful in the cities of China, might well be the product of an awareness of the conflict between Chinese food requirements and the local food-production potential plus what the world can supply. The latter figure presumably takes into account what China can export in other raw materials and manufactures. It is most unlikely that an accurate econometric equation can be constructed to embrace these variables. But Chinese experts have contemplated these matters sufficiently to support extreme measures of population limitation and measures to maximize domestic production, including increased and diverted water supply.

Strangely, there is no book entitled *Who Will Feed India?*, even though all projections show India outstripping China in population by 2050. Perhaps it is because most probers of the future underestimate Indian industrial progress or believe that Indian culture will contain the demand for proteins. Both assumptions are questionable.

But barring a breakthrough in energy that would make desalting commercially feasible, the greatest and most difficult problem will be in Africa, which is not likely to generate by 2050 the capacity to export commercially to the food-surplus countries on the necessary scale. The problem of feeding Africa would then become a political and social-policy problem.

The conclusion to be drawn from these observations for near-term policy is that the present food-surplus countries should focus their foreign economic programs on developing effective water supplies and other policies that would maximize food production in the incipient food-importing countries. Even then, there might be major regional food shortages on the road ahead.

Energy

There is a consensus among experts that there is no energy crisis foreseeable. On an index number basis with 1982–1984 at 100, in July 1997 the figure for energy was only 106, whereas the overall consumer-price index was 161. The price is now relatively low for all forms of energy. The supply is ample; world production is spread about. Saudi Arabian production was 17.6% of the total in 1981; it fell to about 3% by the end of 1985. To reestablish market share, the Saudis lowered prices drastically and came back to 13.3% by 1993. All possible mistakes in projection will be covered by the abundance of coal.

With so much to worry about, why worry about energy? The answer includes but transcends energy. When I took stock of the world's resource problems in 1978 in *The World Economy: History and Prospect*, I concluded that the future depended on two factors: the forehanded action of governments and a breakthrough in cheap, nonpolluting energy based on an essentially infinite natural resource—that is, fusion power. Specifically, it is the cost of removing the pollution potential of coal that casts a shadow on excessive reliance on this form of energy, thus the emphasis placed on the emergence of fusion power to commercial status, although there are several potential competitors (e.g., wind power, solar energy, and powdered hydrogen). Moreover, the ability of advanced industrial powers to reduce fuel consumption has been better than was expected in the 1970s. The main danger appears to be a disproportionate rise in the price of oil, which could arise from political unrest in the present oil-exporting nations of the Persian Gulf. Although these states will continue to have an interest in exporting oil, there might be a traumatic oil crisis that could last some years.

The Environment

Writing almost 20 years ago, I said this about pollution and the environment:

> In talking about the human environment and its problems, one is, of course, dealing with a spectrum including potential dangers to human life on a massive, even global, scale; serious dangers for particular communities; substantial dangers which raise mortality and illness rates in particular regions to a limited degree; progressive degradation of the physical and aesthetic environment in which human beings live; and failures to exploit opportunities to create a more agreeable setting for human life. On an ascending scale, the spectrum has been broadly defined as follows:
>
> Class 1 in which the amenities and aesthetic qualities of life are violated.

Class 2 in which there is injury or death to individuals from environmental contamination.

Class 3 in which whole species are threatened with extinction from disturbances in ecological interrelationships.

Class 4 in which fundamental cycles in the biological pyramid and its natural environment are distorted or destroyed to such a degree that life for whole series of living forms becomes impossible over wide areas and possibly over the globe as a whole.[11]

This listing is useful because it separates problems that are or might be of universal concern (Class 4) from problems that might have their principal impact on particular countries or regions. Classes 1–3 are of the latter type. The "amenities and aesthetic qualities of life" are under strain in all of our cities, notably in the less-developed countries, although some older industrial societies have mounted a successful counterattack. We have seen Class 2 in the Ukraine due to a nuclear accident. Species are widely threatened (Class 3); while they exhibit considerable resilience, they fight a defensive game at best, notably the African mammals.

Of the dangers, the greatest (Class 4) remain the most obscure, namely, that the weather and the climate will be changed irretrievably by the buildup of CO_2 or the attenuation of the ozone layer. Although governments have reacted to both dangers, they both are surrounded, as they were two decades ago, by scientific uncertainty concerning the precise effects of continuing with the status quo.[12] By 2050, two things could happen. We might learn more firmly the impact of our economic activities on the weather, and the presently middle-income countries might become affluent enough (and enjoy population stagnation or decline) to allocate more resources to keeping environmental degradation in check.

FIVE

Cycles

Background

The reason for tracing in this chapter the history of cycles, as a pre-
lude to speculating about the future, lies in two features of cyclical
history: the fact that this history includes the global depression of the
1930s that helped trigger World War II and the fact that a number of
economists have underlined the role of population increase, stagnation, or decline in determining the length and amplitude of depressions and of cycles themselves. Cycles viewed historically, then, are
not irrelevant to the issues of the next century.

Trend periods, treated in Chapter 4, have a rhythm that runs
through a series of business cycles. Trend periods affect the price level,
interest rates, terms of trade, capital movements, and direction of
migration. Business cycles, unlike trend periods, consist of fluctuations in employment and output. The length and intensity of business-
cycle upswings — and the extent of overshooting they yield — are partially determined by the time lags involved in the particular leading
sectors of the boom.

The shortness of the inventory cycle — about three years — is related
to the simple fact that inventories have a short life. Unlike a factory, a

road, or a house, they are used up rather promptly in the production process. Inventory overshooting, therefore, tends to be capable of correction fairly soon. Housing stands at the other extreme. Houses last a generation, and their replacement (relative to inventories) is more postponable.

Against this brief background, the character and timing of business-cycle patterns are examined in four periods: the 18th century, 1783–1914, the interwar years, and post-1945. Then the cyclical problem as now foreseen for 1996–2050 will be discussed.

Cycles in the 18th Century, 1700–1783

Britain is the only country where business fluctuations in the 18th century have been examined in a reasonably systematic, if still explor-atory, way. Moreover, Britain gained primacy in the course of the 18th century and remained at the heart of global cyclical fluctuations through about 1914. T. S. Ashton's chronology of turning points in Brit-ish business fluctuations of the 18th century is given in Table 5.1.

At first sight, one is tempted to treat these fluctuations as cycles of a kind continuous with those before 1914. For example, in setting turn-ing points for British cycles from 1788 to 1913, one emerges with an average duration of 5.25 years. This is just about the average for the 18th century as well. And the building cycle in Table 5.1 averages 17.4 years, close enough to the modern 20-year building cycle to suggest a continuity reaching back to 1700. But domestic harvests and war played a larger role in these fluctuations before 1783 than they did later; tech-nological change and industrial investment certainly played a lesser role. There are, thus, significant differences between pre-1783 fluctua-tions and post-1783 cycles, as well as some elements of continuity.

I conclude that the pre-takeoff British economy contained within it the major elements that were later to yield modern business cycles, except for major industrial innovation. If the evidence were available, one could probably trace out similar erratic but suggestive fluctuations in the French and other continental economies, and one would expect to find reasonably strong inventory cycles in the Dutch economy, given its predominant financial and large commercial role in the 18th-century world economy. I would guess that, given the time and distance involved and the role of credit, there was also an element of inventory fluctuation in the foreign trade of the American colonies through 1775.

Table 5.1. British Business Fluctuations, 1700–1783

Trough	Length of Cycle	Peak	Length of Cycle
1700	—	1701	—
1702	2	1704 (1705?)	3
1706	4	1708	4
1712 (1711?)	6	1714	6
1716	4	1717–1718	3.5
1722	6	1724–1725 (1724)	7
1727	5	1728	3
1730	3	1733	5
1734	4	1738 (1736)	5
1742	8	1743	5
1746 (1744)	4	1746	3
1748	2	1751 (1753)	5
1755	7	1761	10
1763 (1762)	8	1764	3
1769	6	1771–1772	7.5
1775	6	1777 (1776)	5.5
1781	6	1783	5
Average	5.1		5.0

Sources: Reprinted by permission from T. S. Ashton, *Economic Fluctuations in England, 1700–1800,* (Oxford: Clarendon Press, 1959), pp. 172–173; dates in parentheses are from John Parry Lewis, *Building Cycles and Britain's Growth* (London: Macmillan, 1965), p. 14.

Cycles in the Classic Era, 1783–1914

The period 1783 to 1914 was the classic era of business cycles. We shall proceed by first considering cycles in the British economy, which remained throughout a central, if not wholly dominating, force in the world economy. Only then will divergences from the British pattern be considered in the timing and character of business cycles in some other major economies.

Precisely because of Britain's large role in the world economy, its cycles cannot be understood fully except as part of an interacting process in which Britain both reflected forces at work in other economies and acted upon them. The major capital-export booms, for example, were those peaking in 1825 (Latin America: gold and silver); 1836 (United States: cotton), 1854 (United States: railroads), 1873 (United States and Germany: railroads), 1890 (Argentina: railroads), and 1913 (Canada: railroads). In each case, they left their mark clearly on the pattern of British exports. But, of course, increases in British exports were also determined by the more or less autonomous movements of nations into industrialization, such as the United States, Western Europe, Scandinavia, Japan, and Russia. And periods of relatively rising or high foodstuff and raw-material prices were reflected in increased British exports to countries producing basic commodities.

As the railway age came and the metallurgical and engineering industries began to play an increased proportional role in the economy, the long-term investment cycle of roughly nine years became increasingly dominant (Table 5.2). This was the trend not only for Britain but also for certain key British markets on the Continent and in the United States; thus, the longer rhythm suffused not only British domestic activities but also foreign trade.

The changed character of cyclical fluctuations had consequences for the relative impact of the business cycle on the economy and the society as a whole. At the beginning of the era, Britain was, in agriculture, virtually self-sufficient, with only minor capital industries and a foreign trade mainly in consumers' goods. By the end of the era, Britain was heavily in deficit in agriculture, with its industries closely tied, in both their domestic and their foreign markets, to long-term capital development. Undoubtedly, a larger proportion of the population felt the impact of the business cycle on their lives and fortunes in 1910 than in 1790, even though the nine-year cycle was a regular feature throughout.

One of the most consistent cyclical phenomena throughout this era was the tendency in Britain for long-term investment decisions to concentrate in the latter stages of the upswing of the major cycles. This appears to have been true not only of formal fluctuations in the capital markets but also to a considerable extent of other forms of investment, such as housing, shipbuilding, and industrial investment. On the whole, the Industrial Revolution, regarded as a process of plant expansion and the installation of new industrial methods and techniques, lurched forward in a highly discontinuous way, with a relative concentration of decisions to expand or to improve techniques occurring in the latter stages of the major cycle. It was then that confidence was high, the saving pool was replenished, and the scene was propitious for long-term investment.

Table 5.3 sets out the National Bureau of Economic Research (NBER) monthly reference-cycle turning points (where they exist) for the United States, France, and Germany alongside those already given for Britain. For our limited purposes, the central fact is that despite evident deviations, the major cycles of this period identified in the

Table 5.2. British Business Cycle Turning Points, 1783–1914

Monthly		Annual	
Peak	Trough	Peak	Trough
—	—	1783	1784
—	—	1787	1788
Sept. 1792[a]	June 1794	1792[a]	1793
May 1796	Sept. 1797	1796	1797
Sept. 1800	Oct. 1801	1800	1801
Dec. 1802[a]	Mar. 1804	1802[a]	1803
Aug. 1806	May 1808	1806	1808
Mar. 1810[a]	Sept. 1811	1810[a]	1811
Mar. 1815	1816	1815	1816
Sept. 1818[a]	Sept. 1819	1818[a]	1819
May 1825	Nov. 1826	1825[a]	1826
Jan. 1828	Dec. 1829	1828	1829
Mar. 1831	July 1832	1831	1832
May 1836[a]	Aug. 1837	1836[a]	1837
Mar. 1839	Nov. 1842	1839	1842
Sept. 1845[a]	Sept. 1846	1845[a]	1848
Apr. 1847	1848		
1853 3rd qtr.	Dec. 1854	1854[a]	1855
Sept. 1857	Mar. 1858	1857	1858
Sept. 1860	Dec. 1862	1860	1862
Mar. 1866[a]	Mar. 1868	1866[a]	1868
Sept. 1872[a]	June 1879	1873[a]	1879
Dec. 1882[a]	June 1886	1883[a]	1886
Sept. 1890[a]	Feb. 1895	1890[a]	1894
June 1900[a]	Sept. 1901	1900[a]	1901
June 1903	Nov. 1904	1903	1904
June 1907[a]	Nov. 1908	1907[a]	1908
Dec. 1912[a]	Sept. 1914	1913[a]	1914

Sources: Reprinted by permission from T. S. Ashton, *Economic Fluctuations in England* (Oxford: Clarendon Press, 1959), p. 173; A. D. Gayer et al., *The Growth and Fluctuation of the British Economy, 1790–1850* (Oxford: Clarendon Press, 1953), 1:348; Arthur F. Burns and Wesley C. Mitchell, *Measuring Business Cycles* (New York: National Bureau of Economic Research, 1946) p. 79; J. R. T. Hughes, *Fluctuations in Trade, Industry, and Finance* (Oxford: Clarendon Press, 1960), p. 29.

[a]Major cycle peaks.

British evidence—and quite often the minor cycles as well—are also roughly reflected in the turning-point dates for the United States, France, and Germany. In broad terms, there is no doubt that the rhythm of cyclical fluctuations was international.

When the perspective is widened to embrace fluctuations in pre-industrial as well as industrial economies, there is—as one would

Table 5.3. Cyclical Turning Points, Great Britain, United States, France, and Germany, pre-1914 Era

Cycle	Great Britain	United States	France	Germany
Peak	1792	—	—	—
Trough	1793	—	—	—
Peak	1796	1796	—	—
Trough	1797	1798	—	—
Peak	1802	1801	—	—
Trough	1803	1803	—	—
Peak	1806	1806	—	—
Trough	1808	1808	—	—
Peak	1810	1811	—	—
Trough	1811	1812	—	—
Peak	1815	1815	—	—
Trough	1816	1816	—	—
Peak	1818	1818	—	—
Trough	1819	1820	—	—
Peak	1825	1825	—	—
Trough	1826	1826	—	—
Peak	1828	1828	—	—
Trough	1829	1829	—	—
Peak	1831	1831	—	—
Trough	1832	1833	1831	—
Peak	1836	1836	1836	—
Trough	1837	1837	1837	—
Peak	1839	1839	1838	—
Trough	1842	1843	1839	—
Peak	1845	1845	1846	—
Trough	1846	1846	—	—
Peak	1847	1847	—	—
Trough	1848	1848	1848	—
Peak	1854	—	1853	1852
Trough	Dec. 1854	Dec. 1854	1854	1855
Peak	Sept. 1857	June 1857	1857	1857
Trough	Mar. 1858	Dec. 1858	1858	1858
Peak	Sept. 1860	Oct. 1860	1864	1860
Trough	Dec. 1862	June 1861	Dec. 1865	1861
Peak	Mar. 1866	Apr. 1865	Nov. 1867	1863
Trough	Mar. 1868	Dec. 1867	Oct. 1868	1866
Peak	—	June 1869	Aug. 1870	1869
Trough	—	Dec. 1870	Feb. 1872	1870
Peak	Sept. 1872	Oct. 1873	Sept. 1873	1872
Trough	—	—	Aug. 1876	—
Peak	—	—	Apr. 1878	—
Trough	June 1879	Mar. 1879	Sept. 1879	Feb. 1879
Peak	Dec. 1882	Mar. 1882	Dec. 1881	Jan. 1882
Trough	June 1886	May 1885	Aug. 1887	Aug. 1886
Peak	—	Mar. 1887	—	—
Trough	—	Apr. 1888	—	—

(*continued*)

Table 5.3. (*continued*)

Cycle	Great Britain	United States	France	Germany
Peak	Sept. 1890	July 1890	Jan. 1891	Jan. 1890
Trough	—	May 1891	—	—
Peak	—	Jan. 1893	—	—
Trough	Feb. 1895	June 1894	Jan. 1895	Feb. 1895
Peak	—	Dec. 1895	—	—
Trough	—	June 1897	—	—
Peak	June 1900	June 1899	Mar. 1900	Mar. 1900
Trough	Sept. 1901	Dec. 1900	Sept. 1902	Mar. 1902
Peak	June 1903	Sept. 1902	May 1903	Aug. 1903
Trough	Nov. 1904	Aug. 1904	Oct. 1904	Feb. 1905
Peak	June 1907	May 1907	July 1907	July 1907
Trough	Nov. 1908	June 1908	Feb. 1909	Dec. 1908
Peak	—	Jan. 1910	—	—
Trough	—	Jan. 1912	—	—
Peak	Dec. 1912	Jan. 1913	June 1913	Apr. 1913
Trough	Sept. 1914	Dec. 1914	Aug. 1914	Aug. 1914

Sources: U.S. annual turning points, 1796–1832, estimated from a combination of data in Willard L. Thorp, *Business Annals* (New York: National Bureau of Economic Research, 1926), pp. 113–121, and W. B. Smith and A. H. Cole, *Fluctuations in American Business, 1790–1860* (Cambridge, Mass.: Harvard University Press, 1935), pp. 3–84. French annual turning points, 1831–1848, estimated from François Crouzet, "Essai de construction d'un indice annuel de la production industrielle française au XIXe siècle," *Annales, Economies, Societétés, Civilisations*, no. 1 (January–February 1970). German annual turning points, 1850–1866, estimated from Walther G. Hoffmann, *Das Wachstum der Deutschen Wirtschaft seit der Mitte des 19. Jahrhunderts* (Berlin: Springer-Verlag, 1965). Otherwise, dates are taken from Arthur F. Burns and Wesley C. Mitchell, *Measuring Business Cycles* (New York: National Bureau of Economic Research, 1946), pp. 78–79.

expect—a high degree of conformity between British and world fluctuations; but before 1914 there is a marked tendency for world imports, with a strong upward trend, to lag in their cyclical movement at peaks and to lead at cyclical troughs.

Interwar Cycles: 1919–1939

The National Bureau of Economic Research reference-cycle turning-point dates for the four major economies during the troubled interwar years are given in Table 5.4. The aberrations in Table 5.4 relate to the three major factors. First, in Britain they required a wage policy that helped trigger the coal strike and the subsequent general strike. Second, the interwar cycles reflect the character of the trend period, which began with the disproportionate decline of foodstuff and raw

Table 5.4. Business Cycle Turning Points, United Kingdom, United States, France, and Germany, 1919–1939

Cycle	United Kingdom	United States	France	Germany
Trough	Apr. 1919	Apr. 1919	Apr. 1919	June 1919
Peak	Mar. 1920	Jan. 1920	Sept. 1920	May 1922
Trough	June 1921	Sept. 1921	July 1921	Nov. 1923
Peak	Nov. 1924	May 1923	Oct. 1924	Mar. 1925
Trough	—	—	June 1925	—
Peak	—	—	Oct. 1926	—
Trough	July 1926	July 1924	June 1927	Mar. 1926
Peak	Mar. 1927	Oct. 1926	—	—
Trough	Sept. 1928	Dec. 1927	—	—
Peak	July 1929	June 1929	Mar. 1930	Apr. 1929
Trough	Aug. 1932	Mar. 1933	July 1932	Apr. 1932
Peak	—	—	July 1933	—
Trough	—	—	Apr. 1933	—
Peak	Sept. 1937	May 1937	June 1937	—
Trough	Sept. 1938	May 1938	Aug. 1938	—

Source: Adapted from Arthur F. Burns and Wesley C. Mitchell, *Measuring Business Cycles* (New York: National Bureau of Economic Research, 1946), pp. 78–79.

material prices in 1920–1921. Third, also reflected was the underlying shift in economic power from Britain to the United States. This shift was already under way before 1914, but it was much accelerated by the differential impact of World War I. It was the failure of the United States to accept fully its new central position in the world monetary and trading system that helps account for the depth of the world depression and in particular for the fact that the depression brought on a protectionist breakdown in that system.

Despite these powerful structural elements at work on the contours of interwar cyclical fluctuations, there was, in a narrow sense, considerable continuity with a longer past. The immediate postwar pattern of readjustment, boom, and slump (1918–1921) echoed the sequence after the Napoleonic Wars a century earlier (1815–1819), and it anticipated the sequence after World War II (1945–1949). In a fashion familiar since the 18th century, peace brought a powerful wave of residential building. In conventional business-cycle terms, the major interwar peaks (1920, 1929, 1937) came at intervals that gave them a rough-and-ready continuity with the major cycles of the era that began in 1783. The minor cycles, in the United States at least, continued to occur in the shorter rhythm their inventory character would suggest.

The tools of business-cycle analysis generated to explain the sequence from 1783 to 1914 therefore remain relevant to the interwar years despite the average high level of unemployment in the world economy.

Two new elements also anticipated to a degree the 30 years after World War II: the role of the automobile and durable consumers' goods, the latter related to the concurrent expansion of electricity production and consumption, and the effort of governments to counter the post-1929 depression. These efforts were not wholly successful, with the possible exceptions of Nazi Germany and Japan. From 1936 at least, rearmament played a large role in the former case, and military outlays played a decisive role in the latter after 1931 and the Japanese attack on Manchuria. But the German recovery from 1932 to 1936 was closely linked to the rapid expansion in automobile production and road building, as well as the suppression of the independent trade unions.

It was during the depression of the 1930s that governments in the advanced industrial world began to assume political responsibility for the level of employment. In some cases, whatever their intent, these efforts were counterproductive — such as those of the National Recovery Administration (NRA) in the United States and some of the experiments of Léon Blum's government in France. From the perspective of the historical analysis of business fluctuations, however, a probably irreversible watershed had been passed. Somewhat ironically, it was during World War II, in a context of policy designed to control inflation rather than to reduce unemployment, that the statistical tools of national-income analysis were refined and absorbed within the central government bureaucracies.

Cycles in Growth Rates, 1945–1973

From 1945 to the recession of 1974–1975, cyclical fluctuations assumed a new and salutary form in the more advanced economies of the noncommunist world, and they have generated a new literature of cyclical analysis. Cycles became primarily systematic fluctuations in the rate of growth, rarely broken by the absolute declines in output that marked off the classical cycles of the past. The average level of unemployment thus declined markedly, as compared to the pre-1914 era as well as to the interwar years and the time after 1973. The American economy was still abnormally volatile, but GNP in real terms declined only three times between 1947 and 1973: in 1954, 1958, and 1970. And those brief declines averaged less than 1%. Unemployment in the United States averaged only 4.7% for these 27 years, just about the average level for the prosperous 1920s. There was nothing quite like the boom immediately after World War II in the whole modern era.

Within this framework, however, there is much familiar about the minor fluctuations that did occur. The various sensitive business-cycle indicators continued to lead and lag in their old ways; the short rhythm of inventory fluctuations could still be detected and measured; and the various other components of investment remained volatile and still accounted substantially for business fluctuations as a whole, although the economies of Western Europe and Japan now joined North America in experiencing the short-run sensitivity of fluctuations in durable consumers' goods. Still, most analysts considering the period 1945–1973 have echoed Robert A. Gordon's dictum about the American economy: "The business cycle, although in a gratifyingly attenuated form, still exists."[1]

Inflation: The Price of Full Employment

The nations with large private-enterprise sectors paid a considerable price for the rapid growth they enjoyed from 1945 to 1972. The price was a rate of inflation unique in the peacetime history of the modern world economy, one that accelerated dangerously as the period drew to a close.

Table 5.5, covering the period 1955–1974, shows consumer price indexes for a number of the major industrial economies. In different ways, all shared the immediate postwar inflationary boom as well as the Korean War boom and subsequent retardation. The annual inflation rates for the decade after 1955 varied from 1.5% in the United States, damped by low growth rates and then wage-price guideposts, to 4.9% in France, which suffered severe inflation in the late 1950s, as well as two currency devaluations.

The problem of inflation was perceived from the early postwar years to be a potential time bomb in an era of relatively steady, rapid growth. The fact is that over the whole span of the postwar boom of 1946–1974, the political and social task of constraining money wages became increasingly difficult. In part, perhaps, the reasons were technical: The labor surpluses to be drawn into the urban working-force pool from the countryside or from abroad diminished, and the post-1951 damp-

Table 5.5. Consumer Price Indexes in the United States and Other Major Industrial Countries, 1955–1974 (1970 = 100)

Year	Germany	Avg. Annual Rate of Increase (%)	Italy	Avg. Annual Rate of Increase (%)	Netherlands	Avg. Annual Rate of Increase (%)	United Kingdom	Avg. Annual Rate of Increase (%)	United States	Avg. Annual Rate of Increase (%)	Canada	Avg. Annual Rate of Increase (%)	Japan	Avg. Annual Rate of Increase (%)	France	Avg. Annual Rate of Increase (%)
1955	70.1		62.2		57.8		59.0		69.0		69.9		52.6		50.4	
1956	71.9		64.3		58.9		61.9		70.0		70.9		52.8		51.4	
1957	73.3		65.2		62.7		64.2		72.5		73.2		54.4		53.2	
1958	75.0		67.0		63.8		66.2		74.5		75.0		54.2		61.2	
1959	75.7		66.7		64.3		66.5		75.1		75.9		54.7		65.0	
1960	76.7	2.3	68.2	3.4	66.4	3.1	67.2	3.1	76.3	1.5	76.7	1.7	56.7	3.8	67.3	4.9
1961	78.5		69.7		67.0		69.5		77.0		77.1		59.7		69.5	
1962	80.9		72.9		68.3		72.5		77.9		78.0		63.8		72.9	
1963	83.3		78.3		70.9		73.9		78.8		79.4		69.2		76.4	
1964	85.2		83.0		74.8		76.3		79.9		80.8		71.9		79.0	
1965	88.1		86.7		78.7		80.0		81.3		82.8		76.7		81.0	
1966	91.2		88.8		83.3		83.1		83.6		85.9		80.6		83.2	
1967	92.5		91.6		86.0		85.2		86.0		88.9		83.8		85.4	
1968	93.9	3.6	92.8	3.6	89.1	5.7	89.2	5.6	89.6	4.1	92.6	3.8	88.3	5.5	89.3	4.7
1969	96.4		95.2		95.8		94.0		94.4		96.8		92.9		95.0	
1970	100.0		100.0		100.0		100.0		100.0		100.0		100.0		100.0	
1971	105.3		105.0		107.5		109.5		104.3		102.9		106.3		105.5	
1972	111.1		110.9		115.9		117.0		107.7		107.8		111.5		111.7	
1973	118.8	6.8	122.4	8.6	125.2	8.6	126.7	11.7	114.4	8.6	116.0	8.9	124.5	16.9	119.9	10.4
1974	126.8	12.4	140.0	12.4	136.6		145.9		127.0		127.9		152.4		135.5	

Source: *Economic Report of the President* (Washington, D.C.: Government Printing Office, 1975), p. 359.

ing effect on overall prices of relative raw-material and foodstuff prices ceased to operate as the 1960s wore on and stocks were drawn down. And then, under pressure from bad harvests and OPEC's assessment of the world oil market, they gave way to a mighty inflationary push. In part, the reason was psychological: The tendency of inflation to accelerate set up expectations of further inflation. This led union leaders to try, in their current negotiations, not merely to correct for past pressures of inflation on real wages but also to achieve settlements that would hedge their clients' real incomes against expected future inflation. This heightened inflationary pressure. In a sense, failure bred failure: The breakdown of successive income-policy efforts consolidated inflationary expectations in business and labor. And so these rich, comfortable, and rapidly expanding economies became—so far as wages and prices were concerned—like a dog chasing its tail.

But deeper questions were involved. The willingness and ability of various societies to implement successfully a social contract governing price and wage behavior were and remain measures of their political cohesion and sense of common purpose. When the relatively easy phase of postwar growth through 1972 gave way to the more constrained environment of the new trend period, none of the advanced industrial countries—nor all of them together—had yet defined its interests and objectives in ways that made wage restraint acceptable, except by policies that slowed down the rate of growth or raised the level of unemployment. The prospects for the OECD in 1976 appeared to be a rate of growth that would leave unemployment relatively high, combined with an average inflation rate of about 8%. The temperature of a quite sick patient was being lowered at great economic and social cost, but no cure was in sight.

U.S. Stagflation, 1974–1982

There is nothing new about a cyclical recession brought about by balance-of-payments pressures arising from excessive imports during a period of rapid growth. Indeed, a global recession in 1974 was foreshadowed by a deceleration in industrial production and by other leading indicators in the second half of 1973, before the major increase in oil prices of November had significant balance-of-payments effects.

In the short run, the central fact is that worldwide recession among the oil importers did not significantly decrease the net foreign-exchange outlays for oil imports. Therefore, relief from balance-of-payments pressure had to be found in other directions. By and large, the recycling problem—the problem of returning the OPEC surplus to the markets of the world—proved in 1974–1975 more manageable than was at first thought. Increased OPEC imports, foreign aid, and the lending resources of the Eurodollar market provided short-term credits to hard-pressed oil importers. But the various nations exhibited quite unequal capacities to reduce their current account deficits by expanded exports. Germany, Benelux, and Japan did relatively well; Britain, Italy, and France did quite poorly.

But a second problem confronted the United States, Western Europe, and Japan. The rise in oil prices reduced real incomes in the industrialized, oil-importing parts of the world, and it increased the real incomes of oil exporters. To some extent, the industrialized nations could move back toward full employment by exporting relatively less to each other, relatively more to those now richer. But increased exports to oil exporters were not likely to prove a sufficient compensation, in terms of employment, for the weakening of the leading sectors that carried forward U.S., Western European, and Japanese growth up to 1972. Those sectors (automobiles, durable consumer' goods, etc.) were energy intensive.

Meanwhile, in one country after another, a sense was emerging that limits were being approached or had been exceeded in levels of social services provided by public authorities. The expansion of such services was an important source of increased demand and employment in the 1960s and 1970s. Outlays for education, public health, and other welfare services were, to be sure, financed through taxation, but their expansion not only reflected an important aspect of the income elasticity of demand in rich societies during the 1960s but also had spreading effects (notably in education and health) similar to those of other leading sectors. Schools and hospitals were built and supplied with equipment. Their continued expansion provided increased employment indirectly as well as directly.

Then came the second oil-price jump in 1978–1979, triggered by the Iranian Revolution and the cutback of Iranian oil production and exports. There was a second convulsive rise in the inflation rate throughout the world economy. Money-wage increases and a decline in productivity provided a second-stage booster to the behavior of prices in 1979–1980. The decline in productivity was markedly more severe, reflecting the now-protracted prior period of low investment. The global economy began to revive in 1982–1983.

The 1980s

The expansion of the 1980s in the United States is peculiar in a way quite different from in the 1970s, but it was shaped also by a political event: the end of the Cold War. From the deep cyclical trough of 1982, the American economy thus expanded until 1990 in two dramatically different phases, marked by the emergence of Mikhail Gorbachev in the Soviet Union in the mid-1980s.

Through 1986–1987, expansion was carried forward by a powerful military buildup (see Figure 5.1) and a construction boom rooted in tax breaks (see Figure 5.2). As the economy revived, there was also a

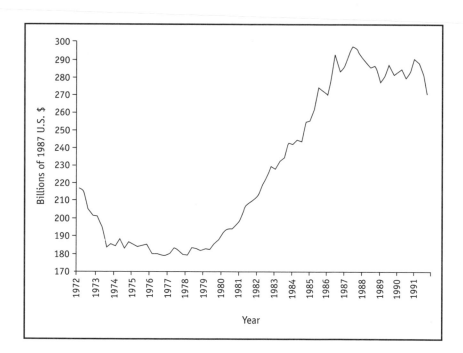

Figure 5.1 Federal Government Purchases: Defense. *Source:* U.S. House of Representatives, *Anti-Recession Infrastructure Jobs Act of 1992: Hearings before the Committee on Public Works and Transportation* (Washington, D.C.: Government Printing Office, 1992), p. 142.

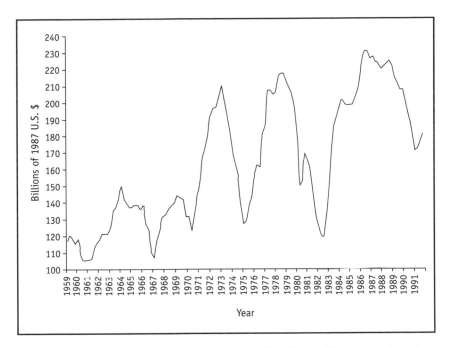

Figure 5.2 Residential Fixed Investment. *Source:* U.S. House of Representatives, *Anti-Recession Infrastructure Jobs Act of 1992: Hearings before the Committee on Public Works and Transportation* (Washington, D.C.: Government Printing Office, 1992), p. 139.

substantial increase in state and local infrastructure investment, which had been in decline from the late 1960s to the early 1980s — part of an overall decline in nonmilitary infrastructure investment from about 4.1% of GNP in 1968 to 2.4% in 1991 (see Table 5.6).

These three expanding sectors (construction, military, and federal and state expenditures) overcame an extraordinary unfavorable shift of the trade balance from plus $31 billion in 1980 to minus $155 billion in 1986. This shift was caused in large part by the tax cuts of 1981–1982 and the consequent high American interest rates and overvalued dollar. The latter priced the United States out of export markets and opened the way for Japan and others to increase their market shares in the United States.

Then things shifted. Construction investment declined after 1986 as tax laws were changed and awareness of the extravagance of the building boom spread. Military expenditure leveled off after 1987 when an astonished world took the measure of Gorbachev. And after the

Table 5.6. Gross Government Nonmilitary Expenditure in Infrastructure as Proportion of GNP, 1950–1991 (Billions of Dollars, 1987 Prices)

Year	Federal	State and Local	Total	GNP	Percent
1950	10.8	32.5	43.3	1,413	3.1
1960	13.9	58.6	72.5	1,955	3.7
1968	15.1	96.8	111.9	2,742	4.1
1977	14.8	67.6	82.4	3,474	2.4
1990	16.9	104.5	121.4	4,885	2.5
1991	14.6	102.8	117.4	4,848	2.4

Source: Unpublished data from John Musgrave, Department of Commerce, Bureau of Economic Analysis.

Plaza Agreement devalued the dollar in 1985, exports expanded strongly and the trade deficit narrowed. In real terms, U.S. exports increased by two-thirds between 1984 and 1991. The export boom was accompanied by a further expansion of state and local infrastructure expenditures.

In 1990–1991, virtually all of the critical sectors declined. Both residential and nonresidential construction declined. The net export position ceased to improve as the dollar strengthened. Military expenditure began what has proved to be a radical and sustained decline. All forms of infrastructure investment declined, including a $15 billion decline in military-infrastructure investment. Ironically, historians might well call this the Peace Dividend Recession as military expenditures fell off but the federal government passively watched the economy fall into depression without compensatory action.

1992–1996

The first half of the 1990s lacked the drama of the oil-price jumps of the 1970s or the end of the Cold War in the 1980s. But long-term forces began to assert themselves.

- The fourth Industrial Revolution, a high-tech phenomenon, became a leading sector on a world scale, causing a split in the workforces of both the United States and Western Europe. The gap in the distribution of income widened, and in Western Europe the rigidity of the economy resulted in abnormally high levels of employment—a phenomenon that had begun to appear in the 1980s.
- The United States rallied from the self-inflicted wounds of the 1980s and reasserted its position in the world economy, while Western

Europe did not move forward with the same élan as the United States in the new technologies; Japan suffered what can only be described as a generational political, social, and economic crisis. It suffered a prolonged depression, but it was too sound a society not to resume growth; perhaps its economic progress will assume European proportions. In any case, the mood that Japan would be dominant, which always had a shallow base, dissipated on both sides of the Pacific.

- All of the advanced industrial countries took stock of the social expenditures to which they became committed in the 1960s and early 1970s and went through, in different ways, the painful, political path of retraction. In part, this uncomfortable experience was a product of the technological revolution and the process of aging in older industrial societies. Historians might well look back on the 1990s as the decade when the 21st century began in Japan and Western Europe.

1996–2050

The first lesson that the 20th century can pass along to the 21st is to avoid a global breakdown like that experienced in the 1930s. It cannot be emphasized too often, notably as time passes and the memories of citizens and governments grow dim, that World War II was a product of the depression of the 1930s and the progressive loss of cohesion among those who ultimately had to fight Hitler and the Japanese military, both of whom were, in different ways, children of depression. More precisely, both the problems of supply and shortage that will emerge in the early part of the 21st century and the problems of demography and demand that will emerge later on will require a high order of international cooperation if fragmentation is to be avoided.

Second, despite just-in-time inventory policies and other informational strategies made possible by computers, it is likely that business cycles will continue. They will be of two kinds: those dominated by leading sectors that aim to increase supply or reduce demand for commodities in short supply (including clean water and other environmental commodities) or leading sectors associated with quality of life that have their own virtues but might be fostered to help compensate for the impact on the investment level of stagnant or falling population. The two types of leading sectors might even operate at the same time, arising from differences in timing of the coming of stagnant or falling populations among the older and newer industrial countries.

With respect to the cycles dominated by sectors where one wishes to increase supply or constrain demand, it is likely that prices of the output of these sectors and the general price level will be rising. It is always possible, as in the 1970s, to use monetary policy to force a recession, unemployment, and a sufficient decline in overall demand to achieve some containment of the inflationary thrust. In the inherently chaotic environment of this clumsy remedy, members of the workforce who can do so will attempt to avoid a fall in real wages, due to increasing prices, by raising money wages, thus imparting a further inflationary element to the system.

This can only be countered with a cohesive, national incomes policy. The lesson of experience is that, aside from the social and political forces evoked, this is most likely to work if three conditions are satisfied:

1. Wages are set by certain large industry and public-sector groups at the same time, usually in the spring, as in Germany and Japan.
2. The general rule is widely understood that average money-wage rates can only be increased to the extent that average productivity is increased. Industries that wish to attract manpower are permitted to exceed this rule; industries that wish to off-load labor are permitted to offer wages below this rule.
3. It is generally understood that monetary authorities will be forced to contain inflation by inducing recession if this rule is, on average, violated.

As the working force is attenuated by demographic factors, some such method of wage setting that will avoid the wastes of crude monetary-induced depression should become more attractive. Thus far, politicians in most of the democracies have preferred an enlarged body of the unemployed to the disciplines of an income policy. But with the passage of time, that judgment might change. This system would give better results in a period like the early 1990s, when the pressure of foodstuff and raw-material prices is not seriously inflationary. By linking wage increases to average productivity increases, it would permit higher levels of growth with less inflation. This would be of particular importance at a time of stagnant or falling population.

J. M. Keynes's *General Theory of Employment, Interest, and Money* and the sharp recession of 1937–1938, long before full employment

had been achieved in Britain and the United States, spurred speculation about secular stagnation in which the possibility of a declining
population figured generally. Keynes's only reference to the economics of population decline in *General Theory* relates to its negative
impact on investments, but it is set in the context of business-cycle
analysis rather than secular stagnation:

> The interval of time, which will have to elapse before the shortage of
> capital through use, decay and obsolescence causes a sufficiently
> obvious scarcity to increase the marginal efficiency [of capital], may
> be a somewhat stable function of the average durability of capital in
> a given epoch. If the characteristics of the epoch shift, the standard
> time-interval will change. If, for example, we pass from a period of
> increasing population into one of declining population, the charac-
> teristic phase of the cycle will be lengthened.[2]

In a subsequent article published in the *Eugenics Review*, Keynes
discussed population in the context of his view of secular stagnation:

- The demand for capital is a function of three variables: the rate of
  growth of population, the rate of growth of "the standard of life,"
  and the rate of increase and character of technology.
- Putting aside the other two variables, a positive rate of population
  increase enlarges the demand for capital by diffusing a hopeful —
  even excessively hopeful — set of expectations among investors, but
  such errors of overoptimism are rapidly corrected. The errors of
  pessimism induced by a falling population correct themselves more
  slowly, and the changeover from optimistic to pessimistic expectations, rooted in population projections, can be "very disastrous."
- In an interesting combination of conventional British and Austrian
  analyses of capital, Keynes argued that, as compared to the long
  sweep of the past, inventions are becoming less capital intensive,
  with a lower "average period of production" due to higher income
  elasticity of demand for services.
- Projecting forward a stationary or declining population plus a decline in the capital intensity of new inventions plus an assumed 1%
  per annum limit on the rise in per capita consumption ("standard
  of life"), Keynes concluded that "to ensure equilibrium conditions
  of prosperity over a period of years it will be essential, *either* that
  we alter . . . the distribution of wealth [to reduce the savings rate]
  . . . *or* reduce the rate of interest sufficiently to make profitable very
  large changes in technique . . . or . . . as would be wisest . . . both
  policies to a certain extent."[3]

Keynes closed by recalling that Malthus focused his work successively around two anxieties: first around the dangers of excessive population (P); later around chronic unemployment (U). "I only wish to warn you that the chaining up of one devil may, if we are careless, only serve to loose another still fiercer and more intractable."

W. B. Reddaway's *Economics of a Declining Population*, first published in 1939, reflects the best systematic interwar British thought on the economic implications of potential population decline implicit in a net reproduction rate close to 0.7. He identifies "the skeleton in the cupboard" in terms similar to Keynes's: "the increased risk of slumps."[4] His proposed remedies, therefore, come to rest on those commonly recommended at the time to avoid general unemployment.

It is useful that the issue that will arise or has already arisen in the advanced industrial countries was debated in the depression of the 1930s. But the issue was not taken very far in the precocious discussions of Keynes and Reddaway, nor by Alvin Hansen in his 1938 debate with Schumpeter. They simply recommended the conventional prescriptions against unemployment.

Table 5.7 exhibits the fertility rate for the industrial countries in 1990. Only Israel, Ireland, Poland, and the USSR were at 2.1 or higher

Table 5.7. Fertility Rate for Industrial Countries, 1990

Country	Rate	Country	Rate
Canada	1.7	Belgium	1.6
Japan	1.7	New Zealand	2.0
Norway	1.7	Israel	2.9
Switzerland	1.5	Luxembourg	1.5
Sweden	1.9	Italy	1.4
United States	1.8	Ireland	2.4
Australia	1.8	Spain	1.6
France	1.8	Greece	1.7
Netherlands	1.6	Czechoslovakia	2.0
United Kingdom	1.8	Hungary	1.8
Iceland	2.0	Poland	2.2
Germany	1.5	USSR	2.3[a]
Denmark	1.5	Bulgaria	1.9
Finland	1.7	Yugoslavia	1.9
Austria	1.5	Malta	1.9

Source: Reprinted by permission from *Human Development Report 1992* (Oxford: Oxford University Press, 1992), pp. 19, 202.

[a]Recent figures for the former USSR show an absolute decline in the European Russian population.

Table 5.8. Keynes' Rough Calculation of the Role of Population Increase: Britain, 1860–1913 (1860 = 100)

	1860	1913
Real capital	100	270
Population	100	150
Standard of life	100	160
Period of production	100	110

Source: Adapted from J. M. Keynes, "Some Economic Consequences of Declining Population," *Eugenics Review* 29, no. 1 (April 1937): 18.

in 1990, and we know that European Russia is already experiencing population decline. I expect that when economists come to grips with this issue in the next century, we shall consider whether pronatalist policies can be induced by the tax system; the remedies will consist not simply of a shift from investment to consumption but increased investment in infrastructure, in the arts, and generally in the quality of life.

The only rough measurement of the employment gap to be filled by increased investment or increased consumption is Keynes's rough calculations for what transpired in Britain from 1860 to 1913, shown in Table 5.8. From these highly approximate calculations Keynes concluded: "It follows that a stationary population with the same improvement in the standard of life and the same lengthening of the period of production would have required an increase in the stock of capital of only a little more than half of the increase that actually occurred."[5]

This awkward problem will require an explicit distinction by public authorities between public investment and current consumption. But that distinction is long overdue and will be required in any case by a fiscal policy for a stagnant or falling population.

The Limits to Growth

Economists have never believed that trees would grow to the sky. They have always assumed, explicitly or implicitly, that some forces from the side of supply or demand would produce limits to growth. In the course of these recurrent speculations, they faced and wrote about many of the issues that the world economy will face, if I am more or less correct, in the century ahead.

The first five chapters of this book dealt with characteristics of growth from the 18th century to the last decade of the 20th. In that interval, by and large, most men and women in the industrial world became accustomed to think that endless growth was more or less normal and automatic. This chapter will be somewhat different. After taking the oscillations of the Chinese dynasties as an example of the limits of traditional societies, it will deal with the reflections on the limits to growth that run sporadically as a minor theme from Adam Smith to John Maynard Keynes and beyond to our own day. I will then turn to what we can say about the next half century in terms of the limits to growth.

The Chinese Dynastic Cycle

Until Europe, after some four centuries of preconditioning, invented via Britain the Industrial Revolution, the long cycle was the normal economic and political pattern of the traditional society. The Chinese theory of the long dynastic cycle, for example, is paraphrased memorably by Mary Wright:

> In brief, the theory was this: A new dynasty at first experiences a period of great energy, and vigorous and able new officials put in order the civil and military affairs of the Empire. In the course of generations the new period of vigor is followed by a golden age. Territories acquired earlier are held, but no new territories are conquered. Learning and the arts flourish in an atmosphere of elegance. Agricultural production and the people's welfare are supported by the maintenance of peace, attention to public works, and limitations of taxes. This golden age, however, carries within it the seeds of its own decay. The governing class loses first the will and then the ability to meet the high standards of Confucian government. Its increasing luxury places a strain on the exchequer. Funds intended for irrigation, flood control, maintenance of public grain reserves, communications, and payment of the army are diverted by graft to private pockets. As morale is undermined, corruption becomes flagrant.
>
> This process of decline may be retarded by the vigorous training of officials and people in the Confucian social philosophy, but the basic direction of events cannot be altered. Sooner or later, the governing class, blind to those reforms which alone can save it, taxes the peasants beyond endurance and fails to attend to the public welfare. Sporadic local rebellions result, necessitating additional taxes and the recruiting of troops from an increasingly disaffected population. Their stake in the existing order gone, the people express their disaffection in a great rebellion. If the rebellion is successful, the "swarming bandits" become in the eyes of history the "righteous forces."
>
> The great rebellion is usually successful. One of its leaders slowly consolidates his power by securing (1) military superiority; (2) support from the literati, to whom he offers a revived Confucian state that they will administer; and (3) support, at least tacit, from the peasantry, to whom he offers peace, land, reduced taxes, and a program of public works to protect the agricultural economy. The new dynasty thus begins where its predecessor began, and its destiny will follow the same pattern.[1]

But there was a more material basis for this cyclical experience than human vulnerability to the temptations of affluence. China produced a Malthus of its own, Hung Liang-chi (1746–1809), who began much as Malthus began and ended on the same pessimistic note on which Malthus ended in his first edition (1798).

> The increase in the means of subsistence and the increase of population are not in direct proportion. The population within a hundred years or so can increase from five fold to twenty fold, while the means of subsistence, due to the limitation of the land-area, can increase only from three to five times.
>
> Some may ask: "Do Heaven and Earth have remedies?" The answer is that their remedies are in the form of flood, drought, sicknesses and epidemics. . . . Some may ask: "Does the government have remedies?" . . . During a long reign of peace Heaven and Earth could not but propagate the human race, yet their resources that can be used to the support of mankind are limited. During a long reign of peace the government could not prevent the people from multiplying themselves, yet its remedies are few.[2]

For our purposes, what is worth noting is that growth in both Wright's and Hung's formulations runs up against a ceiling: an end to the golden age or the "limitation of the land-area" or both in some unspecified relation to one another. In the end, like Adam Smith, the Chinese economists thought diminishing returns would win.

What is left out of this formulation are, of course, two things that distinguish modern growth: the flow of innovations that thus far has defeated diminishing returns and the fact that after real income reached a certain point, the birth rate began to fall, not rise. It was the implacable rise that caused the geometric increase in population that brought down the classical empires, since those empires never reached the point in real income per capita when falling birth rates kick in, as the demographic transition decrees.

Adam Smith's Formulation

Innovation raised its head in Adam Smith's *Wealth of Nations*. But it did not do so in terms of the new cotton factories, the steam engine with a separate condenser, and the iron foundries, all of which were more or less contemporary with Smith as inventions if not commercial innovations. Innovation emerged in the *Wealth of Nations* as productivity-raising improvements as the market was extended and specialization took place. Smith also allowed, as has been pointed out, for the possibility of "philosophers" (i.e., scientists) producing sporadically inventions that involved "new powers not formerly applied."[3]

Adam Smith provided, then, for a systematic advance in output up to a point. His self-reinforcing growth process does not proceed indefinitely. Increased capital investment permits the expansion of the market, which in turn generates increased profits and further investment until a limit is reached. The limit is set by a nation's "soil and climate, and its situation with respect to other countries" as well as by its "laws and institutions."[4] This statement appears to imply diminishing returns to agriculture and to efforts to expand markets by geographic extension.

Smith also made the case strongly for popular education. This could have led to an argument that education would bring down the birth rate, but his population and wage theory assumed a fixed relation between the means of subsistence and population size. Thus his famous conclusion:

> It is not the actual greatness of national wealth, but its continual increase, which occasions a rise in the wages of labour. It is not, accordingly, in the richest countries, but in the most thriving, or in those which are growing rich the fastest, that the wages of labour are highest. England is certainly, in the present times, a much richer country than any part of North America. The wages of labour, however, are much higher in North America than in any part of England. . . .
>
> It is in the progressive state, while the society is advancing to the further acquisition, rather than when it has acquired its full complement of riches, that the condition of the labouring poor, of the great body of the people, seems to be the happiest and the most comfortable. It is hard in the stationary, and miserable in the declining state. The progressive state is in reality the cheerful and the hearty state to all the different orders of the society; the stationary is dull; the declining, melancholy.[5]

Malthus and Ricardo

The first Industrial Revolution actually took place in the time of Thomas Malthus (1766–1834) and David Ricardo (1772–1823). Even in his first edition, Malthus reflected on why the middle men of the highest rank in society and even their servants "may choose to postpone marriage or never marry at all." In the same work, he argued that the cultivation of popular education would maximize the strength of preventive checks to the population by teaching "the lower classes of society to respect themselves by obliging the higher classes to respect them."[6]

More fully, Malthus expounded the demographic transition in a passage in which, at the end, the role of education is evoked.

> In an inquiry into the causes of these different habits, we shall generally be able to trace those . . . which make them [the lower classes] unable or unwilling to reason from the past to the future, and ready to acquiesce, for the sake of present gratification, in a very low standard of comfort and respectability; and those which . . . tend to . . . make them act as beings who look before and after, and who consequently cannot acquiesce patiently in the thought of depriving themselves and their children of the means of being respectable, virtuous, and happy.
>
> Among the circumstances which contribute to the character first described, the most efficient will be found to be despotism, oppression, and ignorance: among those which contribute to the latter character, civil and political liberty, and education.[7]

Ricardo, who differed amiably but seriously with Malthus, has the demographic transition evidently in mind in this passage: "The friends of humanity cannot but wish that in all countries the labouring classes should have a taste for comforts and enjoyments, and they should be stimulated by all legal means in their exertions to procure them. There cannot be a better security against a superabundant population."[8]

It is evident, then, that between Adam Smith and the time of Malthus and Ricardo (about 40–50 years) economists came to perceive that the birth rate might fall as a result of the social as well as economic consequences of a rise in real income per capita and the level of education. In time, working classes, thus elevated, might acquire the habits of "the higher classes" with respect to family size.

J. S. Mill, Karl Marx, and W. S. Jevons

Over a roughly similar interval to that between Adam Smith and Malthus and Ricardo, J. S. Mill and Karl Marx took quite different approaches to the industrial process. They both lived through the diffusion of the next epic innovation: the railroad. They both saw clearly that they were surrounded by an ongoing industrial system; perceived that it produced many horrors as well as progress; were at-

tracted by the socialist ideas that developed at the time; and speculated about the long-run fate of this relatively new system. What divided them, of course, was their view of liberty for the individual. Marx,
a Hegelian, projected a future in which the working class, led by those
who understood history, would overthrow capitalism, install socialism, and in the end achieve a world of affluence under communism.
Marx, in effect, argued that the individual should find satisfaction in
executing the inevitable path of history. Mill saw that, on balance, the
evils of capitalism could be modified and affluence would come to a
world where liberty, as we understand it, was enhanced. For present
purposes, what united these two men was that they saw that the limits
to growth would come not from the supply side—through, for example, a global shortage of food—but from the demand side, from
affluence.

Mill's positive acceptance of the virtues of the stationary state did
not stem, then, simply from a revulsion against materialism. It was
rooted technically in the possibilities opened up in general by the
elevation of the intellectual and social position of the working class
and in particular by birth control. To quote J. R. Hicks, "If the population can once be controlled, there is no need for the economy to go
on expanding, in order that wages should be above the subsistence
level. . . . This is an altogether different, and much more agreeable,
picture. The Stationary State is no longer a horror. It becomes an
objective at which to aim."

Clearly, Mill was premature in asserting this proposition in the mid-
19th century. All classes in the most advanced as well as the "backward" countries still had a great deal more to ask of the economic
system as the flow of new technologies expanded the potentialities for
goods and services, including a remarkable lengthening of life. But
Mill, building explicitly on "the juster and more hopeful anticipations"
of Malthus's later editions, comes closer to foreshadowing the demographic transition of the second half of the 19th and the 20th century
than any of his predecessors or contemporaries. He anticipates, as well,
strands of thought and aspiration that began to appear in the third
quarter of the 20th century as a margin of the population in the most
affluent countries appeared to reject further striving for a higher real
income per capita, defined in conventional material terms. Mill was
also the first major environmentalist. But it should be underlined that
his stationary state implies only a fixed population—technological
change could proceed, elevating real income per capita.

As for Karl Marx, there is little more consideration of where progress will end than this romantic passage from *The Communist Manifesto*.

> When, in the course of development, class distinctions have disappeared, and all production has been concentrated in the hands of a vast association of the whole nation, the public power will lose its political character. Political power, properly so called, is merely the organised power of one class for oppressing another. If the proletariat during its contest with the bourgeoisie is compelled, by the force of circumstances, to organise itself as a class, if, by means of a revolution, it makes itself the ruling class, and, as such, sweeps away by the force the old conditions of production, then it will, along with these conditions, have swept away the conditions for the existence of class antagonisms and of classes generally, and will thereby have abolished its own supremacy as a class.
>
> In place of the old bourgeois society, with its classes and class antagonisms, we shall have an association, in which the free development of each is the condition for the free development of all.[9]

> In a higher phase of communist society, after the enslaving subordination of the individual to the division of labour, and therewith also the antithesis between mental and physical labour, has vanished; after the labour has become not only means of life but life's prime want; after the productive forces have also increased with the all-round development of the individual, and all the springs of cooperative wealth flow more abundantly—only then can the narrow horizon of bourgeois right be crossed in its entirety and society inscribe on its banner: From each according to his ability, to each according to his needs![10]

In the end, Marx's image of human beings "wise, creative, and free,"[11] released from scarcity and the brutalizing imperatives of the class struggle, bears a family relationship, at least, to Mill's stationary state. Both were deeply rooted in the humane values of Western culture and religion. Mill, however, understood well that in the life of societies the results achieved are not independent of the means used to achieve them. One derivation of Marx from Hegel was a separation of ends and means that took communism down a slippery moral slope.

While Mill and Marx were jousting about where this industrial system, carried forward by innovations rooted in science, would end up, some economists were concerning themselves with more mundane short-run matters. In the 1790s, Malthus was certainly affected by the wartime shortage of grain. He countered William Godwin's optimistic view of the future with his "positive" checks to population growth of war, famine, and pestilence.

W. S. Jevons's view in *The Coal Question* (1865) was similar. He contrasted the 3.5% per annum rate of increase in British coal consumption with the inherently transient nature of the thick, accessible, high-productivity seams of coal on which that rate of expansion was based. After an interesting, not wholly optimistic canvas of the implications for a society of constant population and standard of living, Jevons reluctantly concluded: "Our motion must be reduced to rest."[12]

Keynes and Robertson in the Third Kondratieff Cycle

J. M. Keynes and Dennis Robertson were concerned with the implications for Britain of both the upswing and the downswing of the Kondratieff cycle from 1896 to 1920 to 1933. Like the classical economists and like their teacher, Alfred Marshall, they felt acutely the ultimate vulnerability of Britain to the relative price of imports and the likelihood that diminishing returns to agriculture would triumph in the end.

They were, thus, much affected by the Kondratieff upswing from 1896 to World War I. The terms of trade turned against Britain. Keynes published a note on the subject in the *Economic Journal* in 1912. He presented calculations that showed that Britain was £37 million worse off than it would have been if import and export prices had moved equally between 1900 and 1911. His note included the following passage:

> The deterioration—from the point of view of this country—shown above is due, of course, to the operation of the law of diminishing returns for raw products which, after a temporary lull, has been setting in sharply in quite recent years. There is now again a steady tendency for a given unit of manufactured product to purchase year by year a diminishing quantity of raw product. The comparative advantage in trade is moving sharply against industrial countries.[13]

In his *Study of Industrial Fluctuations* (1915) Robertson explored various consequences of shifting relative prices for basic commodities, coming to rest on the same terms of trade data Keynes had used. He concluded forcefully as follows:

> The general conclusion to which these figures, taken as a whole, lead is that the normal tendency for the ratio of exchange to alter against

the manufacturing and in favour of the agricultural communities was in force in the seventies, was suspended in the eighties and nineties, and is now once more on the whole triumphing. This is perhaps the most significant economic fact in the world today. . . . But the fact is clearly of secular rather than cyclical importance.[14]

This preoccupation was carried over directly by Keynes as a basis for Chapter 2 of his *Economic Consequences of the Peace*, where, thinking again of the prewar movement of the terms of trade, he wrote: "Taking the world as a whole, there was no deficiency of wheat, but in order to call forth an adequate supply it was necessary to offer a higher real price." Later, in summing up, he referred to "the increase in the real cost of food, and the diminishing response of nature to any further increase in the population of the world" as one of two fundamental problems of post-1919 Europe.[15] It was in large part on these analytic foundations that Keynes contrasted the precariousness of Western Europe's economic position in the world with the cavalier political surgery of the statesmen of 1919.

But the trend did not continue. Relative prices shifted favorably for Britain in 1920. Keynes, fast on his feet, switched promptly to a new definition of the terms of trade: the income terms of trade. In this new definition, he multiplied relative prices for imports and exports by the relative volumes of trade. His brisk and unembarrassed switch is to be understood by reference to his deeply held view as the probability theorist he was before he became an economist:

> We cannot expect to legislate for a generation or more. The secular changes in man's economic condition and the liability of human forecast to error are as likely to lead to mistakes in one direction as in another. We cannot as reasonable men do better than base our policy on the evidence we have and adapt a measure of prevision; and we are not at fault if we leave on one side the extreme chances of human existence and of revolutionary changes in the order of Nature or of man's relations to her.[16]

In 1919–1920, the high price of British coal exports cushioned the terms of trade against the high price of food and other raw material imports. In the general price collapse of 1921, the fall in Britain's import prices substantially exceeded that of its export prices, including coal. The terms of trade stood 41% higher in that year than in 1913. In the period of relative world recovery down to 1929, the terms of trade fell somewhat for the industrial, food-importing countries, but at their interwar trough, the terms of trade were still almost 20% more favorable than in 1913. This change, however, was accompanied by a "disastrous falling off in the volume of British exports." In a typically swift adjustment to new circumstances, Keynes then bridged the diverse movements of the terms of trade, prewar and postwar, with a concept that defined Britain's difficulties in both cases: "We are no longer able to sell a growing volume of manufactured goods (or a volume increasing in proportion to population) at a better real price in terms of food."[17]

Economists concentrated on how the British economy should react to its sudden increase in real wealth. It proved rather an embarrassment when Britain had to subtract the loss of exports from the fall in prices. In his "Reply" to William Beveridge, Keynes discussed the probable elasticity of demand for British exports, concluding that an attempt to restore their volume and thus to eliminate unemployment in the export industries might involve a sufficiently serious deterioration in the terms of trade to cause also a fall in real wages, a view symmetrical with his conclusions on the German-reparations transfer problem.

Robertson continued this phase of the discussion by defining three alternative methods of adjustment: "a contrived fall in the ratio of interchange," as Keynes had proposed; a shifting of labor from export industries to production for the home market; or an increase in capital exports that would stimulate goods exports. On the whole, he leaned toward stimulus to the home market. In the course of his exposition, Robertson underlined the critical role in the outcome of an economy's capacity to shift its resources rapidly from one sector and occupation to another:

> The general conclusion is that if a country's resources in capital and labour were completely mobile between different occupations, an improvement in the ratio of interchange would be an unmixed blessing, even though it led to a reduction in the volume both of exports and imports. If we could costlessly erect a vast sausage-machine which would grind shipyards into cottages and cotton-spinners into plasterers, we should be wise to do so. I am not sure that even as it is we ought not, so far as labour is concerned, to take a leaf out of Germany's book, and make a far more decisive move in that direction than we have yet done.[18]

Aside from terms of trade analysis, two aspects of this story are worth noting. First, Keynes and Robertson were conscious that they were evoking an old classical doctrine when they viewed with alarm the unfavorable pre-1914 movement in the terms of trade, but they did not review the historical oscillations of relative prices and the terms of trade over the previous century nor explore the corrective mechanism that had operated in the past nor ask whether that mechanism might again operate. When the pre-1914 trend was unfavorable, they assumed, implicitly at least, that it would continue into the indefinite future. When the interwar trend was favorable, they generally assumed that it would persist over the time period relevant to current policy. They did not follow Marshall, who, in his "Fiscal Policy of International Trade" (1908), devoted more than five pages to "wheat prices in England since 1820" and sought systematically to put his conclusions in a long historical perspective.

Second, Britain learned something of a lesson about the intense interdependence in the world economy. The negative impact on Britain's overseas-export markets of excessively favorable terms of trade was, indeed, a puzzlement. Mainstream economists had not generally contemplated this problem before, and they did not turn their minds to it again until the United States of the early 1980s behaved in such a way as to generate a dollar some 30% overvalued, which damped domestic inflation at home while contributing to a radical loss in U.S. export markets.

The Hansen-Schumpeter Debate: The Demand Side

There are essentially three perspectives on the limits to growth: failure of the economic system to generate sufficiently high levels of demand to avoid abnormally high and protracted unemployment, diminishing returns and relatively rising prices for basic commodities, which come to rest on the supply side, and the need to restrain growth in order to elevate the quality of life. To these we can add Joseph Schumpeter's vision of a clash between the dynamics of democracy and the imperatives of viable capitalism, although this is, at its core, an argument for the demand perspective.

Here, the focus is a particular phase of the first type of anxiety—limits to growth on the demand side—and on the heightened concern with "secular stagnation" that followed the sharp recession of 1937–1938 after a cyclical upswing that had failed to bring the economies of Western Europe (except Germany) and North America back to full employment. Alternative perspectives are provided by Alvin Hansen's presidential address at the 51st meeting of the American Economic Association, December 28, 1938, entitled "Economic Progress and Declining Population Growth," and Schumpeter's quite explicitly different view of the meaning of "the disappointing . . . Juglar [business cycle]."[19] More than any other occasion, this debate anticipates some of the key issues of the 21st century.

Hansen perceived clearly that to grapple effectively with the problem of secular stagnation, he had to bring together the tools of both growth analysis and Keynesian short-run income analysis—or, in Hansen's vocabulary, "structural change" and "fluctuations." Hansen's thesis was as follows:

1. The 1930s represented a new era, not yet definable: "We are passing, so to speak, over a divide which separates the great era of growth and expansion of the nineteenth century from an era which no man, unwilling to embark on pure conjecture, can yet characterize with clarity or precision."

2. "Overwhelmingly significant" was the decline by one-half of the increase in U.S. population in the 1930s as opposed to the rate of increase in the 1920s and pre-1914.

3. Taking a positive, Smithian rather than negative, Malthusian view of the role of population increase, we can identify two additional "constitutent elements of economic progress . . . (a) inventions, (b) the discovery and development of a new territory and new resources. . . . Each of these in turn, severally and in combination, has opened before 1914 investment outlets and caused a rapid growth of capital formation."

4. In the 19th century, "investment outlets were numerous and alluring." The business cycle was the preeminent problem of that century. Now we suffer from "secular stagnation—sick recoveries which die in their infancy and depressions which feed on themselves and leave a hard and seemingly immovable core of unemployment, . . . the main problem of our times."

5. The fall in the rate of population increase has reduced the demand for investment and thus contributed to chronic unemployment by cutting requirements for housing, utilities, and manufactured consumer goods. Rough estimates suggest that in the last half of the 19th century, the growth of population was responsible for about 40% of the total volume of capital formation in Western Europe and 60% in the United States.

6. "Thus the outlets for new investment are rapidly narrowing down to those created by the progress of technology." We need an acceleration in the rate of progress of science and technology.
7. Hansen estimated current U.S. full-employment national income at $80 billion, suggested strong government action should it fall "materially below" $65 billion, and commended a "tapering off" of government stimulus at about $70 billion to avoid inflationary pressures.
8. The pursuit of such a policy, Hansen recognized, posed major questions that economists as of 1939 could not answer. He pointed, in particular, to the fact that government measures to stimulate consumption and public investment not only would confront political difficulties but also might diminish the incentives for private investment in various ways. He concluded: "The great transition, incident to a rapid decline in population growth and its impact upon capital formation and the workability of a system of free enterprise, calls for high scientific adventure along all the fronts represented by the social science disciplines."[20]

Given the great global boom of the 1950s and 1960s, some of Hansen's analysis seems quaint and off the mark. Evidently, he did not perceive the extraordinary interdependence that would evolve between the advanced industrial and developing regions in the five post-1945 decades. But his argument remains a rare bringing together of the terms of growth and of short-run income analysis—multiplier, accelerator, and so on. It also, of course, captures a perspective widely shared both as World War II broke out and in the early postwar days, and it may well become a central preoccupation of the coming century.

But this view was not shared by Joseph Schumpeter, who devoted the final chapter of *Business Cycles* to specifying the area and character of his disagreement, a view later elaborated in his *Capitalism, Socialism, and Democracy.* Schumpeter's thesis was, in the end, simple enough: "The balloon shriveled, not from causes inherent to its structure [as Hansen argued] but because the air was being sucked out of it" by the psychological impact on American capitalists and their willingness to invest of various New Deal policies and the hostile atmosphere they created.[21] In short, Schumpeter was prepared to argue that Hansen's final question about the compatibility of a vigorous competitive capitalism and an active if selective interventionist government of the kind commended by Hansen had already been answered negatively.

Schumpeter's conclusion is less important than how he made his case, for, once again, his argument foreshadows the debates of the next century. Focusing like Hansen on invention and innovation, Schumpeter viewed the 1930s as a phase in which the economy was carried forward by the diffusion of the increasingly mature but still vigorously unfolding technologies of its long Kondratieff cycle: in this case, electricity, motor vehicles, and chemicals. He concluded his interpretation of this Kondratieff downswing in terms quite different from Hansen's:

> Having thus satisfied ourselves that the processes which in the past used to carry prosperitys have not been absent in the present instance, we have established a right to speak of a Juglar prosperity and to infer from experience that it would have asserted itself without any external impulse being imparted to the system by government expenditure or any other factor. In particular, there is nothing to indicate that objective opportunities were smaller or capitalist motivation weaker than they had been, say, in 1925. The problem why that prosperity was so weak, and why it should have been followed by so severe a slump now emerges in its proper setting.[22]

After reviewing various monetary and fiscal developments, he concludes that the government's role was "singularly infelicitous—its high-water mark came exactly at the time when the economic process could most easily have done without it and its cessation exactly at the time when the economic process was in its most sensitive phase."[23] But he argues that infelicity of fiscal and monetary policy does not wholly account for the severity of the recession of 1937–1938.

After reviewing Hansen's thesis in typically judicious style, Schumpeter identifies two further areas of agreement with the secular-stagnation doctrine: "Sometime in the future investment opportunities may vanish," and they might vanish "through saturation." This permits him to isolate lucidly his area of disagreement by questioning

> the relevance of those [long-run] considerations for the diagnosis of the situation of 1938. . . . We are less than ten years removed from as vigorous a prosperity as was ever witnessed and from a depression probably due, in the main, to the pace of preceding "progress." It did not differ in character from the comparable Juglar prosperitys of the preceding Kondratieff downgrades, and therefore does not indicate any fundamental change in the working of the capitalist organism. . . .
>
> [But] capitalism produces by its mere working a social atmosphere—a moral code, if the reader prefer—that is hostile to it, and this atmosphere, in turn, produces policies which do not allow it to

function. . . . This is what, to a certain extent and presumably not yet for good, has happened in this country.[24]

Schumpeter, now freed to expound his own thesis, argued that it was the sudden change in policy and attitude of the government toward American private capitalism that produced the radical inhibition of investment. Changes in tax, labor, utilities, and antimonopoly policy, which Schumpeter reviewed, explain part of the problem because they "tended to reinforce each other." Their combined effect was enhanced by the suddenness of the change in 1933 and the manner of administration of the new measures.

Thus, Schumpeter concluded: "There should not be left much doubt as to the adequacy of the factors external to our process to account both for the disappointing features in the current Juglar and for the weakness of the response of the system to government expenditure, in particular for the failure of the latter to affect investment and employment more than it did."

In a final footnote, Schumpeter prepares the way for his next book (and foreshadows something of the rationale for the enormous deficits of the Reagan administration):

> The pattern resulting from the action of inhibiting factors would in all respects be similar to the pattern envisaged by the saving-investment theory; it would display the same lack of resilience and the same tendency toward sub-normal quasi-equilibria; in particular, it would always produce or reproduce extensive unemployment. Therefore, government spending would . . . always suggest itself as a remedy for shortrun difficulties each application of which would impose, under penalty of breakdown, the application of the next dose. Fear of such breakdowns may in the end become the dominant motive even among those who on principle are most strongly opposed to spending policies.[25]

Now, and even more so in the future, Japan, Western Europe, and North America might be caught up in a new version of the Hansen-Schumpeter debate, with the presently underdeveloped world joining in sometime later.

The Environmentalist Debate: The Supply Side

Rachel Carson's book *Silent Spring* might have started the current debate about the environment in 1962. In many versions since then, from Dennis Meadows's *Limits to Growth* (1972) to the annual volumes on the *State of the World* edited by Lester R. Brown, environmentalists have carried forward a systematic questioning, sector by sector. Starting with the kinds of population and industrial growth rates experienced in the world economy over recent decades, they ask: For how long can such rates continue on a physically finite planet?

Among those answering that question, there are, again, pessimists and optimists. The best-known pessimistic analysis is in *The Limits to Growth*, in which Dennis Meadows and his colleagues elaborated computer methods pioneered by Jay Forrester to confront a geometric increase in population with an arithmetic increase in supplies. They came to an apocalyptic conclusion: "If the present growth trends in world population, industrialization, pollution, food production, and resource depletion continue unchanged, the limits to growth on this planet will be reached sometime within the next one hundred years. The most probable result will be a rather sudden and uncontrollable decline in both population and industrial capacity."[26] They arrived at this result by setting up a computerized model that sought to interrelate the key variables: population, food availability, industrial raw-materials requirements, and pollution. The model treated the world as a single economic unit and predicted the future by projecting forward past movements of the variables and assumed relations among them. The "World Model Standard Run" came out of the computer with a crisis in agriculture and industry early in the 21st century, population and pollution peaking later, due to inherent lags.[27]

Out of this exercise, the analysts commend the earliest possible achievement of a state of equilibrium in the world economy in which capital plant and population are maintained at constant levels, as are food and industrial production per capita, while pollution is contained at low and manageable levels. This requires both the acceptance by the more advantaged of radical income redistribution and the acceptance by all of a standard of living less dependent on industrial output. In short, they argue that the world community should quickly abandon the concept of progress and the pursuit of affluence as they have come historically to be defined, radically alter the social values of modern life as it has emerged, and make all of the necessary adjustments required to achieve soon and maintain an egalitarian steady state on a global basis.

As one reads these passages in *The Limits to Growth*, one cannot avoid a sense that the authors regard this outcome as good as well as necessary. With W. S. Jevons, they believe "our motion must be reduced to rest"; but unlike Jevons, they regard this as an unmitigated good thing. Thus, there are some unstated value judgments embedded in the book.

The Meadows study has been examined carefully and subjected to the acute criticism appropriate to so fundamental a theme. In my view, *The Limits to Growth* has the virtue of posing and dramatizing effectively a real set of problems. Moreover, its emphasis on the interconnections among the problems of population, food, energy, raw materials, and pollution is salutary in a world where specialization is the reigning intellectual, professional, and bureaucratic mode. But it suffers from five serious weaknesses.

First, the calculations are global. Acute limits-to-growth crises can occur—indeed, are occurring—in some parts of the world while others go forward. Second, the factual basis for the system model is exceedingly weak. Only the population equation is reasonably satisfactory, but it is subject to the kind of common ignorance we all share. The data on pollution, which plays a critical role in frustrating growth if other limits are expanded and population constrained, are fragmentary. From the incomplete evidence now available, the containment or even rollback of air and water pollution is an expensive but economically manageable task.

Third, the handling of technological and resource constraints is misleading. A once-over expansion in limits will merely postpone a crisis when confronted with a geometric increase in requirements. An incremental expansion of both resources and technology, of the kind to be observed over the past two centuries, need not yield a crisis.

Fourth, this model includes no price system to increase incentives to invent or discover, to constrain consumption of scarce items, or to find substitutes. The relative-price mechanism was, for over two centuries, a powerful engine for setting in motion compensatory action in the face of resource constraints.

Finally, there is no evidence that the Meadows prescription is politically, socially, and psychologically viable. On the contrary, the thrust for affluence of less-advantaged groups and nations is one of the most powerful forces operating on the world scene, as is the determination of advantaged nations and social groups to sustain and even improve their material status. Thus far, the tensions generated by these ambitions have been softened because the pie to be divided was expanding. It is one thing to quarrel about fair shares when all are gaining in real income, the struggle for fair shares is a more dour matter in the face of a static or low growth rate in income per capita.

Among the critics of *The Limits to Growth* are relative optimists about the prospects for the world economy over the next century. The optimists recognize the reality of present and prospective problems of population pressure, food and energy supply, as well as certain environmental dangers. They also recognize that at some time in the future not only population but income per capita will level off. After all, the birth rate is already falling quite fast in the developing world, and the average death rate has almost reached a minimum. But they hold that technological performance over the past two centuries, present scientific capacity, and future prospects all justify faith that people can find or create the new resources and the methods of conservation and pollution control to continue to go forward. They foresee the achievement, no doubt with many vicissitudes and setbacks, of a plateau of more or less universal affluence, achieved at different times for different nations, as a possible and statistically more likely outcome of industrial civilization than either a great, convulsive global crisis and decline or an early and purposeful adoption of a no-growth, income-redistribution strategy. The relative optimists, too, tend to have an ideological bias. There are some at least who hold with undiminished faith to the old optimism about the constructive and human possibilities that will be opened up in the future by the further development of science.

In the end, this debate takes its place with four previous debates, each occurring during a Kondratieff upswing, of which three have already been reviewed. A fourth period of anxiety came after World War II, when food and raw-materials prices continued to rise relatively. In the United States, the apparent scarcity stimulated the massive report of 1952 by the President's Materials Policy Commission, chaired by William S. Paley. The commission was luckier than some of its predecessors in this field. Relative prices broke favorably for the industrial nations in 1951, and the commission's final report (*Resources for Freedom*, 1952) was written in the altered price setting. It took the temperate view that resources should be reviewed in terms of the cost of acquisition rather than in terms of absolute depletion and that the unfolding of technology was a powerful force in fending off classical diminishing returns. In its wake, a permanent institution to monitor the problem was created, Resources for the Future, which continues to do authoritative studies in this field.[28]

There is, then, nothing new about anxieties stimulated by the projection of geometric increases in demand against absolutely limited or arithmetically expanding supplies, shadowed by diminishing returns. It figured in the work of Hung Liang-chi and later in the first edition of Malthus. Between the end of the 18th century and the end of the 20th, such pessimistic predictions were belied by the coming in of new supplies or substitutes or economies or the development of new technologies. That fact is no cause for complacency now. But the undulating sequence of scarcity and oversupply does raise the question of how useful long-run projections of current situations and trends really are.

I believe they are of some use. After all, most public policy is made in response to immediate pressures on the political process. It is rare for democratic governments to act with even a 5- or 10-year horizon in view, except with respect to weapons systems. For just this reason, the attempt to predict or even to speculate systematically about the world 50 or 75 years from now is not an empty intellectual exercise. It might force governments to think and act within a longer perspective. This is necessary because there are significant lags at work in some of the critical problems faced in the world economy. The lag is long between the achievement of a net reproduction rate of 1.0 (or a gross fertility rate of 2.1) and a constant population, given population age structures in the developing world inherited from the past. The lag is also long in creating and diffusing new technologies in energy, agriculture, pollution, and other fields that might be required urgently in the time ahead. Above all, attitudes must change and suffuse the net judgments of the majority before measures even the optimists regard as necessary (e.g., resource conservation) can be effectively carried out in democratic societies; and here the lag can be long indeed.

The critical question still remains: How do we get from here to there? What must we begin doing now to maximize the chance that these challenges can be overcome and that the optimists' vision of the 21st century will come to pass? In this book's first six chapters, I have tried to answer the question: Is a favorable outcome technically feasible? Furthermore, if solutions are technically feasible, what is the character and order of magnitude of the economic problems they pose for the world? I shall conclude by probing what I judge to be the ultimate question: What are the changes in American public policy and in social and psychological attitudes at home as well as abroad required for a favorable outcome? Thus, we turn now to how the resolution, one way or the other, of America's deepest domestic problem will affect its foreign policy in the 21st century.

SEVEN

The Role of the United States in the Post–Cold War World

As in the other chapters in this book, it is wise to begin by recalling the past. In this case, I begin with the history and concepts that have guided U.S. foreign policy. This historical survey is useful first because the issues we will confront in the next half century, while distinctive, will not be wholly new. Americans have wrestled with them, wisely or otherwise, in the past, and that should help provide perspective as we face the future on the other side of the Great Spike.

Second, looking forward, it is necessary to see the past as objectively as we can. There are endless aphorisms about the usefulness of history to illuminate the present and the future, as well as many concerning its lack of usefulness. In general, the use of history as a guide to the future has a bad name. Samuel Taylor Coleridge in one century and Lewis Namier in another both asserted that humanity could only look at the past and was incapable of looking forward. But in a book about the future, there is virtue in trying to belie Coleridge and Namier and, looking backward as well as forward, in trying to clarify where we have come from and what we face in the time ahead.

From British Colonies to Hemispheric Dominance, 1775–1823

In the half century from the Revolutionary War to President James Monroe's message to the Congress in 1823, the United States evolved from a group of colonies to a nation-state. In this half century, the United States gained its independence with the decisive aid of France. It struggled through another war with Britain over a neutral country's right to freedom of the seas. In 1823, it moved to guarantee the independence of its hemisphere against military intrusion from outside.

There was an abiding security as well as an ideological component in the Monroe Doctrine. As for security, it warned the nations of Europe, including Russia, not to extend their military presence in the hemisphere. John C. Calhoun, then secretary of war, wished the United States to guarantee not merely the independence of Latin America from any extension of European power but also Latin America's movement toward democracy. John Quincy Adams, then secretary of state, had two objections. First, he felt that "the feudal and clerical heritage" of Latin America would render its movement toward democracy problematic. Second, the enunciation of such an ideological doctrine would lead the United States to become embroiled in the current struggle of Greece for independence against the Turkish Empire. He felt it was wrong for the United States to let its ideological sympathies involve the nation in Europe at a time it was restricting Europe's further involvement in this hemisphere. Adams won on both counts: The Monroe Doctrine was limited to guaranteeing the states of Latin America their independence, and the United States committed itself not to engage itself in European quarrels or wars. The Monroe Doctrine proved a halfway house—still grounded in Washington's farewell address—between the nation's initial effort at neutrality and the global responsibility it was to assume in the 20th century.

From the Monroe Doctrine to the Partial Assumption of Global Responsibility, 1823–1890

With its ideological base in the Monroe Doctrine, the United States pushed westward. That historic march was broken by the Civil War. France and Britain, looking backward, took that war as an occasion to undo the Monroe Doctrine; indeed, with the outcome undecided, a split of the United States and an opening for Europe in Latin America seemed possible. But the Emancipation Proclamation and the Union victories at Gettysburg, Vicksburg, and Atlanta washed out the visions of the past. Their place was taken by visions of the future whose author, in a sense, was the ambitious but still cautious Otto von Bismarck. He capped his quick victories over Austria, Denmark, and France with the creation in 1870 of a united German empire in the center of Europe.[1] But a new perspective took hold in the German camp when the less cautious Kaiser Wilhelm dispensed with Bismarck in 1890.

In the United States, the transition was fitful and complex, and there were many cross-strains, but 1890 is a reasonable benchmark. During that year, the director of the census announced the closing of the American frontier, and Admiral Alfred T. Mahan published his remarkable book *Sea Power and History*. Meanwhile, a new generation of Americans—mainly professionals and intellectuals—began to argue that it was no longer realistic and appropriate for Americans to rely on others for national security. The United States had to protect its Atlantic and Pacific approaches itself, given the declining relative power of Britain. This was the view, however, of a handful of leaders, not of the average citizen. E. V. Rostow captured this gap between what was happening and the world of ideas: "Certain actions took place . . . which turned out to be constructive factors in the evolution of American foreign policy. But while one could detect slight movement in the intellectual content of the American foreign policy tradition, Washington's Farewell Address and the Monroe Doctrine still had so much prestige as icons, and so much inertia, that they easily resisted the forces for change."[2]

The Uneven Performance of the United States on the World Scene, 1890–1945

Like the other periods into which I have divided the past two centuries, 1890 to 1945 was marked by an uneven transition toward a relatively clear-cut position. This transition began with American participation in the last year and a half of World War I. The war ended with some 2 million armed Americans in Europe. They were the critical margin between Allied victory and defeat. But the period between 1890 and April 1917 was profoundly schizophrenic. The United States was caught between an old attachment to Washington's Farewell Address and the Monroe Doctrine and the realities of a world where an American president sent the great White Fleet around the world and settled at Portsmouth, New Hampshire, a war between Japan and Russia (1905). This schizophrenia was settled for a time not by a mannerly or even raucous American debate on the national interest but by a German declaration of its right to impose unrestricted submarine warfare in the Atlantic—a felony the Germans compounded with the Zimmermann telegram, which promised Mexico a return of its empire in the Southwest of the United States if it sided with Germany in a German-American war. A neutral country's right to sail the seas safely was as old and deep in American history as Washington's Farewell Address, but President Woodrow Wilson rationalized American participation in the war not solely in terms of freedom of the seas but as the struggle for a peaceful, democratic world rooted in the universal acceptance of international law. The symbol was to be American membership in the League of Nations, but an ailing Wilson failed to carry his country.

Historians differ as to what caused Wilson's failure: his unwillingness to compromise with Republican members of the Senate, the pro-German bias of J. M. Keynes's *Economic Consequence of the Peace*, the pedestrian nationalistic concerns of the European leaders at Versailles. In any case, America went from Wilson's internationalist, idealistic rhetoric to a pragmatic isolationism that hardened after the Great Depression produced a major domestic crisis. When war broke out in 1939, the United States, led by a determined Congress hardened by its isolationism, declared its neutrality. The survival of Britain in 1940 was enough to loosen the bonds of neutrality and induce Congress to pass the Lend-Lease Act early in 1941. But it took the catastrophe of Pearl Harbor on December 7, 1941, to bring the whole nation together to fight a two-front war from an initially weak position.

Most Americans were conscious of the costs to the nation and the world of acute nationalism during the depression and of isolation from 1939 to Pearl Harbor. They tried to make sure that history would not repeat itself. The United States had pulled its short-term loans home from Europe in 1928–1929 to make a profit in the stock market in New York. Thus, a central world bank, the International Monetary Fund, was created to provide short-term lending that would not be affected by such short-term considerations. The New York market had suddenly ceased to lend abroad on the long term, again due to the appeal of the stock market. Thus, a long-run global lending agency, the World Bank, was created. Tariffs had proved an illusory device for shielding nations from the vicissitudes of international trade. Thus, the General Agreement on Tariffs and Trade (GATT) and a commitment to negotiate for an approximation of free trade were made. A heavy price was paid by all for the failure of America to join the League of Nations. Thus, long and careful efforts with the Senate in support of U.S. membership in the United Nations were made by Presidents Roosevelt and Truman. It is difficult if not impossible to find in history so clear an example of a nation making systematic amends for its failure — and the common failure — in the interwar years. In Coleridge's phrase, America tried to "learn from history."

In 1945–1946, however, the United States as a political community showed every inclination to return to isolation. In November 1946, the armed forces having been substantially dismantled, congressional election battles were fought primarily on the issue of meat rationing, and the Democratic administration lost ground. But meanwhile, a view was forming in the executive branch and among congressional leaders that under Stalin's leadership the Soviet Union was going to press to the West as far as it could safely advance. General George Marshall rejected Washington's Farewell Address and the limitations of the Monroe Doctrine: "It no longer appears practical to continue what we once conceived as hemispheric defense as a satisfactory basis for our security. We are now concerned with the peace of the entire world."[3] Along the way, George Kennan's "Long Telegram" from Moscow in February 1946 and, even more, Clark Clifford's canvassing of high-level thought in the executive branch in September 1946 helped crystallize opinion within the government. Above all, it was decided that it was only a matter of time before the Soviet Union acquired nuclear weapons.

The first secretary of the British Embassy delivered to the State Department on February 21, 1947, word that Britain could no longer hold the line alone against the communist guerrilla warfare mounted against Greece and provide the external support needed by Turkey as it faced protracted Soviet pressure. By that time, the executive branch was in much better shape to deal with the crisis than a year earlier. On March 12, 1947, the American response was laid before Congress, the Truman Doctrine was launched, and, with Marshall's unsatisfactory talks with Stalin on Germany in the early spring of 1947, the Cold War was joined.

The Cold War, 1945–1989

The various stages in the Cold War not only have been the subject of a mountainous literature but also are, on the whole, fresh in mind.[4] I shall focus, therefore, on one important point about the Cold War that is often overlooked and that bears directly on the theme of this chapter—namely, that the Cold War and the policy of deterrence were conducted by the United States while pursuing a larger policy rooted in the United Nations charter, which called for organizing the international community in peace and under law. That was the job that America, despite Wilson's urging, failed to undertake in 1919. That was the job that, under Franklin Roosevelt's leadership, America did undertake during World War II and that President Truman and his successors carried forward in the half century after 1945.

This thesis needs some explaining. It is a fact, of course, that many of the policies pursued to move the world toward the larger vision were also touched by a Cold War dimension. For example, the Marshall Plan was, in part, an instrument of containment. But it, along with the North Atlantic Treaty Organization (NATO) and, indeed, the European Community, were institutions meant to solve once and for all the long-run instability of Europe and the French-German rivalry. In the language Jean Monnet used with Konrad Adenauer on May 23, 1950, in Bonn with respect to the proposal for a Coal and Steel Community: "The aim of the French proposal, therefore, is essentially political. It even has an aspect which might be called moral."[5]

Monnet, the acknowledged father of a united Europe and, after World War I, a deputy secretary general of the League of Nations, ended his *Memoirs* with a paragraph that reaches beyond Europe. It captures well the view that in his mind—and the minds of others— the Cold War was incidental to the achievement of "the organized world of tomorrow."

> Have I said clearly enough that the Community we have created is not an end in itself? It is a process of change, continuing that same process which in an earlier period of history produced our national forms of life. Like our provinces in the past, our nations today must learn to live together under common rules and institutions freely arrived at. The sovereign nations of the past can no longer solve the problems of the present: they cannot ensure their own progress or control their own future. And the Community itself is only a stage on the way to the organized world of tomorrow.[6]

The American ultimate commitment to a democratic world, at peace under law, was and is an honest reflection of the interests of the nation. It is not simply high-minded Wilsonian rhetoric. America is part of a large island off the mainland of Eurasia. The Monroe Doctrine declared that no extracontinental power could extend its military power into this hemisphere. In return, Latin Americans exacted in time from the United States a commitment to live by the dictates of treaty arrangements that denied the United States the exercise of its military power against Latin American states—a dictum violated occasionally and mainly in the Caribbean and, when Wilson was president, in Mexico. The result of this arrangement, nevertheless, is that Latin America spends about 1.5% of its GNP in military outlays; Africa about 4%; Europe 4.7%; the Middle East 20.1%; and North America 4.7%. This relationship was put to the test in the Cuban missile crisis, and Latin America backed Kennedy's position with greater unanimity and strength than did Western Europe. The Latin Americans, on the whole, would prefer dealing with the major power they know, bound by treaty and common law to be a good neighbor, than to become a bear pit among major contending powers.

In Europe, America alone had the capability to protect the West against nuclear blackmail by the Russians or any other nuclear power. Moreover, the American presence in NATO was assurance to the lesser states of Europe against eventual German domination. However, as the Bosnian crisis demonstrated, there is not yet a European foreign policy. In the end, NATO and the United Nations have been able to operate effectively only with a strong, positive U.S. position.

In Asia, similarly, the United States stood against whatever power sought hegemony in the region, whether Japan, China, or the Soviet Union. As in Europe, the United States was the friend of the smaller nations by advocating and bringing to life a larger policy of regional unity. That was what the smaller nations wanted rather than to be the pawns of the larger regional powers. Even Vietnam has followed this course and joined with the smaller and middle-sized powers in the Association of Southeast Asian Nations (ASEAN).

In terms of its narrow national interests, the U.S. role of critical margin vis-à-vis Europe and Asia prevented an unfriendly power from taking over the Atlantic or the Pacific. This role might be assumed someday by another major power, but that moment is not yet in sight. This might well still be true for the middle of the next century.

The United States as the Critical Margin in the Post–Cold War World, 1989–2050

The UN charter has built into it a deep-rooted problem that is un-likely to be remedied by 2050. The preamble of the charter is pro-claimed by the "Peoples of the United Nations," but the document was signed by representatives of governments who carefully preserved their sovereignty. Thus, the United Nations was not designed as a world government but, in its own phrasing, as "a center for harmonizing the actions of nations in the attainment of . . . common ends." "Nations" is the critical word.

This problem has had wide ramifications. The United Nations (and the League of Nations before it) has been, on the whole, impotent in preventing conflict. In the Cold War, the Western powers had to provide alternative regional arrangements to those developed by the United Nations, such as the Organization of American States (OAS) in Latin America; the OECD and NATO in Europe; and now ASEAN and the Asia-Pacific Economic Cooperation (APEC) in Asia and the Pacific. In all cases, economic and other regional instruments of the United Nations existed.

Although it was the unilateral American decision to deal with the incursion into South Korea that was decisive, the role of the United Nations, to put it politely, was made more possible by the temporary withdrawal of the Soviet Union from the Security Council. In the Gulf War, again, ad hoc relations were worked out in the military coali-tion that forced the withdrawal of Iraqi forces from Kuwait. In the crisis over the successor states to Yugoslavia, the problems have only been dramatized by the awkward relations between the United Nations and NATO.

Why has this clumsy dual system been permitted to persist? In the short run, the cross-purposes of major members of the United Nations varied from time to time and with the problems confronted. Some of those problems represented "common ends" that could be pursued through UN channels. Moreover, in a precarious world that contained the possibility of nuclear war, each side in the Cold War felt the United Nations represented a safety net for contact if the normal workings of diplomacy failed or were insufficient. In the long run, it was at least the hope of the Western nations that the Cold War would in time give way to the "harmonizing" of national interests over a broad front on which the viability of the United Nations ultimately depended. And so this peculiar system continued, although, in 1995, the 50th anniversary of the United Nations was the occasion for much angry and disappointed rhetoric, which had its origins in debates in San Francisco in 1945 over the role of the nation-state.

In the light of experience with both the League of Nations and the United Nations, these are the principles needed to get us safely to 2050.

1. A *credible framework of "uniting for peace"* by the United Nations Security Council, especially its permanent members, is needed to *undo acts of aggression should they occur.* In South Korea some 45 years ago and more recently in the Persian Gulf, the Security Council proved this could be done, albeit at great cost. On both occasions, the United Nations was saved from the fate of the League of Nations when the latter failed to deal with the Japanese invasion of Manchuria in 1931. The United Nations, however, did not provide effective machinery for deterring aggression in either 1950 or 1990, and it has failed systematically in this respect since 1945, including the recent failure in what was Yugoslavia, which it subsequently attempted to redress.

2. Therefore, the second dimension of rules for the future is *the provision of systematic and organized regional efforts to maintain balances of power that make regional aggression grossly irrational.* These arrangements should embrace, where acceptable, a role for interested nations outside the regions, whose work in this regard should be linked closely, if possible and effective, with that of the Security Council. That happened in what was once Yugoslavia, but it did not happen until, under American leadership, NATO came alive in 1995.

3. These rules require *systematic regional as well as global economic and technological cooperation,* including sustained efforts by the more-advanced nations to assist the less-advanced ones in moving forward in economic and social progress, including also the preservation of a viable environment for future generations. Global and regional efforts now exist with these purposes but on a scale that evidently does not match the size and importance of the problems.

4. Stubborn efforts by governments and their citizens are required to continue the trend toward increased *democratization and the further extension of human rights,* including respect for "the dignity and worth of the human person."

5. This effort to achieve a civilized and humane world order must be underpinned by *a heightening of those strands in our respective cultures and religions that enjoin the individual to care for the fate of others as well as our own.* Without leadership and will, rooted in

such values, this multipolar world can become a scene of chaotic violence rather than an increasingly credible approximation of the ideal expressed in the UN charter.

As earlier underlined, neither the League of Nations nor the United Nations took account of the importance of successful regional arrangements. There were UN institutions in the various regions, for example, in Geneva, the Economic Commission for Europe, and, in time, parallel organizations in Santiago, Bangkok, and Addis Ababa. In the cases of Latin America, Asia, and Africa, there now exist regional development banks that are tied loosely to the United Nations. But the more vital regional functions have been carried out in the Western Hemisphere by the OAS and in Europe by the elaborate set of regional institutions that developed into the European Union and NATO, and in the Pacific, APEC also arose independent of the UN system. Thus, ad hoc arrangements linking the United Nations to other regional arrangements were sometimes created, as in the cases of the Gulf War and, more recently, the civil war in former Yugoslavia. Taken overall, the deterrence of conflict, which is often regional in the first instance, has been done poorly.

The experiences of post-1945 Europe, stripped down to essentials, suggest the general character of the problem and its long-run solution. Europe managed to create over the past 50 years a reasonable if still somewhat fragile approximation of the international "peace and security" for which the UN charter calls. It did so by acting effectively, in collaboration with the United States and, in recent years, with the Soviet Union, in three critical dimensions:

1. It provided solutions to critical political questions, notably, in Germany and Eastern Europe. Germany appears embedded in the institutions of Europe, and, although Hitler is not forgotten, it is unlikely to make a third thrust for European hegemony.
2. It enacted arms-control measures ruling out the possibility of military hegemony.
3. The more-advantaged nations provided assistance to the less-advantaged nations of the region, notably, to countries in Southern and Eastern Europe and Africa.

The whole process was moved forward by regional progress on human rights via the Helsinki Accords and, since 1989, by the explicit triumph of democracy in most of Eastern Europe. One key to the triumph of democratic principles in Europe was the decision to make loyalty to those principles a criterion for membership in the European Community. This device could not immediately undergo global application.

Despite some dangerous European crises over the past two generations, the perhaps-abating crisis in the Balkans, and the still-unresolved question of extending NATO to the east, these constructive objectives have been reasonably well fulfilled as of the mid-1990s, although the balance achieved will evidently have to be watched and nurtured, not taken for granted, over the generations ahead. Among the palpable dangers is the reassertion of potentially explosive schismatic strands of nationalism, often with ancient roots. In the end, only a heightened sense of the potentialities of a great East-West Europe within which old historical attachments have a proper but limited place will permit these fragmenting impulses to subside.

In the case of the Middle East, there is a rough consensus that regional peace and security require special versions of the three conditions required in Europe:

1. A settlement of the problems of Palestine, Lebanon, and Syria and other major unresolved political questions within the area.
2. A reliable arms-limitation-and-control agreement, backed by external powers, that would rule out the temptation for any Middle Eastern nation to seek regional hegemony by military means.
3. A regional development bank to accelerate the economic and social progress of the less affluent, financed, in part at least, by oil revenues provided by the nations richly endowed with oil reserves.

Obviously, none of this is possible unless the governments and people of the Middle East—looking back over more than 40 years of bloody struggle; looking at the tragedy all around them; looking at their children and heeding their possible fate—decide that enough is enough, that it is time to make peace, as Central Europe did in 1648 when the Treaty of Westphalia brought a period of terrible bloodletting toward a close. We are, perhaps, halfway there.

The Western Hemisphere is, of course, a quite different case than the Middle East. On the political side, the historical equivalent of the German problem in Europe has been, in a sense, the problem of the United States. How could unilateral intervention by a more powerful United States in Latin America be deterred? How could the inescapable interdependencies of the more- and less-developed parts of the hemisphere be dealt with through dignified partnership rather than through excessive dependence on the United States?

Over the decades, substantial progress has been made on both scores, as both Latin America and the United States matured within the deceptively somnolent framework of the OAS and the principles it incorporates. These principles also provide a basis for dealing with a problem much on Latin American minds but not much discussed, if at all, in official public discourse within the hemisphere: How, in the long run, can the small and medium-sized Latin American states deal with the three largest states, Brazil, Mexico, and Argentina?

The achievements in the hemisphere thus far are generally ignored or taken for granted by the American public. The greatest possibilities in the hemisphere, however, are creative. They arise from the surge of democratic aspiration and the emergence of a new generation of Latin American leaders determined to break out of the economic and political distortions that stem from the birth of Latin American industrialization in the Great Depression of the 1930s. Protectionism is giving way to more liberal trade and state autarchy to more competitive private markets and the welcoming of foreign private capital. The new directions have been strengthened by demonstrations of economic vitality in the noncommunist world, notably in East Asia, and the palpable bankruptcy of the communist states. The end of the Cold War contributed to the outcome by reducing the leverage of Third World bystanders and encouraged these nations to begin to face up to domestic problems only they could solve.

If the three major powers in Latin America—Argentina, Brazil, and Mexico—could sustain self-disciplined economic performance plus continued democratic government, some rather remarkable innovations might become possible in time. For example, there might emerge serious movement toward an extension of the North American Free Trade Agreement (NAFTA) into a Hemispheric Common Market—a hemispheric version of the OECD to work on such problems as assistance to the weaker economies; financial cooperation among the central banks; concerted work on environmental problems; the buildup of Latin American scientific and technological institutions and their opening to students from the small and medium-sized Latin American countries; and full participation in the dynamic development of East Asia. As for democracy and human rights—which are still fragile—the heartening progress made in recent years could be strengthened and consolidated by a unifying hemispheric program of this kind.

On November 9, 1989, 12 nations meeting in Canberra set APEC in motion. That was also the day the Berlin Wall came down. On a TV program that night, I expressed the view that in the long sweep of history, the modest birth of APEC might well outrank the dramatic end of the Berlin Wall. The creation of APEC was a collective, first formal step toward one of the most important goals of the 21st century: to assure that the governments and peoples of the Pacific Basin, in the language of the UN charter, "maintain international peace and security . . . practice tolerance and live together . . . as good neighbors."

In terms of population, economic and technological momentum, and military potential, the Pacific Basin in the next century is likely to remain the most important single community on earth. It contains not only China, Japan, and ASEAN but also Russia and the United States. Moreover, a number of Latin American countries will almost certainly join APEC. The Pacific Basin is also inevitably linked by geography with South Asia. And in the course of the coming decades, that linkage could become increasingly important, especially if South Asia's affairs could be stabilized in the spirit of the organization of South Asian Regional Cooperation (SARC), created in 1983.

On the other hand a considerable array of dangerous political problems must be settled in Asia:

- Cambodia has not yet achieved stable peace.
- Vietnam has not yet found the road to civilized and efficient modernization that its talented people are clearly capable of traveling, although it has entered its natural home in ASEAN, and foreign investment and trade are rising.
- The issue of unity is still to be settled peacefully by Koreans, and the ambiguity of North Korea's nuclear status is among the most acute regional nuclear issues.
- Formal peace still does not exist between Japan and Russia.
- China's post–Cold War domestic evolution remains incomplete, and question marks remain concerning the fate of Hong Kong and Taiwan.

Overall, however, the scene is relatively tranquil compared to the recent past, and the time is propitious to act with stubborn patience on this ample political agenda.

As for the arms-control agenda, the transformation of Russia's relationship to the world has greatly eased tensions. This is, of course, less true in the Pacific than in the Atlantic, as the considerable list of unresolved political problems in East Asia cited above suggests. Definitive arms-control agreements might well be possible when those problems are resolved and when China, North Korea, and Vietnam move toward approximations of liberal democracy. But right now, with sophisticated military equipment in gross oversupply, China continues to arm in a substantial way. The present network of security relations in the Pacific Basin, reflecting a wide range of concerns, is best left alone. But, in the end, APEC will not fulfill its destiny unless it engages this complex diplomatic and arms-control agenda.

This is not a banal or pious conclusion. As China moves toward a role as a great world power, acquiring in the two generations ahead all the technologies that will be then current, with a population of perhaps 1.5 billion, it is important that it accept the verdict of the 20th century: Efforts at regional or global hegemony end badly, as Germany, Japan, and Russia progressively discovered. A Chinese thrust for control of the South China Sea and the Malacca Strait—the key to the Asian balance of power—would find Russia, Japan, India, and the members of ASEAN against it, and probably the United States as well. With the capacity to produce nuclear weapons and other instruments of mass destruction spreading, we should not risk another world war. On the other hand, a modern China surrounded by comfortable and secure neighbors would be a great world power.

Americans have a special reason for concerning themselves with these matters. We have no cause for condescension or self-congratulation. We have only slowly and painfully learned a simple lesson: We cannot be a significant factor on the world scene if the smaller nations near us are not comfortable and secure. Specifically, this, above all, has meant that Canada and Mexico should be comfortable and secure.

This is, as well, the lesson that India and Russia must learn. India cannot fulfill its global possibilities unless Pakistan, Bangladesh, and Sri Lanka are comfortable and secure in the face of India's size and expanding technological prospects. Similarly, the dream of a peaceful Russian confederation will not be advanced for long by a series of Chechnyas. Russia, as it finds its feet economically and technologically in the next century, will have to make its neighbors in the commonwealth comfortable and secure if it is to play its part as the great world power it could surely become again.

Without extending the analysis to Africa and the Indian subcontinent—which can easily be done—I conclude that if chaos is avoided and the objectives of the UN charter gradually approximated, a flexible federal structure is likely to emerge. That structure will provide for an array of purely global, purely regional, and mixed enterprises.

Relations between non-UN regional institutions and the United Nations will vary, but we live in a world where the large objectives of the United Nations cannot be achieved by it alone, and this inelegant state of affairs is likely to be generally accepted.

The Role of the United States

If this is a roughly correct view of the common task in a world of accelerated diffusion of power that has succeeded the Cold War, what is the appropriate role of the United States, given its abiding interests? Once again, those interests are that no single nation dominate the balance of power in Europe or Asia and thereby gain control of the Atlantic or the Pacific; that no major external power emplace itself in the Western Hemisphere with substantial military force; and that the United States deter the use of weapons of mass destruction. The United States is also committed by the binding core of our nation's creed to support peacefully the causes of economic and social development, human rights, and political democracy.

But these objectives have, somehow, an empty ring. Groups large and small, sophisticated and unsophisticated, ask themselves: "What are we going to substitute for the full-blooded, unambiguous enemies we enjoyed during the world wars and the Cold War?" It was much easier to fight the Kaiser, Hitler, Tojo, or Stalin than to rally around a banner inscribed with abstract, positive objectives. It was much easier to rally an unarmed nation to fight its way back from near defeat early in 1942 than it is to pursue patiently and stubbornly the small preventive steps by which large positive goals are achieved in the post–Cold War world.

This transformation, however, must take place if the United States is to play steadily a constructive role on the world scene. There is much glory for America in contemplating its role in the 20th century. But there is also a strand of immaturity in its performance. America believed in isolationism and acted on that belief. Its enemies systematically took steps assuming that the United States was irrelevant to their seizing the balance of power in their respective regions. In Andrei Vichinsky's phrase (in the context of Korea) as reported to Dean Rusk: "The U.S. deceived them."

The continuance of that convulsive pattern into the 21st century will be exceedingly dangerous. The diffusion of power palpably under way will increase the number of nations who command weapons of mass destruction. They must see in the United States a mature, well-armed nation that stands steadily by the concepts that define both its own and the common interest. As we have seen, these interests can be stated positively as an interest in global peace under law and movement toward the UN goals of human rights and political democracy. This is what the political slogan the "New World Order" was all about.

But how much influence on the course of events does the United States command? A few years ago, there was a good deal of talk in the United States and around the world about the decline and fall of the United States as a great power. After the Gulf War, there was a good deal of talk about the United States as the single remaining superpower. With the unnerving stubbornness of the 1991–1992 recession and a certain loss of poise and sense of direction in the executive branch as the general election approached, the image of a fading America reemerged. The period 1993–1997 provided evidence that was taken to mean that the United States was both a fading giant and the sole superpower. Both images of the United States are, I believe, misleading.

Seizaburo Sato, a Japanese foreign-policy expert, once defined "the greatness of a power as measured by four things: wealth, military strength, political ideas and the will to impose them, and a culture that appeals to other people and can influence them. The United States is the only super power on all four counts. Japan, says Sato, has the wealth, and may come to have some cultural sway. But it lacks the political will and the military strength."[7]

There is a certain neatness about Sato's definition that doesn't quite fit the dynamics of the diffusion of power that will mark the 21st century. The United States has had and still has a considerable array of serious domestic problems, but it is a resilient, creative, continental society, with many centers of initiative and experiment and a saving, skeptical sense of humor. We are committed by our origins as a nation to ideals beyond our reach — perhaps beyond human reach — but we keep striving. On our most serious social problem — the building of a multiracial society of equal opportunity in the cities — some progress has occurred in the past several generations, but the cities are still deteriorating. The increasingly multiracial character of American society poses considerable challenges in the short run. It could prove a source of strength in the intensely multiracial global arena of the next century, but that depends in large part on finding a solution to the acute urban problem.

As for being a superpower, it is now clear in retrospect that in a world of diffusing power, the notion of a superpower has been an illusion and is becoming progressively more so. The United States does represent a significant margin of power and influence, but if it seeks to do something that runs against the grain of majority thought and feeling in the world, it can be easily frustrated or, indeed, vetoed. When its view of things conforms to the common view or majority interest, the United States can still play a critical catalytic role in the enterprise.

We are, in short, as I have argued, the "critical margin." At the margin, the quiet, purposeful presence of the United States is required to sustain the balance of power in Europe, the Middle East, Latin America, and the Pacific; I think the case could be made, as well, for Africa. The United States cannot impose its will on others as a hegemonic power. Powers large and small can tell us to go to hell and regularly do. But major diplomatic or military objectives are difficult to attain in the world community without our active participation. And there is no contemporary power that can now perform our role. Europe is not yet sufficiently unified to do the job on its own, as the crises in the Persian Gulf and what was Yugoslavia underlined; Russia, in extraordinary disarray as it makes the triple transition from single-party dictatorship to democracy, from central command to a market economy, from an empire maintained by force to a federal system governed by consent, cannot yet play this part, nor can Japan by reason of its history in the 20th century and because its rapid transition from a state of insular isolation to status as a comfortable leader in the world community is still incomplete, nor can China or India. It is not likely that any other nation can play this role of critical margin for some time.

If the United States fails to assume the responsibilities of the critical margin, the alternative is likely to be chaos dangerous to the interests of all. Despite the higher priority certain domestic problems clearly deserve, this is not a world from which the United States can safely withdraw. It remains, as Dean Acheson once said, an arena in which we must continue to pursue our purposes "like the pain of earning a living."[8] But we cannot pursue our purposes abroad if we cannot resolve our greatest domestic challenge: the urban problem, to which I shall now turn.

EIGHT

The Critical Margin and America's Inner Cities

There is no extravagance more prejudicial to the growth of national wealth than the wasteful negligence which allows genius that happens to be born of lowly parentage to expend itself in lowly work.

Alfred Marshall, *Principles of Economics* (1890)

The slums . . . constitute America's main domestic challenge today.

Economist, March 20, 1992

I agree with British economist Alfred Marshall about the high costs of "wasteful negligence" of the poor and with the *Economist* that the slums in our cities constitute "America's main domestic challenge." But those judgments alone would not justify making the urban problem the subject of the final substantive chapter of this book. What argues for coming to rest here on the contemporary urban problem is the view that it will be impossible, over a period of time, for the United States to play the role of critical margin on the world scene if we do not solve the urban problem.

By "solve," I do not mean a reduction of the social pathology within the inner cities to the level of the more affluent counties that surround them. That will take time, perhaps a generation or more. Indeed, it might never happen. In any case, there is no quick fix. By "solve," I mean the bringing about of a systematic and substantive process of decline in the social pathology of the inner city. That demonstration will convince those who live there and the community as a whole that the job is doable. Right now, the greatest obstacle to a solution of the problem is the belief both in the inner city and the community at large that the job is not doable.

As I said on another occasion:

> When I am asked how I would rate the urban problem on the agenda of national-security problems, I reply it is our number one national-security problem. If we succeed in mastering the current urban problem of our country, we shall strengthen our hand on the world scene. We shall demonstrate that we can be a truly multiracial society, which is at the same time true to the international ideals to which we as a nation have long been committed. Nothing constructive can be accomplished in this dynamic, contentious, aspiring world without the active participation of the United States. But, if we fail to master the urban problem, we shall, I fear, turn inward, away from the world. We shall be unable to play our part at the critical margin. And we shall risk a world environment of chaos.[1]

What is the basis for this apocalyptic conclusion? First, the demographic factor provides a basis for this conclusion. At the present time, some 40% of the entrants into the U.S. workforce are immigrants. And these proportions are on the rise since the 1970s, as Table 8.1 indicates. More than half those who attend public schools in our major cities are minorities.

This point can be driven home by examining the Texas A&M study of prospects for Texas, where the proportional rise of the Hispanic population is substantial.[2] First, the pessimistic base projections. If the trends of 1980–1990 persist, by 2030 the total population of the state would increase by 99% to 34 million. The increase, however, would

Table 8.1. Immigrants as Proportion of Those Entering U.S. Work Force, 1951–1993

Time Period	Annual Percent Change in Civilian Labor Force	Number of Immigrants as a Percentage of Labor Force Growth
1951–1960	1.8	33.0
1961–1970	1.9	27.0
1971–1980	2.6	20.0
1981–1990	1.6	36.0
1991–1993	1.0	a

Sources: Adapted from Frank D. Bean, Robert G. Cushing, and Charles W. Hayes, "The Changing Demography of U.S. Immigration Flows: Patterns, Projections, and Contexts," in Klaus J. Bade and Myron Weiner, eds., *Migration Past, Migration Future: Germany and the United States* (Oxford: Berghahn Books, 1997), table 6; U.S. Department of Commerce, *Monthly Labor Review of Bureau of Labor Statistics* (Washington, D.C.: Government Printing Office, various years); U.S. Immigration and Naturalization Service, *Statistical Yearbook of the United States* (1994).

aIncludes Immigration Reform and Control Act–adjusted immigrants. The 1991–1992 figure was as high as 90%, due to the regularization permitted by that act.

Table 8.2. Composition of U.S. Population by Race, 1990–2030

Anglo		Black		Hispanic		Other	
1990	2030	1990	2030	1990	2030	1990	2030
64.6%	37.5%	10.8%	9.1%	22.3%	45.6%	2.3%	5.2%

be dominated by minorities, Hispanics above all. Anglos would increase by 20%, Hispanics by 258%. The Anglo population, almost 60% in 1990, would fall to 37%, while Hispanics would account for 46% of the population in 2030.

Under the rigid and linear assumptions used in this exercise in forecasting, the shift would profoundly affect the structure of the working force as well as the expenditures on AFDC (cash assistance to mothers with preschool children), Medicaid, and food stamps. The proportion of Texas citizens below the poverty line would rise, average household income would fall, and total state taxes would increase by less than the population. A marked further polarization of incomes between the minorities and the Anglos would take place. Texas would contain, in this scenario, a somewhat poorer population in 2030 than in 1990, with a larger proportion of its people ill trained.

The labor force on a national basis would undergo the change shown in Table 8.2.[3] The Texas A&M authors then make an alternative optimistic linear assumption. They assume that between 1990 and 2020 there is "total closure in the difference in rates among Anglos, Blacks, and Hispanics." This calculation demonstrates the cost to the community of the underclass insofar as it is made up of minorities.[4]

- Public-school enrollment increases by 59% from 1990 to 2030, compared to 61% under the base projections.
- College enrollment increases by 103% from 1990 to 2030, compared to 50% under the base projections.
- Aggregate income would increase by 151% versus 99% from 1990 to 2030.
- The rise in poverty would be reduced from an increase of 165% from 1990 to 2030 to an increase of 44%.
- The number of Texas Youth Commission enrollees would decline by 22% rather than increase by 81%.
- The number of persons in prison would decline by 21% from 1995 to 2030 instead of increasing by 68%.
- AFDC would decline by 21% from 1990 to 2030 rather than increase by 131%.

- The number of food-stamp recipients would decline by 26% from 1995 to 2030 rather than increase by 109%.
- Medicaid enrollees would decline by 1% from 1995 to 2030 rather than increase by 102%.
- Average household income would increase by 14% rather than decline by 9%.
- Consumer expenditure would increase by 133% from 1990 to 2030 rather than increase by 106%.
- State tax revenues would increase by 139% rather than increase by 98%.

It should be emphasized that these two projections are linear. Specifically, our analysis emphasizes the extent of intermarriage among the young in the presently minority populations and the possibility that the demographic situation in Mexico and the rise in income per capita there might lessen the pressure to migrate to the United States.

But these two linear projections reflect an authentic challenge. Passivity and hoping for the best will, as Paul Waggoner wrote, "butter no parsnips." Just as the current differentials between minority status and socioeconomic resources might lead to increased dependence and poverty in the underclass, so an alteration of such patterns could lead to enhanced socioeconomic conditions and increased independence. It is obvious that addressing such differences is critical to the state's long-term economic and social well-being. Specifically, the systematic exploitation of these possibilities would have a high rate of return. It would return big monetary profits to the Texas community as a whole.

Second, *education and high-tech jobs* provide a basis for my conclusion. A generation ago, those coming north from the southern United States or from abroad without an advanced education could still qualify for blue-collar manufacturing jobs. Innovation took place slowly and with little change in the skills required. Factories were organized from the top down with ample mid-level management. Now, however, there has been a polarization of skills and wages. Half of the widening of the wage-skill gap has been measured as a question of computer literacy. Personnel managers look for men and women who will pick up new skills as emerging technology dictates; who have mathematical skills up to the algebra level (if not differential calculus); who will contribute ideas leading to increases in productivity; who work well with others; who can write a coherent memorandum; who will report for work on time and regularly. This is the kind of workforce that will permit the thinning out of mid-level management.

The operational link to the abnormally high inner-city unemployment lies in the fact that, for whatever reason, the public-school system does not prepare young women and men for the modern workforce. In part, this has been the fault of the private sector. Preparation for the workforce historically has been the function of the school system, which in turn was adequate for the workforce of previous generations. The dropouts from middle school and high school — indeed, a majority of the young who persevere — usually regard their schooling as dull and irrelevant to their futures.

But behind the current failure to prepare young men and women for jobs in the modern world lies the progressive weakening of the family, notable throughout the Western world but particularly marked under the pressures of life in the American inner cities. Since a return to the romanticized family of Norman Rockwell's *Saturday Evening Post* covers seems unlikely — in the short run, in particular — the argument that follows looks to the creation in the inner cities of an extended family built up out of neighborhood institutions.

American cities need a quiet revolution that would link systematically the private sector and the school system from kindergarten to the workforce and professions. This does not require an educational system that separates early those who will seek a college degree (about 30%) from those who will pursue a technical track. The last thing the private sector wishes the school system to do is to introduce the student at length to a particular technology. Technology changes so fast that the student's knowledge will be overtaken by the time he or she enters the workforce. Thus, the final stage of training is done at the plant by the private sector.

Simon Head has argued persuasively that two technological gaps must be overcome.[5] One is the gap just referred to — namely, the need for training a workforce that can easily assemble a group of components, is flexible, and can work with a just-in-time inventory system. But Head also describes the rapid rise of outsourcing in the 1980s and 1990s. Earlier, some 70% of component production was unionized. This percentage has dropped radically in the United States, and this work now takes place under the threat of outsourcing the manufacture of components to overseas, low-wage plants. This method is made possible, Head argues, because new software permits production of satisfactory components by semiskilled labor.

Thus, industry faces two distinct problems related to the new technology: the problem of making the educational system turn out workers who can operate successfully in the computerized world of modern industry and the problem of unionization, wage settlements, and outsourcing to foreign plants in the component industry. The second problem will be eased in the long run by the rise of wages in the developing countries, which is beginning to happen; the first problem will be solved by an improved educational system in the United States. There is every reason to think that high-tech plants will be opened in time to take advantage of well-trained American labor if a rational educational policy is followed.

Meanwhile, however, there is a strong xenophobic reaction to the rise of the Hispanic and Asian populations in the United States, and the number of African Americans in the prison population is disproportionately large. A reaction by the Anglo majority is under way against the high cost of an underclass in welfare and other expenditures. In state elections as well as national politics, the key issues relate mainly to the pathology of the inner cities: crime, welfare, and education. Above all, in many American cities the linear projection of present acute trends has produced a strand of raw fear that not only has changed the character of American politics but also will alter the nation at home and its image and role abroad. Behind the fear is the notion that, with the Anglo population on the way to becoming a minority, American society will become unrecognizable. Frightened people do not lead well or comfortably.

It is true that there is a surge of Latin Americans and Asians in the U.S. population. It is true that the proportion that we now call Anglos will fall from 75% to 59% by 2040, and before that date certain of the states, notably California and Texas, will have Anglo minorities. As noted earlier, on present evidence, one-third of the younger Hispanic population will marry Anglos, as will 22% of the Asians. Mixed-race marriages are also on the rise among young African Americans.

This is not merely a matter of statistics and projections but a living reality. On Sunday, May 12, 1996, a newspaper in Austin, Texas ran five pictures of the week's brides. Two marriages were between Anglos. The other three were marriages between a Mexican bride and an Anglo, a young Indian woman and an Anglo, and an Anglo woman and a man from Sri Lanka. No doubt their children and grandchildren will be good Texans and thrive on barbecue.

Moreover, the birth rate in Mexico is falling rapidly. The social problem of the future will be the cost to the community of the retired population in Mexico, not of those looking for work. Since 1940, the

Mexican average per capita rate of growth has been at more than 2% per annum. By the middle of the next century, Mexico should attain at least the present level of New Zealand. The push of overpopulation and poverty might wane in time. There is every reason to have faith for the long term in the continuity of the principles that have guided the United States for more than two centuries.

But right now, the urban problem that fans out from the inner city to state and national politics cannot be understood except as a vicious circle that embraces the whole life of these neighborhoods and the larger society. I believe, then, that what we do or fail to do about the urban problem in the time ahead will determine whether we can play the international role envisaged for the United States through 2050.

The Dynamics of the Vicious Circle in the Inner City

Like many major phenomena, the present deteriorating state of the inner cities results from the convergence of a number of independent, powerful forces, in particular the following:

- The World War II and postwar large-scale migration of African Americans from the rural south to northern cities and an accelerated flow of immigrants from Latin America. On the whole, both groups were initially poor and not well educated.
- Nevertheless, until the coming of the microelectronics revolution in (approximately) the mid-1970s, a good many migrants commanded sufficient skills to find places in the manufacturing workforce. The new technologies widened the gap in required areas of competence (and in wage rates) between skilled and unskilled labor and raised the skill requirements for many service jobs.
- As this process proceeded, the average level of unemployment in the United States rose from 4.7% in the 1950s and 1960s to 7.1% in the 1970s and 1980s. As Tables 8.3, 8.4, and 8.5 demonstrate, "Black" unemployment ran at about twice the level of "White"; for males 16–19, the "Black and Other" proportion of that group more than doubled over this period relative to "White."
- The adjustment of the inner-city workforce to the imperatives of the new technologies from the 1970s forward was gravely impeded by the sluggish response of the public-school system to the new environment and by the almost equal sluggishness of private and public employers in cooperating intimately with the school systems in training the young for good entry-level jobs upon graduation from

Table 8.3. Cyclical Behavior of Black and Other Relative to White Civilian Unemployment, 1948–November 1995

	All Workers	White	Black[a]	Black and Other/White
Peak 1948	3.8%	3.5%	5.9%	1.7%
Trough 1949	5.9	5.6	8.9	1.6
Peak 1953	3.0	2.7	4.5	1.7
Trough 1954	5.5	5.0	9.9	2.0
Peak 1956	4.1	3.6	8.3	2.3
Trough 1958	6.8	6.1	12.6	2.1
Peak 1960	5.5	5.0	10.2	2.0
Trough 1961	6.7	6.0	12.4	2.1
Peak 1969	3.5	3.1	6.4	2.1
Trough 1971	5.9	5.4	9.9	1.8
Peak 1973	4.9	4.3	9.0	2.1
Trough 1975	9.5	8.9	13.8	1.8
Peak 1979	5.8	5.1	11.3	2.2
Trough 1982	9.7	8.6	17.3	2.0
Peak 1989	5.3	4.5	10.0	2.2
Trough 1992	7.4	6.5	12.7	2.0
Peak 1995[b]	5.6	5.0	8.9	1.8

Source: Economic Report of the President to the Congress (Washington, D.C.: Government Printing Office, 1996), p. 320.

[a]"Black" after 1972.

[b]Latest date available, November 1995.

high school. Under these circumstances, the verdict of inner-city youth was overwhelmingly that their schooling was unrelated to any credible path to an attractive future. The adjustment to the realities by both public schools and employers is slowly changing, but change does not yet match the scale of the problem.

• This complex of circumstances heightened in the inner city the endemic pressures on conventional family life. These pressures were induced throughout the advanced industrial world by a change in sexual mores and the increased role of women in the workforce. In different ways, these circumstances in the inner city tended to reduce the inhibitions against teenage pregnancy and increased the attractiveness of gangs as a substitute for gravely weakened or nonexistent families.

• To an extent difficult to measure when multiple forces are at work, welfare policies might have compounded inner-city problems (as well as cushioning their impact) by providing what appeared to some a subsidy for creating a single-parent household and, more generally, by strengthening a sense of neocolonial dependence,

Table 8.4. Civilian Unemployment Rate, 1955–1995 (Monthly Data Seasonally Adjusted)

Year	All Civilian Workers	Males Total	Males 16–19 Years	Males 20 Years and Over	Females Total	Females 16–19 Years	Females 20 Years and Over	Both Sexes, 16–19 Years	White	Black and Other	Black	Experienced Wage Workers	Married Men, Spouse Present	Women Who Maintain Families
1955	4.4%	4.2%	11.6%	3.8%	4.9%	10.2%	4.4%	11.0%	3.9%	8.7%	—	4.8%	2.6%	—
1965	4.5	4.0	14.1	3.2	5.5	15.7	4.5	14.8	4.1	8.1	—	4.3	2.4	—
1975	8.5	7.9	20.1	6.8	9.3	19.7	8.0	19.9	7.8	13.8	14.8	8.3	5.1	10.0
1985	7.2	7.0	19.5	6.2	7.4	17.6	6.6	18.6	6.2	13.7	15.1	6.8	4.3	10.4
1995	5.6	5.6	18.4	4.8	5.6	16.1	4.9	17.3	4.9	9.6	10.4	5.4	3.3	8.0

Source: Adapted from *Economic Report of the President to the Congress* (Washington, D.C.: Government Printing Office, 1996), p. 324.

Table 8.5. Civilian Unemployment Rate, by Demographic Characteristic, 1955–1995 (Monthly Data Seasonally Adjusted)

Year	All Civilian Workers Total	White							Black and Other or Black						
		Total	Males			Females			Total	Males			Females		
			Total	16–19 Years	20 Years and Over	Total	16–19 Years	20 Years and Over		Total	16–19 Years	20 Years and Over	Total	16–19 Years	20 Years and Over
1955	4.4	3.9	3.7	11.3	3.3	4.3	9.1	3.9	8.7	8.8	13.4	8.4	8.5	19.2	7.7
1965	4.5	4.1	3.6	12.9	2.9	5.0	14.0	4.0	8.1	7.4	23.3	6.0	9.2	31.7	7.5
1975	8.5	7.8	7.2	18.3	6.2	8.6	17.4	7.5	14.8	14.8	38.1	12.5	14.8	41.0	12.2
1985	7.2	6.2	6.1	16.5	5.4	6.4	14.8	5.7	15.1	15.3	41.0	13.2	14.9	39.2	12.4
1995	5.6	4.9	4.9	15.6	4.3	4.8	13.4	4.3	10.4	10.6	37.1	8.8	10.2	34.3	8.6

Source: Adapted from *Economic Report of the President to the Congress* (Washington, D.C.: Government Printing Office, 1996), p. 325.

humiliation, and bitterness, weakening a view that greater control over one's destiny was possible. That, too, might be changing, but not rapidly enough to undo the vicious circle. The welfare legislation of 1996 might alter this situation; but this is still to be seen.
- The dynamics at work in the inner cities were complicated greatly by drugs and the fact that dealing appeared to be a realistic alternative to the more conventional career pathways, even though it carried a high risk of incarceration or early death.

Looked at in this way, the problem can be stated as follows: A powerful converging set of economic and technological forces sharply raised the level of unemployment in the inner city and simultaneously reduced in the minds of young men and women future prospects for good jobs. This perceived narrowing of realistic options led many young people to accept life on the streets. This led, in turn, to an increase in teen-age pregnancies, often associated with low birth weights. More generally, inexperienced and hard-pressed young mothers did not provide their children with the physical care, continuity of affection, and stimulus required for proper development in these early critical years. As a result the children often entered school with little self-esteem or confidence. They regarded themselves as losers.

In schools dominated by the principle that time should be the independent variable and learning the residual one, many students fall behind as problems of discipline eat up the time available for teaching. This lag plus the gathering sense that school offers no credible, attractive future yields a decision to drop out and surrender to the real-enough attractions of the streets: gangs, crime, sex, drugs. For some the attractions included money. The surrender to street life, in turn, constitutes a powerful negative feedback. It not only adds to the flow into the system of teenage mothers but also enlarges the pool of young people ill-equipped for decent entry-level jobs in an increasingly high-tech world. And so the vicious circle continues.

It cannot be said too often that our present social policy organized by public and private authorities is primarily after-the-fact damage limitation rather than a preventive policy. This kind of primarily remedial social policy would only be acceptable for the long run if some other forces were bringing forward the young out of inner-city poverty into the mainstream. For previous generations of immigrants, there were three such forces: the family, the churches, and an educational system that effectively equipped its students for a workforce demanding only modest skills, although some schools of an earlier era prepared many immigrant children for business and the professions.

In fact, the underdevelopment of American inner cities has a great deal in common with underdevelopment abroad. The major difference—more important than initial income per capita—is the greater weakness of the families in the American inner cities. For many contemporary inner-city children, viable families do not exist, and sufficient education is not acquired to enter the workforce or the professions at a satisfying level. As a matter of long-term trend, the old dynamics do appear still to be working—that is, the proportion of African Americans and Hispanics entering the middle and white-collar classes appears to be rising. But for a large number of minority children, men, and women, the system of institutions from prenatal care forward fails, bringing about great human tragedy, which transmits itself to American society as a whole.

In the short run, society is protected from the full, potentially disruptive consequences of this failure only by enormous safety-net and remedial expenditures that mitigate but do not solve the problem. Something like 40% of the entrants into the workforce are minorities, and this proportion is rising. In the longer run, the size and productivity of the effective workforce will be reduced, and the unity of our communal life placed at risk. This is probably the greatest foreseeable danger to our national security, for a divided nation, its cities driven back to tribalism and fear, is unlikely to be able to protect its vital interests, including those of allies, on a still-treacherous world scene.

The Present State of Urban Policy

Thus, the United States lacks a coherent urban strategy that would reverse the vicious circle I have described. Lacking a coherent strategy, our skills and resources have been overwhelmingly applied to limiting or mitigating the symptoms of prior failure—from neonatal clinics to prisons.

For example, Head Start is a quite useful preschool system. At its best, it engages children and their mothers in constructive programs, but only 40% of those who should be in Head Start now get that experience in the United States. Also the amount of job-readiness training linked to the private sector and thus leading to job offers immediately following incarceration is confined to a relatively few hopeful experiments.

An exact categorization of the content of social expenditures with respect to prevention versus damage limitation is, of course, impossible. But a 1992 evaluation of social expenditures during the Bush administration is suggestive. Increases of $54 billion were cited: 85% were damage limitation (Medicare and food stamps) mandated by law and the product of rising medical costs and unemployment and only 15% might be regarded as investments in prevention (elementary education, school nutrition, Head Start). Something like that proportion is probably typical of American cities. Martin Gerry made some parallel calculations for children's services nationwide. He found that "approximately 60% have been allocated for maintenance [income subsidy], 30% for treatment, and 10% for prevention."[6] Well over half of the public funds expended for maintenance are spent to cover costs that are clearly preventable. From the insurance standpoint, what is needed is a serious effort to manage against the downstream risk by significantly increasing our investment in prevention activities.

In Austin, the title of a key urban public-service program was changed in 1992 from "Youth at Risk" to "Opportunities for Youth," but the damage-control character of the enterprise and its fragmentation by symptom are apparent in the following list of areas addressed:

Unhealthy infants

Child abuse

Physical and mental disabilities

Low self-esteem and poor physical fitness

Teenage pregnancy

Hunger

Illness

Substance abuse/addiction

Drop out/insufficient education

Inadequate child care

Unemployment

Youth crime

Fragmentation has been exacerbated by four further factors. The first is the almost incredible multiplicity of worthy private social agencies at work in our cities, drawing on public as well as private funds,

About 300 are engaged in youth programs in a typical city of a half million.

Second, the current highly specialized nature of the social sciences in the United States reinforces these tendencies. The field of urban studies has experts on young children and families, dropouts and gangs, drugs and crime, teenage pregnancy and health, education and the inner-city economy, and many even narrower specialties. The proportion of creative effort devoted to intellectual or policy synthesis—to viewing the inner city as an intimately interacting dynamic system—is low.[7]

Third, the private foundations, each with an independent board of directors, have a long, historical interest in one facet or another of the urban problem: young children; medical and health problems; more advanced education; families; minority neighborhoods; teenage pregnancy; gangs; and so on. At the same time, they lack the resources to undertake large, coherent urban programs. They are understandably anxious to disengage their resources after a time, in the hope that the experiments they have fostered will be taken up and carried out at full scale by public authorities. This does not happen often.

Finally, Congress has passed much categorical legislation that provides funds for specific purposes if certain conditions are met. By its nature, the urban problem spreads wide. The many congressional committees engaged have thus contributed a further element to this bewildering mélange. Perhaps this will change with the devolution to the states and the block grants of the 1996 welfare legislation.

The de facto American policy toward its inner cities now consists of a massive array of fragmented, ill-coordinated, mainly damage control programs. There was never any reason to believe that a policy of this sort could break the vicious circle at work in our inner cities. Experimental preventive programs of real promise exist in every city, but none exists on a scale that matches the scale of the problem to which it is addressed. And it is still to be seen whether the state governments can do better.

Above all, there is no coherent national or state policy to create in the inner-city neighborhoods a substitute for the old-fashioned nuclear family. It is unlikely that there will be, for some time at least, a return to such a family. What is needed are institutions created by a partnership between the community as a whole and those who live in the inner city. In time, these institutions ought to be run entirely by men and women of the inner city. Only thus will the sense of neocolonial dependence be broken and the people of the inner city gain a sense that control of their own destiny is possible. One would hope that the welfare legislation of 1996 will do that job. Its element of attack on the most vulnerable among us — the children — does not bode well. In the end, though, it is on the local communities, not on the national or state governments, that devolution will depend it if is to be successful.

How Can the Vicious Circle Be Reversed?

To break the vicious circle, then, three principles must be applied systematically:

Prevention: a maximum of action in an urban program must be directed to prevention rather than damage control.

Continuity: An urban program should extend without break from prenatal care to the workforce or professions.

Scale: Preventive investment must be built up to match the scale of the problem. There is not a major city in the United States that does not have a substantial preventive program. But there is no city in the United States that has built up preventive programs to match the scale of the problem. This is the greatest and most immediate problem faced by the United States.

The objectives of an urban policy, thus defined, might be set out operationally as follows: to mobilize the public and private sectors of the community in order to reverse the decline of the disadvantaged inner city neighborhoods in the next several years and to set in motion a process that would bring the men, women, and children who live there fully into the mainstream of American society.[8] The first objective might take five years of concerted work; the second might take at least a generation's sustained effort.

To supplant a vicious circle with a benign self-reinforcing one requires that the forces of fragmentation be confronted and that the proportion of preventive investment be radically increased so that the investment in prevention matches the scale of the problem. Fortunately, this shift from damage control to prevention is a shift from social expenditure to investment with a high rate of return over cost.

Let me be more specific by citing The Austin Project. Its view of how the cumulative process can be rendered benign is symbolized by two figures. The first, shown in Figure 8.1, appears on the cover of

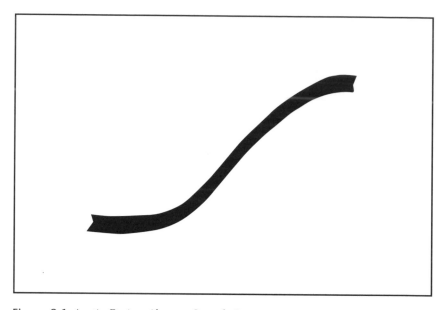

Figure 8.1 Austin Project Abstract Growth Curve

The Austin Project: First Phase Plan. The abstract growth curve in the figure dramatizes the importance in human development of the individual's earliest years and consequently the high rate of return on investment in child development in the period from prenatal care to the age of eight. As the late Barbara Jordan, who was on The Austin Project board, said: "If you don't start at the beginning, you'll never get there."

It is also necessary to accept the principle of continuity throughout the whole path to the workforce or the professions. As that principle is applied, the operational meaning of preventive investment changes. In the early phases of life—say, through Head Start—prevention means direct interventions engaging the parents in prenatal care, guidance in parenting, early immunization, continuity of affection, early social experience, pre-school education, and so on. From entrance into the school system, prevention increasingly takes the form of efforts to enlarge the young person's skills, confidence, and view of the realistic options for the future, such as computer-assisted accelerated learning and visits to industrial plants. Direct interventions, of course, do not cease (e.g., in the form of school nurses and advisers), nor do activities that maintain the ties between parents and children.

They should be enlarged and extended. But there is a difference between the direct interventions of early childhood and the widening of options that the emerging young individual will regard as realistic. Among other elements in this program are academies for chip manufacture for computers, the health professions, and financial operations; summer apprenticeship jobs; a large-scale course to prepare young men and women for construction jobs; a development bank; and guidance officers attached to every high school.

The concern is that the boom in prospects in Austin might well draw its labor from other parts of the country and Mexico, bypassing the still large body of local unemployed. This happened in the 1980s. Many in the local pool of unemployed labor would not now qualify for the jobs likely to be available. We have, therefore, pursued a policy that would give local labor a training in what is required for job readiness by intimate cooperation between schools and the private sector. The authorities of the Austin community have supported this job-readiness program fully: the middle and high schools under the Austin Independent School System, and the Austin Community College, which has undertaken the job of teaching the job-readiness component and the scale problem, which is still to be solved by public authorities. As I have already indicated, job creation in the United States might well be thrown back on the cities and the local communities, the ultimate home of devolution. But that is still to be proved.

Whatever the political outcome of welfare reform, however, the inner-city problem will not soon be solved unless unemployment is radically and permanently reduced; and that, in turn, requires both intensified training and retraining from the supply side of the labor market and a high, sustained level of effective demand for labor. The reason for this view is, simply, that some unmeasurable but high proportion of the cause of the closely related complex of inner-city social pathologies lies in chronic unemployment. Just as unemployment is a powerful negative feedback heightening the familiar array of social disorders, a sustained decline in unemployment could constitute a positive feedback in breaking the vicious circle.

Thus, a second diagram of The Austin Project, or similar comprehensive efforts, simplified down to its three large components, might look like Figure 8.2. These preventive operations for young children and their families and a linking of the private sectors and the school system must be developed in the neighborhoods if they are to have their full effects. It is only in the neighborhoods that one

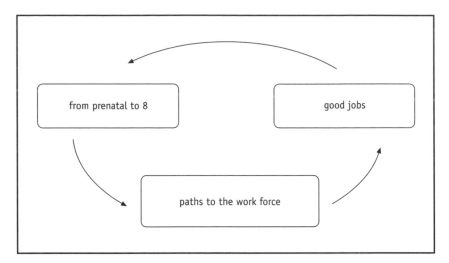

Figure 8.2 Austin Project: Key Interconnections

can build a set of institutions that constitute an extended family. It is only in the neighborhoods that men and women can, in time, take control of these institutions and shape their own destinies. Thus, a coherent urban plan must have three components: It must work with young children and their parents; it must, by the joint work of the schools and the private sectors, provide good jobs to the young; and it must bring these two functional aspects of the job to bear on the neighborhoods.

I have said thus far nothing about the professions and higher education. About a third of Americans now acquire higher degrees. The figure in the inner city is about 9%. If the latter should move toward the average, still there would be two-thirds who are headed for the workforce. The question is: Does society have to decide early, as some industrial societies do, whether a young man or woman is headed for the workforce or college? The answer is no, because the preparation for a college career and the preparation for a place in the modern workforce are essentially identical. They both require solid training in mathematics, an ability to write, a substantial degree of computer literacy, an ability to work with colleagues and to take the initiative, and an ability and will to get to work on time. The upshot is that students can postpone the choice of track they will follow, and the criteria will be their own preference, talents, and ambition, not a decision made too young.

The Role of the Federal Government

In the welfare reforms of 1996, Congress appeared to wash its hands of the urban problem and to hand it to the states. As I have already emphasized, this might get rid of the categorical projects, as they are partially replaced by block grants from Washington. The states, in turn, might exercise some influence on urban plans, pushing them in the direction, for example, of regional operations. But in the end, if the urban problem is to be solved, it will be in the urban communities themselves. It is in those communities — both Anglo and minority — that one finds the ideas, initiatives, hard work, and dedication that, when mobilized around a comprehensive plan, have some chance of solving the urban problem of the United States.

The first task of the federal government is to dramatize and then support a comprehensive preventive strategy for the nation, as opposed to the fragmented application of damage control. President Clinton began well enough in presenting a plan for empowerment and enterprise zones on May 7, 1993.

> Our proposal recognizes that long-term, stable economic growth in severely distressed areas must be achieved through a coordinated plan of economic, human, and physical development. And it recognizes that the answers to a community's problems must be generated by that community. Under our program, not a single dollar will go out without a coordinated strategy developed at the grassroots level.[9]

The statement seemed, with a few words, to change fundamentally the whole nature of urban policy in Washington from fragmented categorical grants to comprehensive urban plans. In the upshot, this proved not to be the case. Whatever the criteria were for awarding the empowerment/enterprise zones, they were not embraced by this definition.

This raises a second role for the executive branch of the federal government: to convince the Congress that investment should be clearly separated from current expenditures. This separation was attempted and failed in the early days of the Clinton administration. But the policy is right and should be attempted again. More than 40 states and virtually all other advanced industrial countries make this budgetary separation. There is no stronger case for treating productive investment and current consumption expenditures in the same category in the public sector as in the private one. Economically, an increase in public investment can have the same or greater impact on employment, GNP, and productivity. The lion in our path is simply a product of bad public bookkeeping in Washington.

Finally, it is time thoughtfully to take stock of our present policy for controlling inflation. At the present time, the primary instrument for keeping unemployment and inflation at a low level is monetary policy. Fiscal policy has been substantially ruled out since the sharp rise in federal deficits of the 1980s, which have not yet been remedied. Since 1951, the most important inflationary pressures confronted by the American economy have arisen from supply shocks—notably, the two oil-price explosions of the 1970s and, more quietly, the earlier inflationary impact of the cessation in the mid-1960s of the 1951–1964 price decline in basic commodities. As the fall of prices ended, stocks of commodities were depleted and idle land reduced. But the possibility of demand-induced inflationary pressure cannot be ruled out in circumstances of protracted low unemployment when money-wage increases might occur in excess of the average rate of productivity increase.

In such circumstances, both monetary and fiscal policy can, of course, play a restraining role on demand and prices, especially if we can bring federal current expenditures and outlays into balance and thus recapture fiscal policy as a vital instrument of government. Operating on its own, monetary policy has proved a blunt and costly instrument in constraining inflation. These familiar devices should, however, be supplemented by some form of income policy that gears money-wage increases to an approximation of the average rate of productivity increase.

It is a fact that certain democratic, capitalist countries have exhibited for quite long periods a capacity to reconcile low levels of unemployment with low levels of inflation: notably, Japan, Germany, Austria, and Switzerland. How they have managed to achieve this result has been widely studied. A recent, quite persuasive analysis argues that the success stories can be attributed primarily to three characteristics of the wage-setting process: First, wage changes are synchronous (i.e., made at approximately the same time); second, changes are centralized in the sense that changes throughout the economy are related to those in a key sector or group of sectors; third, if the working force attempts to achieve wage increases in excess of productivity increases, the authorities will invoke as a last resort monetary deflation and a rise in unemployment.

A successful income policy must, of course, be related to the peculiar circumstances of each country. Nevertheless, the proven compatibility of income policies with free-enterprise systems, the heavy economic and human costs of excessive reliance on monetary restraint, and the immense rewards for sustaining low unemployment levels, low interest rates, and high growth rates justify thoughtful exploration of the possibilities of an income policy in the United States.

The Larger Setting of the Urban Problem

In the preface to the third edition of *Stages of Economic Growth* (1990), I made this observation on the paradox of our times:

> On the one hand, powerful forces are leading nations to accept participation in larger international groupings in order to assure their security and well-being in an increasingly inter-dependent world. On the other hand, heightened schismatic forces of differing intensity and violence are also at work within a good many nations, tending to dilute or fracture national unity. . . . It is as if the credibility of the nation state is being attenuated from above and below.[10]

Indeed, the central fact all peoples must confront is that, as the 20th century has evolved, the old-fashioned nation-state by itself cannot guarantee its people's security, economic welfare, or even protection of the physical environment.

We turn finally, therefore, in larger terms to the pace of a resolution of the American urban problem seen against the simultaneous struggle to make sense out of the post–Cold War world. What outcomes can we envisage? As I have emphasized from the beginning, chaos is evidently a quite possible result, for it is obvious that the smaller units now claiming national status are even less able to deal effectively with the forces at work in the world arena than the larger units from which they emerged. Another more hopeful scenario is that, with the passage of time, people in the fragmented states or those threatening to fragment will come to their senses. They will enter into constructive relations with their neighbors, regional organizations, and the world community. They would confine their loyalty to neighborhood or regional or ethnic cultures and to roles within them.

But there is something missing here if we are to draw citizens into a sustained effort of this kind. The missing element is a vision. The character of this missing element is suggested by the meeting of Konrad Adenauer and Jean Monnet in Bonn on May 23, 1950, to which I have already referred.[11] The subject was the Schuman Plan, which was to be translated into the European Coal and Steel Community. The proposal had arisen to cope with strong gathering pressure in French political life to limit the dramatic recovery of Germany after the currency reform of 1948. The operative issue was the disposition of the Saar. Nightmarish memories shadowed a reviving Europe, memories of French insistence on permanent unequal treatment for Germany and the predictable German nationalist reaction. A hopeful outcome for post–World War II Europe and, more immediately, the viability of NATO appeared at stake.

Presenting the Schuman Plan to Adenauer, Monnet made clear that its purpose was political and moral, not economic. Its aim was to calm French anxieties, meet the German need for equal treatment, and permit both to work side by side to build a Europe that could stand in dignity in dealings with the United States and in confronting and negotiating with the Soviet Union—a Europe living with pride in continuity with its old variegated cultures. Adenauer had not expected all of this or had not quite believed in the sincerity of the French proposal. He was evidently moved and concluded: "Monsieur Monnet, I regard the implementation of the French proposal as my most important task. If I succeed, I believe my life will not have been wasted."[12] This conversation was the birth of Europe as we know it and of the path on which it is still evolving.

The present stage of the movement for European unity is not, however, controlled by any such grand vision. It arose in the early 1980s from Euro-pessimism—a fear that unless Europe moved toward much closer unity, it would never be able to catch up with the United States and Japan in the surging new technologies rooted in microelectronics and genetic engineering. Europe's leaders have permitted the larger vision of the leaders who knew the world before 1914 to fade. The vision I have in mind is global but requires a strong united Europe, real enough and strong enough to capture the imagination of the Europeans and keep within tolerable limits the ethnic and regional appeals that abound in that region. The region requires that concept if its grand purposes are to be achieved and if the 21st century is not to repeat the tragedies of the 20th century—or worse.

We need statesmen to remind their fellow citizens that there is hardly a national border in the world that is not bloodstained, the product of violence and inequity almost too painful to contemplate without seeking redress. But there can be no redress, no rerunning the tape. Ethnic cleansing is a satanic, impossible scheme. History has decreed an extraordinary interweaving of races and peoples, and the differential demographic and industrial pressures in different regions of the world decree this process will continue in both hemispheres. The skein of history cannot be unraveled. This Monnet and Adenauer understood. They knew we must move forward from where history has brought us, and living peacefully with one another is the condition for survival.

My simple point is that, at the core, the problem that must be solved in American urban communities is precisely the problem that must be solved in Western Europe and what used to be Yugoslovia, in what used to be the Soviet Union and in the Indian subcontinent, and in the many other places where races and peoples are commingled and can't be disentangled. The uniqueness of our various cultural heritages—much less pure than we often suppose—can and will be preserved. But like Monnet and Adenauer in 1950, we must join, in the United States and everywhere else, to bring to life the larger vision that must underpin the American effort at home and abroad if we are to get through the 21st century in good style.

NINE

Conclusions

I have tried in this book to summarize where the world economy has come from in the past three centuries and to set out the core of the agenda that lies before us as we face the century ahead. This century, for the first time since the mid-18th century, will come to be dominated by stagnant or falling populations. The conclusions at which I have arrived can usefully be divided in two parts: one relates to what can be called the political economy of the 21st century; the other relates to the links between the problem of the United States playing steadily the role of critical margin on the world scene and moving at home toward a solution to the multiple facets of the urban problem. As for the political economy of the 21st century, the following points relate both to U.S. domestic policy and U.S. policy within the OECD, APEC, OAS, and other relevant international organizations.

General Conclusions

There is a good chance that the economic rise of China and Asia as well as Latin America, plus the convergence of economic stagnation and population increase in Africa, will raise for a time the relative prices of food and industrial materials, as well as lead to an increase in expenditures in support of the environment. This should occur in the early part of the next century. If corrective action is taken in the private markets and the political process, these strains on the supply side should diminish with the passage of time, the advance of science and innovation, and the progressively reduced rate of population increase.

The government, the universities, the private sector, and the professions might soon place on their common agenda the delicate balance of maintaining full employment with stagnant or falling populations. The existing literature, which largely stems from the 1930s, is quite illuminating but inadequate. And the experience with stagnant or falling population in the the world economy during post–Industrial Revolution times is extremely limited. This is a subject best approached in the United States on a bipartisan basis, abroad as an international problem. It is much too serious to be dealt with, as it is at present, as a domestic political football.

The economics of a pronatalist policy might well be explored as well as the experiences of various countries with such policies. Again, the existing literature is quite thin. All of this, too, is inherently a bipartisan task.

In different ways, the United States, Great Britain, Japan, and continental Western Europe are caught up in the immigration problem. In each country, this problem takes different courses but has two common features. There is some fear in the host county that the demographic character of the country is being significantly altered and unskilled immigrants might add to long-term unemployment and welfare costs. The extent to which immigration can fill the gap in the workforce is thereby limited.

The African situation — now and in the future — should be explored carefully. As at present, the situation in some countries is unmanageable unless there is a consensus that the leaders and the people assume more responsibility for their long-run destiny. We need to gear our policies to this objective. Increased aid may be a part of that policy, although outside forces cannot substitute for a lack of what development economists chastely call "absorptive capacity."

Water

Both at home and abroad, more rational water policies are needed that will lead to a higher proportion of water available for irrigation. Water is a key bottleneck to agricultural expansion.

Fusion Power and Its Alternatives

Many of our resource problems could be much eased in the 21st century if we had a cheap, inexhaustible, nonpolluting source of electricity. This should be a global priority in the time ahead. For economic and noneconomic reasons, the United States should allocate increased public resources to R&D for this purpose, including, of course, R&D for fusion power if that is judged a practical objective.

Genetic Engineering

Genetic engineering R&D is overwhelmingly in the hands of the old industrial countries and, for understandable market reasons, devoted mainly to medical objectives. Given the likelihood of regional food shortages, R&D addressed to basic grains should be pursued on a larger scale by public agencies. The demand for grain exports is likely to expand in the early part of the 21st century.

Expansion of the Working Force

The American prospect is for a somewhat higher rate of growth of population in the near term due to immigration. This will shift the racial balance of the country, as it is now doing. In the long run, the United States will face the same problem as other old industrial countries—that is, how to maximize the size and skill of the working force as the population ages and stagnates or declines. (The U.S. population will peak around 2020–2030 according to UN projections.) A large, ill-trained underclass cannot be afforded. Therefore, a low rate of unemployment and a high degree of training will become necessary and hopefully the object of bipartisan public policy.

The Inadequacy of Contemporary Federal
Reserve Policy and the Installation of a
Supplementary-Income Policy

At the present time, the Federal Reserve System bears an unnatural burden. It aims to maintain a low rate of inflation by maintaining a higher level of unemployment than is justified by the trend of prices. As labor becomes scarce, this crude method might well be supplemented by an income policy that will gear average money-wage increases to the average increases in productivity. It has been proved that this can be done in countries with a strong commitment to private capitalism, such as Japan, Germany, Austria, and Switzerland.

International Cooperation

One of the overriding lessons of the 20th century for the 21st is the need to avoid what happened in the 1930s: the breakup of the world economy, the retreat to beggar-thy-neighbor nationalist policies, and the consequent rise of aggressive military powers. This requires an endless attention to international cooperation and endless war against international disintegration.

In short, the political economy of the 21st century consists of three major parts:

1. *Dealing with the resource strains in the early part of the 21st century*. These are likely to come to rest on the supplies of water and dealing with the degradation of the environment.
2. *The expansion of the working force*. This embraces the extension of the working age; enlarged training of the potential workforce under the guidance of the sectors that will hire the trainees; a public policy that will not tolerate pools of the unemployed; and a pro-natalist policy that will assure a constant population for the long run.
3. *Filling the gap in investment and the enlargement of the population of the elderly who cannot enter the workforce*. The former will call for increased outlays for infrastructure and training; the latter will call for enlarged outlays to support the elderly.

It will take some time and experiment to find the appropriate level of requirements for these large purposes and to identify the extent to which public R&D will be required to supplement private sector R&D.

So much for the political economy of the 21st century. I have stated my conclusions flatly and clearly. What I am sure about is that this transition will require a politics of community at home and abroad. In order to succeed, the policies of the New Deal or the Great Society will not suffice, nor will policies that would uproot all that has transpired in social legislation since the Great Depression. We shall have to look afresh on a bipartisan basis at the challenges to the United

States and to the world that the 21st century will bring. In this effort, we have the great advantage of time to explore the alternatives and to experiment. But we had better start now.

The Larger Conclusion

Moving beyond political economy, the largest conclusion of this book can be tersely stated in two propositions:

1. From now to 2050, there is no likely alternative to United States playing the role of critical margin in the world's affairs except chaos contrary to our own and the global interest. Others might play that role in the distant future, but they are, for a variety of reasons, not yet ready.
2. Our ability to play that role steadily depends on our society finding ways to deal with the urban problem. I do believe that Hamish McRae was right when he wrote that this is "the greatest single challenge the U.S. will face in the coming generation. Failure would destroy the American dream."

I would like to think that we will meet that challenge — that we will leave for those who come after us a world more secure both abroad and at home. The challenge is, at once, international and domestic. It is held together by the perspective in the following lines from Walt Whitman's *Leaves of Grass*, to which I have often been drawn:

One thought ever at the fore —
That in the Divine Ship, the World, breasting Time and Space,
All peoples of the globe together sail, sail the same voyage,
Are bound to the same destination.[1]

Appendix A

A Historical Analogy

The argument of this book is essentially simple. It envisages in the 21st century an initial period of strain on resources and the environment followed by a long period in which a good many new countries will both enter industrial maturity and be forced to come to grips, like the older industrial countries, with stagnant or falling populations. First will come measures to increase the size of the working force, including immigration. Then, pronatalist policies might be installed as these countries face the diminishing size of the workforce in confrontation with the society's commitments to the enlarging population of the still-dependent elderly. This assumes that the effort to raise the retirement age will still leave an increasing number of the elderly outside the workforce. The world will be aided by the continued unfolding of R&D. It will be challenged, however, by the need to fill the gap left by the declining demand for investment.

The analysis is not as precise about the earlier period of 1996–2025—a period of maximum strain on resources and the environment when global population is still expanding, the youthful cadres are still large, and the relative population-growth rates reflect the economic momentum of the latecomers to industrialization relative to the established powers.

This Appendix is, therefore, devoted to the problem in the first quarter of the next century, when the strain on resources and the environment might be at a maximum, if, indeed, it does not produce a global crisis with Malthusian consequences for the size of the world's population or a Ricardian crisis due to sharply diminishing returns to the natural-resource base for a still-expanding industrial civilization. Perhaps both forces will assert themselves in certain regions.

There are no neat or complete analogies in history. But past experience can be suggestive. Following a recommendation by David Kendrick at the University of Texas at Austin, this Appendix summarizes the experience of Britain and, to some extent, the world economy from 1873 to the beginning of World War I in 1914.[1] Although the period from the mid-1890s to 1914 is the main subject of this analogy, that analogy cannot be well understood without going back to the boom which ended in 1873. But the rough analogy here that is of central concern is between Britain during the rising prices of the period 1896–1914 and the United States during the possibly rising prices of the period 1997–2025.

1873–1914

Population and Stages of Growth

In terms of stages of growth, a whole new group of then-developing countries began their sustained industrialization and urbanization in the pre-1914 decades: Sweden (1868–1890); Japan (1886–1905); Russia (1890–1905); Italy (1895–1913); and Canada (1896–1914). The forthcoming period in the United States will be like the period in Britain in 1896–1914 in the sense that new countries will be entering the world economy as industrialized societies. The British proportion of world industrial production fell from 20% to 14% from 1896–1913. The American proportion might well fall from 1997 to 2025 as China, India, and others come forward at higher rates of growth.

These two factors—the continued urbanization of the older industrial countries and the accelerated urbanization of the newer industrializing countries—increased the demand for wheat. This was the prevailing form of foodstuffs, both for making bread and processing into dairy products and meat. The same factors could act in the world economy of 1997–2025.

Technology and Relative Prices

The period 1873–1894 saw three innovations that profoundly affected the supply of food for the urban populations of the advanced industrial world: the coming into production and export of the grain fields of the American West in response to the vast railway net and the immigration that helped populate that region; the steel revolution that led to the dominance of the steel ship on long-distance routes and brought down radically all freight rates; and the electric revolution that made possible, through refrigeration, the long distance shipping of meat and dairy products from North America, Argentina, Australia, and New Zealand. The fall in steel and freight rates leveled off in the 1890s. In 1890 also the controller of the census announced in the United States an end to the sale of federal land at $160 per acre. No major technological breakthroughs in agriculture occurred at this time, and the American capacity to export, even at rising prices, leveled off. Table 4.3 shows the break in the direction of raw-material price movements in the mid-1890s. Table A.1 shows the relative growth in wheat production outside the United States on which the increased supply of foodstuff exports from other countries depended from the mid-1890s to 1913.

The second Industrial Revolution had consisted of the diffusion of the railways and of steel, which affected not only the railways themselves (steel rails) but shipping, machinery, construction, and other fields. The third Industrial Revolution, coming into being on both sides of 1900, consisted of electricity, the internal-combustion engine, and new chemicals including but not confined to those associated with

Table A.1. Wheat Production Growth Rates, 1885–1919 (Annual Average Rates of Change)

	World	Europe except Europe	Russia	USA	Canada	Argentina	Australia	India
1885–1889/1889–1894	1.26%	0.27%	0.11%	4.01%	1.53%	18.64%	3.58%	−1.47%
1889–1894/1894–1899	1.65	0.92	4.66	1.81	4.87	5.01	−2.73	−0.49
1894–1899/1899–1904	1.94	1.26	3.81	0.77	9.17	9.16	9.75	0.66
1899–1904/1904–1909	1.50	0.60	2.61	−1.21	6.20	11.18	6.53	3.93
1904–1909/1909–1914	2.64	1.25	5.02	0.65	13.63	−1.43	9.05	3.11
1909–1914/1914–1919	−0.73	−4.59	−2.19	3.22	4.71	2.58	3.68	0.06

Source: Reprinted by permission from W. W. Rostow, *The World Economy: History and Prospect* (Austin: University of Texas Press, 1978), p. 167.

automobiles (gasoline, rubber tires, etc.). These innovations, however, did not dominate the world from the mid-1890s until 1914; capital exports did. They flowed especially to the new exporters of wheat who filled the gap left on the supply side by the closing of the American frontier in 1890: Canada, Russia, Argentina, Australia, and others. This process is reflected in Table A.1. British capital exports, which had been running at about £50 million for most of the 1890s, rose after the Boer War to £235 million. By 1913, they accounted for more than 9% of GNP. The producers of foodstuffs and raw materials did very well in this interval, enjoying as they did both high prices and an increased volume of exports. In the period 1996–2025, a question mark hangs over the role in food production of genetic engineering. It might or might not produce another Green Revolution. With respect to water, we do not know whether an efficient desalting method will be found. There will certainly be a compensating factor in the fall of birth rates. But a regional food crisis in Africa seems most likely, on balance, to affect global food prices.

Business Cycles and the Period of Falling Prices, 1873–1896

From the business-cycle trough in 1868, the world economy moved to a dramatic peak in 1873. The four-year capital-export boom in Britain (1868–1872) was focused around the pushing to the West Coast of the American railway net and the German railway boom after Bismarck's victory in the Franco-Prussian War. This led to an extravagant rise in prices. There was even an energy crisis in 1872–1873 and an accelerated rise in coal prices and coal miners' wages. There followed a great prolonged depression to 1879 in the United States. Through 1877, Britain, and to a degree Germany, was shielded by a housing boom, held off by previous high interest rates, and France was shielded by the deflationary effect of the indemnity it was forced to pay Germany. The French did not participate fully in the boom of the early 1870s or in the slump that followed, notably in Germany and the United States.

The business expansion from 1879 to 1883 was focused around the coming of electricity and an array of cost-reducing innovations in British industry. But low interest rates were eased (for lenders) at the end of the 1880s by the boom focused on Argentina and the building of the railways into the pampas, cleared ruthlessly of Indians by President Julio Roca. This boom ended in financial crisis centered about the House of Baring, which was rescued by a consortium organized by the Bank of England, a consortium that was not made available to Baring in its more recent embarrassment. But Argentina was soon enjoying an extravagant boom that lasted until World War I as it exploited the high prices of exports that flowed into Buenos Aires by rail from the pampas.

The period 1873–1896 was, then, peaceful and marked by falling prices and interest rates except for the Argentine boom of the late 1880s. It saw the full absorption of the railway and steel revolutions in the industrial parts of the world, as well as the maturing of the steel revolution. Real wages rose rapidly as food prices fell, and the diet of the working classes in the industrial part of the world came to include meat and dairy products for the first time. By and large, agriculture was depressed as the American West poured out a remarkable flow of wheat and cut existing prices; and this development was only partly compensated by tariffs. This period bears a family relation to the 1980s and first half of the 1990s in that real food prices fell and the internal terms of trade turned against the farmer.

1896–1914 in Britain versus 1996–2025 in the United States

The two decades between the mid-1890s and the coming of World War I were the polar opposite of the previous period. They saw a series of minor wars: the war between Italy and Ethiopia; the Spanish-American and Boer Wars; the war between Japan and Russia; and the two Balkan wars. In the background of all of this was the Anglo-German naval arms race.

The prices of foodstuffs and raw materials rose absolutely and relatively, as did interest rates. Capital flowed to produce the grain that Europe needed from sources other than the United States. The new technologies moved forward, but they were not sufficiently mature to dominate the growth of the world economy. Real wages decelerated in Germany and the United States and declined slightly in Britain. Income shifted to the wealthier segment of the population. In response, the working classes turned to politics for redress. Not only did membership rise in the unions as well as in labor and social democratic parties, but the funds flowing into social services increased. In Britain, social services rose from 1.9% of GNP in 1890 to 4.1% in 1913; in Germany, social-insurance outlays doubled in this interval. In France and the United States, where the population was on balance more rural, the increases were much less impressive, but both countries saw an expansion of the unions.

The major differences between 1896–1913 and 1997–2025 are these:

1. Population and the stages of growth on a world basis will have greater momentum in the 1997–2025 period, notably because India and China will be moving to full industrialization and urbanization.

2. For two reasons, technology will have greater momentum in the 1997–2025 period. First, because the second Industrial Revolution, was rapidly waning in 1896–1914 while the new technologies of the third revolution were still at an early stage. In 1997–2025, the fourth Industrial Revolution should still have great momentum. Second, the increase in the links between science and technology and the absolute increase in R&D available in 1997–2025 compared with 1896–1914 could mean that technology will play a larger role than in the earlier period. There is, however, no Argentine pampas or Western Canada to open up.

3. The populations of the older industrial countries will decelerate in 1997–2025. These are countries, except Japan, that have developed exportable food surpluses. The world food price might well rise in this interval, as could the cost of water, but it is unlikely that politics will permit these surplus countries to go hungry, as might happen in other regions. The rise in food prices, should it occur, would, however, bear down on the real wages in advanced industrial countries as in 1896–1914. This means that the greater technological resources available to the private sectors and the governments in the later period should be used to the full to ease the pressures and strains of that period, notably with respect to genetic engineering and the water supply. The special regional dilemma of Africa should be anticipated not least by Africans, for even with the most generous goodwill efforts, the food-surplus countries cannot redress the balance without great and purposeful African effort.

In general, the period 1997–2025 will differ from 1896–1914 in that vast capital exports were mobilized in the earlier period to open up new areas in Latin America, Canada, Russia, Australia, and elsewhere. The equivalent in 1997–2025 will be exports of surplus food, especially from the United States, Canada, and Europe, plus whatever technology can help carry the burden of feeding the still-enlarging but decelerating global population. If the environment comes under great strain in this period, which is quite possible, increased capital exports may be required to less-developed countries where environmental degradation has global significance.

These two periods can undoubtedly be modeled and compared econometrically. Although a good many factors are involved, they can be expressed numerically. Given our ignorance, however, such quantitative estimates are subject to great variation. Rough suggestive analogy is probably the most honest form of comparison available.

Appendix B

The Demography of the People's Republic of China

The Chinese Data

The course of population on the Chinese mainland is of general interest for at least three major reasons. First, the population of China constitutes a large proportion of the world's population, and its course will help determine the peak population of the world in the 21st century. Second, mainland China is undergoing rapid industrialization and urbanization. It gives every sign of becoming a major industrial power in the course of the next century. The impact of this process on Chinese population is of great interest to demographers and social scientists generally. Third, since the 1980s, the Chinese have pursued a policy of population limitation. This policy has been more effective in the cities than in the countryside, where it is economically more advantageous to have large families, especially families with male members; but the gap between urban and rural population rates of increase has narrowed perceptibly. This Appendix focuses primarily on the course of Chinese population in the highly dynamic 1990s.

As a historical framework to the narrow focus of this Appendix, I begin with Figure B.1, covering the period 1949–1985. This figure shows that, after many vicissitudes, China's population at the period

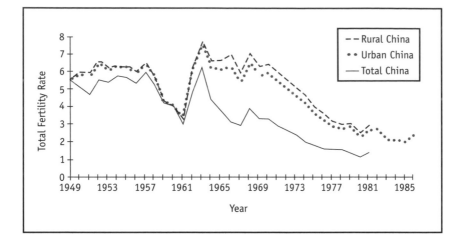

Figure B.1 Total Fertility for China, 1949–1985. *Sources:* Dudley Poston and David Yaukey, eds., *The Population of Modern China* (New York: Plenum, 1992), p. 278; Susan Greenhaigh, "Sexual Stratification: The Other Side of 'Growth with Equity' in East Asia," *Population and Development Review* 2 (1985): 265–314.

of the communist takeover fluctuated around a high base fertility rate of 5–7. A grave demographic crisis took place with the failure of the Great Leap Forward in 1958. After recovering in 1963–1964, China experienced a dramatic, erratic fall in the fertility rate.

There was an upward break in the population figures in 1985–1987. This upward break could be associated with a mild relaxation of the birth-control policy (called the "open a small hole" policy). The subsequent sharp downward break in the total fertility rate might be associated with the appointment of Peng Peiyun as minister-in-charge of the State Family Planning Commission in 1988 plus the accelerated rate of growth and urbanization. In any case, the decline from that time to the 1992 population survey (based on 1991 data) is substantial, steep, and regular.

Figure B.2 shows the remarkably consistent results of three surveys and the 1990 census. The course of the total fertility rate over the period 1979–1995 is calculated in Table B.1.

A Chinese expert has presented the population pyramids shown in Figure B.3 covering the calculations made, respectively, in 1953, 1964, 1980, and 1982. These pyramids are quite persuasive. They show the progressive narrowing of the pyramid as the decline in the total fertility rate takes hold, and they reflect the increase in deaths that

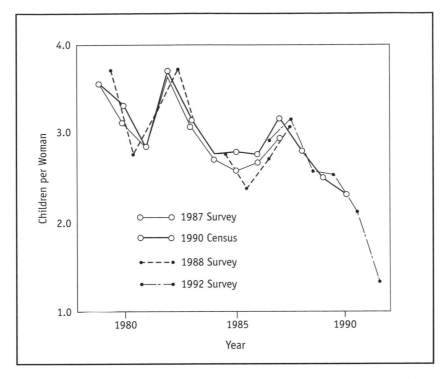

Figure B.2 Total Fertility for China, 1979–1990. *Source:* Griffith Feeney and Jian Hu Yuan, "Below Replacement Fertility in China?: A Close Look at Recent Evidence," *Population Studies* 48 (1993): 384.

followed the Great Leap Forward (1958) and the bad harvests up to 1961; the relaxation of Family Control Policy during the Cultural Revolution; and the success of the Family Control Policy and other population restraining forces from the late 1980s to the present.

After lengthy, subtle, but indecisive speculation about under-reporting of births, which is a possibility in China's rural areas, Griffith Feeney and Jian-Hua Yuan conclude:

> Chinese fertility may very well have fallen below replacement level during the early 1990s, even allowing for substantial underreporting of births in recent years. The possibility of severe underreporting of births in the early 1990s does not on balance counteract the consistent picture of very low, fluctuating, but generally declining levels. . . . The low level of fertility is due in part to large numbers of one-child families. . . .

Table B.1. Total Fertility Estimate, China, 1979–1995

Year	Total Fertility
1979	2.88
1980	2.46
1981	2.54
1982	2.67
1983	2.30
1984	2.28
1985	2.13
1986	2.29
1987	2.43
1986	2.40
1987	2.48
1988	2.27
1989	2.24
1990	2.09
1991	1.75
1990	2.2000
1991	2.0008
1992	1.8222
1993	1.8691
1994	1.7879
1995	1.7630

Source: Adapted from Griffith Feeney and Jian Hua Yuan, "Below Replacement Fertility in China?: A Close Look at Recent Evidence," *Population Studies* 48 (1993): 387. 1979–1987 series computed from unit record data of the 1988 two per thousand fertility survey conducted by the State Family Planning Commission; 1986–1991 series computed from unit record data of the 1992 survey conducted by the State Family Planning Commission.

Near replacement level fertility in China raises numerous questions that can be touched on only briefly here. First and most obviously, will the current low level be sustained, or will there be a rebound? Mme Peng's remark that "family planning is still a long-term and difficult task" suggests that Chinese officials have some doubts on this point, and not unreasonably so, given the sharp rise of fertility levels following the "open a small hole" initiative.

Will the Chinese leadership continue the pursuit of ever lower fertility levels, pushing total fertility closer to one child per woman? . . .

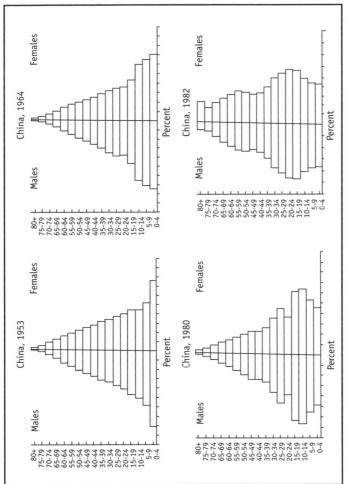

Figure B.3 Mainland China's Age Pyramid. *Source:* Rui-Chuan Zha, "Some Issues in Age Structure of China's Population," in *Population and Economy* 2 (1996): 6 (in Chinese).

Finally, and perhaps most importantly, what are the implications of very low fertility for economy and society in China? The young age distributions characteristic of less developed countries pose a formal demographic trade-off between rapid fertility decline in the near term and rapid population aging in the long term. . . . . If continued fertility decline were to push annual numbers of births substantially below this level, the evolution of China's age distribution over the next half century would be characterized by numbers of older persons that not only equal, but exceed numbers of younger persons. For the longer-term future, then, the cost of reducing future population growth will be a population in which persons of labour force ages will be required to support historically unprecedented numbers of older persons.[1]

Table B.2. Projected Elderly Population (Aged 65 and Over) and Dependency Ratios, China, 1985–2050

	One-Child Projection[a]			Two-Child Projection[b]		
Year	Elderly as % of Total	Dependency Ratio[c]	Elderly as % of Dependents	Elderly as % of Total	Dependency Ratio[c]	Elderly as % of Dependents
1985	5	54	15	5	54	15
1990	6	41	20	6	47	18
1995	7	35	25	6	46	21
2000	8	30	33	7	45	23
2005	8	29	38	8	43	27
2010	9	29	42	9	42	29
2015	11	29	50	10	43	33
2020	15	32	60	12	48	38
2025	17	35	67	14	51	41
2030	22	42	74	16	55	46
2035	28	55	79	19	61	51
2040	34	69	83	22	66	51
2045	38	79	85	22	67	55
2050	41	89	87	22	67	54

Source: Judith Banister, *China's Changing Population* (Stanford: Stanford University Press, 1987), p. 372.

[a]The one-child projection assumes a total fertility rate of 1.0 birth per woman from 1990 to 2050. The total population would peak at 1.11 billion in the year 2005 and decline to 708 million by 2050.

[b]The assumptions of this projection are that a two-child policy is gradually implemented in both urban and rural areas between the years 2000 and 2010 and then maintained to 2050, that urban areas have a total fertility rate of around 1.3 from now to 2000, rising to 1.8 births per woman from 2010 and rises to 2.5 for the period 2010–2050. This projection results in a total population size for the China mainland of 1.24 billion in the year 2000, rising to 1.44 billion in 2020 and peaking at 1.56 billion in 2048. A slow decline in population size then begins.

[c]The population in the dependent ages (under 15 and 65 and above) per 100 people in the working ages (15–64).

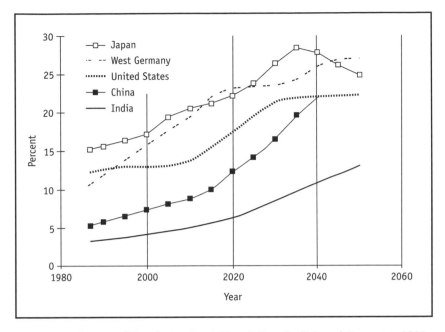

Figure B.4 Percent of Population Aged 65 and Over for Selected Countries, 1987–2050. *Source:* Judith Banister, *China's Changing Population* (Stanford: Stanford University Press, 1987), p. 372.

The balance of the evidence, then, reveals that the Chinese mainland total fertility rate is under the replacement rate for the long run; that this will impose on the Chinese authorities the same choices that confront the more industrialized countries; and that Peng is correct: "Family planning is still a long-term and difficult task." This dictum is underlined by the public awareness of the prospective aging of the Chinese mainland population: "As we watch the emergence of an aging population, it's easy to see how serious the problems become. Predictions show that the percentage of the population over the age of 60 will reach 10% by the year 1997. In China by the year 2030, 339 million people will be over 60, accounting for 21% of the population. At that time one-fourth of the world's elderly will be in China. Just thinking of the huge figure of 339 million elderly is enough of a prediction to impress us with the immensity of this number."[2] This is peculiarly true of the Chinese mainland because it is experiencing two forces tending to reduce the total fertility rate: the official population policy and the rapid industrialization and urbanization of the country.

This is the issue now being debated openly in China. Will the fertility rate rise if policy relents and permits a two-child family? Behind this question is how much of the remarkable fall in the fertility rate is due to public policy as opposed to the burst of growth that has lifted both Chinese affluence and Chinese urbanization. Postan concludes judicially, tentatively supporting the latter view: "The very preliminary review we have undertaken . . . appears to suggest the more influential effects that the socioeconomic variables by and large, compared to the family planning variables, have on changes between 1981 and 1989 in the crude birth rate and the natural increase rate. It would appear from our cursory study that in the 1980s in China the more socioeconomically developed provinces experienced more profound reductions in fertility than the less developed provinces, and as we have just observed, the family planning variables had nowhere as important an effect."[3]

Table B.2 and Figure B.4 put in context the aging process in China and four other major countries in the course of the 21st century.[4]

After surveying the evidence of China and countries elsewhere, I am inclined to report again in this context: "Affluent urban life has not been the friend of large, cohesive families."

Notes

Preface

1. The reader might be interested in the degree of continuity between *Theorists of Economic Growth from David Hume to the Present: With a Perspective on the Next Century* (New York: Oxford University Press, 1990) and the present book. In Chapter 20, I made the following observation on the course of and prospects for world population: "The trend in the net reproduction rate had fallen by the 1970s below 1.0 in seventeen advanced industrial countries; by 1986, of the nineteen industrial market economies listed by the World Bank, all but one (Ireland) had total fertility rates under 2.0. A figure of 2.1 is roughly required for long run population stability. From such data the World Bank has provided, under stylized arbitrary assumptions, the hypothetical size of a stationary population for each country and the assumed date at which it will be reached. . . . The fact is that the 1980s has seen the emergence of the strongest surge of anxiety and analysis of the implications of population decline since the 1930s; and the beginning of pronatalist public policies in some advanced industrial countries. For the moment it is sufficient to note that the world community is likely to confront simultaneously in the several generations ahead anxieties centered, in different parts of the world, on excessive increase and excessive decrease in population; that the richness of contemporary statistical data is not yet matched by firm knowledge of the determinants of fertility; and it is likely—perhaps certain— that the old unresolved issue of how to define an optimum population level will arise again, if it is not already upon us" (p. 451). In Chapter 21 of that

work, there is a more spacious passage on future population prospects and environmental strain in both developed and developing countries (pp. 490–495).

Chapter One

1. This chart includes on the vertical axis the rate of growth of population. On the assumption of a stagnant population (including Africa by the end of the next century), the population chart therefore returns to zero. In fact, if we maintain a stagnant population for the long pull, say 10 billion men, women, and children might inhabit the planet—as opposed to, say, 750 million before the Industrial Revolution. Robert Gates, "A Thread through Time," *Daedalus* (Summer 1996): sees world population responding respectively to three technological revolutions: tool making pre-5000 B.C.; the move to agriculture, 5000 B.C. to 1700 A.D.; and the Industrial Revolution, 1700 A.D. to 1990 A.D.

2. This formula for a static population that permits innovation to proceed is associated with J. S. Mill. See my *Theorists of Economic Growth* (New York: Oxford University Press, 1990), pp. 115–117.

3. J. M. Keynes, "Economic Possibilities for Our Grandchildren," in *Essays in Persuasion* (London: Macmillan, 1931), pp. 365–366, 371–372.

4. W. W. Rostow, *The Stages of Economic Growth* (Cambridge: Cambridge University Press, 1990), pp. 90–92.

5. *Proceedings of the American Philosophical Society* 139, no. 3 (September 1995): 19–264.

6. See, for example, "Will the World Starve?" *Economist*, June 10, 1995, pp. 39–40.

7. Fisher is quoting W. T. Pecora, "Proceedings Limitations of Earth," *Texas Quarterly*, no. 2 (1968): 148–154.

8. William L. Fisher, "Rethinking Resources," *Transactions of the Gulf Coast Association of Geological Societies* 44 (1994): 12.

9. "The Liberation of the Environment," *Daedalus* (Summer 1996).

10. Klaus Michael Meyer-Abich, "Humans in Nature: Towards a Physio Centric Philosophy," *Daedalus* (Summer 1996): 232.

11. Paul A. Waggoner, "How Much Land Can Be Spared for Nature?" *Daedalus* (Summer 1996): 80–81.

12. Hamish McRae, *The World in 2020* (London: HarperCollins, 1995), p. 272.

Chapter Two

1. Hamish McRae, *The World in 2020* (London: HarperCollins, 1995), p. 97.

2. The most useful summary of Gregory King's work on national income in Britain in 1688 is Phyllis Deane's in Phyllis Deane and W. A. Cole, *British Economic Growth, 1688–1959*, 2d ed. (Cambridge: Cambridge University Press, 1969), pp. 1–4.

3. Alfred Sauvy, "Development and Perspectives of Demographic Research in France," in Philip M. Hauser and Otis Dudley Duncan, eds., *The Study of Population* (Chicago: University of Chicago Press, 1959), p. 181.

4. There was an interesting exception to this generalization. After the defeat of France and the formation of the German empire by Otto von Bismarck, the French began to take seriously their inferiority in population and the slow increase in their population vis-à-vis Germany's.

5. Gunnar Myrdal, *Population: A Problem for Democracy* (Cambridge, Mass.: Harvard University Press, 1940), p. 203.

6. The decline in birth rates has been somewhat faster than demographers originally calculated and the increase in world population somewhat slower. The figure of 10 billion as the probable peak is a fair but probably somewhat high estimate. An extremely interesting article on population projections is Cesare Marchetti, Perin S. Meyer, and Jesse H. Ausubel, "Human Population Dynamics Revisited with the Logistic Model: How Much Can Be Modeled and Predicted," *Technical Forecasting and Social Change*, no. 52, (1996): 1–30.

7. Jesse Cheng, "More Senior Citizens, Fewer Kids," *Free China Review* 45, no. 12 (December 1995): 42–45. Similarly, the Korean *News Review* of October 28, 1995, carried the following item: "The growth of the South Korean population is predicted to increase zero percent in 2021 and the nation's population is expected to reach 50.58 million if the total fertility rate continues to be kept at 1.63 until that year, the Korea Institute for Health and Social Affairs said last week. . . . The institute said the fertility rate was 2.1 in the mid-1980s. It declined to 1.6 in 1988, but rose slightly back to 1.75 in 1993. Officials of the government-financed think tank forecast that the fertility rate will hover around 1.75 in the future. It means that the population growth rate remains at zero percent on a long-term basis. The officials said that when the fertility rate of 1.63 continues to be maintained, those aged 65 or more will account for 22.8 percent of the nation's population in 2040, more than five times as many as in 1990." (p. 5).

The *Economist* of December 16, 1995, carried the following item: "The world's population is growing more slowly than at any time since the second world war, says the United Nations. In 1990–94 annual population growth averaged 1.57% a year, compared with 1.73% over the previous 15 years. Many countries in Africa and Asia are starting to see lower total fertility rates. . . . Kenya's rate has dropped from more than eight children per woman in the late 1970s to 6.3 in 1990–95; in Algeria the fall has been even faster, from 6.3 children in 1980–85 to 3.8 in 1990–95. But in several African countries, including Nigeria, Zaire and Ethiopia, fertility rates show no sign of dropping" (p. 98).

8. UN Development Programme, *Human Development Report, 1992* (New York: Oxford University Press, 1992), p. 40, contains a useful summary.

9. Ibid. See also Chester Crocker, "Why Africa Needs Our Attention," *Cosmos* 5 (1995): 60–66. Crocker deplores the tendency to write off Africa and to caricature the whole continent as an unrelieved horror. His is a rare portrait by a sympathetic, constructive, but realistic observer.

10. Jeffrey Sachs and Andrew Warner, "Sources of Slow Growth in the African Economies," Harvard Institute for International Development, February 1996, summarized by Jeffrey Sachs in *Economist*, American edition, June 29–July 5, 1996, pp. 19–21. A more elaborate version of this article was published under the same title as Discussion Paper 100.546, July 1986, by the Harvard Institute of International Development.

11. Ibid., p. 20.

12. *Wall Street Journal*, July 8, 1996, p. A-1.

13. The situation of Japan was captured in a long, vivid article in the *New York Times*, international edition, October 6, 1996, p. 3. Briefly summarized, here are the main points:

- The fertility rate is now 1.4. If that rate is sustained, the Japanese will have 55 million inhabitants as opposed to 125 million now.
- Prizes up to $5,000 per child are being offered by local authorities to those who have children, but there are strong objections to a pronatalist policy.
- Objections include the following: The subsidies offered are insufficient; more children would eat up women's "spare time"; men don't like "annoying things" around and would not help raise the children; women have "advanced" and do not wish to endanger their educations, prestige, and incomes.
- The government might take this issue more seriously, although the first effort of Prime Minister Ryutaso Hashimoto was to propose discouraging young women from higher education. This did not go over well, provoking "a furor."

The director general of the Institute of Population Problems in Tokyo is openly pessimistic about reversing the trend in fertility, which he attributes to the fact that "women have advanced." In short, it will take time and a persistence of present trends to change attitudes in Japan and elsewhere.

14. Hamish McRae, *The World in 2020* (London: HarperCollins, 1995), p. 101.

15. Barbara Beck, "Economics of Ageing," *Economist*, American edition, January 27–February 2, 1996, pp. 3–16. This useful survey acknowledges the assistance of various OECD papers on this subject and, in particular, three recent sources: World Bank, *Averting the Old Age Crisis* (New York: Oxford University Press, 1945); Lei Delsen and Genevieve Reday-Mulray, eds., *Gradual Retirement in the OECD Countries* (Brookfield, Vt.: Dartmouth Publishing Company, 1996); and Susan A. Macmanus, *Young and Old* (Denver, Colo.: Westview Press, 1996).

16. See also "Aging World, New Wrinkles," *New York Times*, September 22, 1996, pp. 1, 5, and *Wall Street Journal*, September 11, 1995, p. 1.

17. Beck, "Economics of Ageing," p. 9. *The Economic Report of the President to the Congress* (February 1996) contains a useful section, "Long Term Demographic Trends" (pp. 95–105). This section reveals a rise in the median age in the United States from 33 in 1985 to 39 in 2030. This rise is seen as a result of a combination of falling fertility and an extension of life. Aver-

age life expectancy has risen since 1950, seven years for men, eight years for women. The fertility rate in the United States is about 2.0, with a higher rate for Hispanics and Asian Americans, a lower rate for African Americans and Anglos.

The dependency rate for those 0–20 will fall from about 40% at the peak of the baby boom to just over 20% in 2050; the rate for those over 65 will rise in that time from about 10% to 20%. The cost of dependency is much higher for those over 65 than for those under 20. There will be a rise in elder-dependency rates for Japan, Europe, and the United States over the period 1995–2050. Elder dependency is projected to rise higher and faster in Japan than in the United States or Europe. The report speculates indecisively on the effects of these demographic changes on productivity, reflecting conflicting views in the current literature.

As for the federal budget, the three main government-income streams to the elderly are Social Security, Medicare, and Medicaid. The aging of the population and the changing proportion in the working force of those over 65 will require in time modifying these programs and putting them on a sound fiscal basis for the long run. The report recommends that these modification be made on a bipartisan basis. Aside from this policy recommendation, the report explores indecisively the question of whether an increase in longevity will permit net increases in work effort, assuming the age of retirement is extended beyond 65.

The point is driven home by "Japan's Debt-Ridden Future," *Economist*, August 3, 1996: "The problem starts and stops with the speed at which Japan is greying. Although still among the younger of the OECD countries with only 14% of its population aged 65 or over, some 26% are likely to fit that description by 2025. Japan will then have a higher proportion of elderly people than any other country in the world, including even Germany and Sweden. And although today there are still 5.1 people who are working and contributing to a national pension scheme for every person collecting an old-age pension, by 2025 there are likely to be only 2.4 workers per pensioner. The implications are clear. Either the pension contributions that working people make will have to rise from today's 16.5% of salary to around 35% by 2025, or pensioners will have to accept far lower benefits. As in most things, the outcome is bound to be a bit of both" (p. 31).

See also Sandro Gronchi, "Demographic Changes and Pension Reforms in Italy," *Banco di Roma*, no. 1 (January–June 1996): 107–117. The demographic background to pension reform in Italy is evoked by Gronchi as follows: "Pension systems represent a problem common to all of Europe, and the reforms being carried out as this century draws to a close constitute fruitful 'national experiments' which may one day merge into a 'single European model.' . . . It is well known that social security systems all over the western world have been hard put to come to terms with the demographic developments of the last few decades, and will be even more so in the next half-century. The Italian case is more serious than the others because our birth rate has been, for some time, the lowest in the world while life expectancy is advancing rapidly towards 76 years for men and 83 for women. . . . As adults, the babies born now will witness a 'demographic scenario' that is completely different from the present one: on the basis of population projections recently developed by the Ministry of the Treasury, the Italian population will diminish by 23 percent between 1994 and 2044. The number of elderly persons (65 and older) for every working person will grow by 133 percent while that of young people will diminish by 22 per cent. . . . We are dealing with demographic changes on a grand scale, which are probably destined to generate equally radical alterations in the production and distribution of income along with saving capacity and thus the rate of economic growth. It would be comforting to say that economists are ready to face the emergencies implicit in the situation by providing governments with ready remedies, but I fear that this is not so. We must ask what 'technical progress' and what increase in productivity will be necessary to come to terms with such substantial aging of the population" (117).

18. The major argument of this passage is derived from Frank D. Bean, Robert G. Cushing, and Charles W. Hayes, "The Changing Demography of U.S. Immigration Flows: Patterns, Projections, and Contexts," in Klaus J. Bade and Myron Weiner, eds., *Migration Past, Migration Future: Germany and the United States* (Oxford: Berghahn Books, 1997), pp. 120–152. This chapter contains an exceedingly useful bibliography. See also a somewhat out-of-date but classic study: Laurence J. Kotlikoff and Daniel E. Smith, *Pensions in the American Economy* (Chicago: University of Chicago Press for the National Bureau of Economic Research, 1983). Of continued relevance is the discussion of disincentives to working beyond the age of retirement (and incentives to early retirement) in existing pension schemes in the American private sector (pp. 16–18).

19. Bean, Cushing, and Hayes, "Changing Demography," Table 5.

20. W. Arthur Lewis, *The Theory of Economic Growth* (London: Allen and Unwin, 1955), p. 371.

Chapter Three

1. See, for example, the following passage from my *Theorists of Economic Growth from David Hume to the Present: With a Perspective on the Next Century* (New York: Oxford University Press, 1990): "In short, a modern economy is not driven forward by some sort of productivity factor operating incrementally and evenly across the board. It is driven forward by the complex direct and indirect structural impact of a limited number of rapidly expanding leading sectors within which new technologies are being efficiently absorbed and diffused. And it is this process of technological absorption that substantially generates, directly and indirectly, the economy's flow of investment via the plowback of profits for plant and equipment, enlarged public revenues for infrastructure, and enlarged private incomes for residential housing. Clearly, macroeconomics as conventionally expounded requires revision to take these realities into account" (pp. 467–469).

2. See Part 5 ("Aggregate and Sectoral Growth") of my *The World Economy: History and Prospect* (Austin: University of Texas Press, 1978),

pp. 365–568, which tells the story and plots the aggregate and sectoral data for 20 countries that represent the bulk of the world's population and industrial production. For full data on Britain, see p. 375.

3. For a full elaboration of the reasons for the breakdown of the Soviet Union, see my *The Stages of Economic Growth*, 3d. ed. (Cambridge: Cambridge University Press, 1990), pp. ix–xix.

4. For my own view, see *How It All Began* (New York: McGraw-Hill, 1975).

5. Newton, *Principia*, ed. Florian Casan (Berkeley: University of California Press, 1962), p. xiii.

6. R. V. Jones, Brunei Lecture, p. 2. Jones's specific reference is to the traditional mind of the Chinese state and the collective mind of its civil servants.

7. Charles G. Gillispie, "The Natural History of Industry," *Isis* 48, pt. 2 (1957): 401–402, repr. in A. E. Musson, ed., *Science, Technology, and Economic Growth in the Eighteenth Century* (London: Methuen, 1972), p. 126.

8. Quoted in Donald Fleming, "Latent Heat and the Invention of the Watt Engine," *Isis* 43, pt. 1, no. 131 (April 1952): 5.

9. I am particularly conscious of this debate because I was writing a book in its midst: *Getting from Here to There* (New York: McGraw-Hill, 1978). I devoted two chapters to this question: Chapter 8, "Productivity: Decline or Transition?," and Chapter 9, "Science, Invention, and Innovation: Is Human Creativity on the Wane?"

10. Edward F. Renshaw, "Productivity," in *U.S. Economic Growth from 1976–1986: Prospects, Problems, and Patterns*, vol. 1, *Productivity* (Washington, D.C.: Government Printing Office, Oct. 1976), p. 56. These are studies prepared for the use of the Joint Economic Committee.

11. Quoted in Rostow, *Getting from Here to There*, p. 150.

12. Barry Minkin, *Future in Sight* (New York: Macmillan, 1995), p. 155. Minkin's book is a rather detailed and market-oriented book about future technical priorities for businesspeople.

13. Robert J. Gordon, *The Measurement of Durable Goods Prices* (Chicago: University of Chicago Press, 1990), p. 188. The quotation is given the following provenance by Gordon: "This was a remark of Norbert Wiener's apparently quoted with approval by Oskar Morgenstern in his work on the accuracy of economic statistics. Gordon demonstrates that the improvement of technology has systematically increased the quality of services provided by consumers' durables and lowered prices. Conventional price indexes therefore underestimate the volume of investment, consumption, and GNP.

14. Nineteen sixty-five is when the sales of minicomputers started; 1975, when microcomputers started. Gordon remarks: "This study develops price indexes for computer processes displaying enormous changes over time: a price index that shrinks from 10,000 to 100 over a span of thirty-three years is probably unprecedented in economic history." Ibid., p. 191.

15. Ibid.

16. V. Szebehely, "New Non-deterministic Celestial Mechanics," in K. B. Bhathagar, ed., *Space Dynamics and Celestial Mechanics* (Dordrecht,

Holland: D. Reidel, 1986), pp. 12–13. For Poincaré's fundamental demonstration of the indeterminacy of the problem of three bodies, see H. Poincaré, *Les Méthodes nouvelles de la mécanique céleste* (Paris: Brautheier-Villars, 1892, 1893, 1899; repr. New York: Dover, 1957), vol. 1, pp. 61–63.

17. Hamish McRae, *The World in 2020* (London: HarperCollins, 1995), p. 175.

18. Nicholas Negroponte, *Being Digital* (New York: Alfred A. Knopf, 1995), p. 5.

19. Ibid., p. 3.

20. Ibid., p. 7.

21. Ibid., pp. 230–231.

22. Clifford Stoll, *Silicon Snake Oil* (New York: Doubleday, 1995), p. 223.

23. *Economist*, June 10, 1995, pp. 39–40.

24. McRae, *The World in 2020*, p. 39.

25. Lester R. Brown and John E. Young, *The State of the World* (New York: World Watch Institute, 1990), p. 68.

26. *Agricultural Biotechnology: The Next "Green Revolution"?*, World Bank Technical Paper no. 133 (Washington, D.C., 1991), p. 51.

27. *Global Outlook, 2000* (New York: United Nations Publications, 1990), p. 142.

28. This process and its implications for the exports from developing countries of copper, zinc, tin, bauxite, and aluminum are spelled out in some detail in ibid., pp. 152–155.

29. J. R. Hicks, *Classics and Moderns: Collected Essays in Economic Theory* (Cambridge, Mass.: Harvard University Press, 1983), vol. 3, pp. 68.

30. J. S. Mill, *Principles of Political Economy* (Toronto: University of Toronto Press, 1965), pp. 750–751, 756–757.

Chapter Four

1. Eli Heckscher, *The Continental System* (Oxford: Oxford University Press, 1923), pp. 248–254.

2. The recovery in Germany from 1933 through 1935 was, however, mainly civil but dependent on the destruction of the trade unions.

3. Miyosei Shinohara, *Structural Changes in Japan's Economic Development* (Tokyo: Kinokuniya Bookstore, 1970).

4. In a view apparently different from McRae's, the Food and Agriculture Organization (FAO) ends up in much the same place. The FAO produced in October 1995 a useful report by Mark W. Rosegrant, Mercedita Agcaoili-Sombilla, and Nicostrato D. Perez, *Global Food Projections to 2020: Implications for Investment*. The projections are based on an econometric model called IMPACT (International Model for Policy Analysis of Agricultural Commodities and Trade). It is disaggregated to yield both global figures and figures for 35 countries and regions as well as for 17 agricultural commodities.

The conclusions of this analysis are somewhat paradoxical. First, the aggregate global supply-and-demand picture is relatively good. If governments and the international community maintain recent levels of commitment to agricultural growth through cost-effective investment in agricultural research, extension, irrigation and water development, human capital, and rural infrastructure, there will not be overwhelming pressure on aggregate world food supplies from rising populations and incomes. Projected per capita availability of food will increase slowly, and real world food prices will continue to decline for the main food crops.

Nonetheless, despite gains from trade and the ability of the world's productive capacity to meet effective global demand for food, many regions will experience virtually no improvement in food security. The most dramatic evidence of this result is the projection that there will be very little reduction in the number of malnourished children in the developing world as a whole. In Sub-Saharan Africa and parts of South Asia, the number of malnourished children will actually increase.

If national and international institutions further cut their investments in agricultural research, health, nutrition, and education instead of maintaining recent levels, the relatively favorable aggregate food situation will worsen significantly. World price declines could reverse, and the already bleak nutritional picture in the developing world will be made even bleaker.

In detail, the regional conclusions are much like those in the text with the exception of the possible water bottleneck, which is not dealt with.

In Sub-Saharan Africa, imports of cereal according to this model will have to increase from 9 million tons in 1990 to 27 million tons, despite a 23% assumed rise in local production. Both are exceedingly optimistic estimates given export capabilities of the region. Thus, the pessimistic conclusion: "Bridging the food import gap in Sub-Saharan Africa would require very rapid production increases. Moreover, it will be difficult to finance cereal imports from domestic Sub-Saharan African sources. The international community will need to devise appropriate combinations of financing and food aid to bridge these gaps in the foreseeable future. . . . As a result, there will be a large increase in the number of malnourished children in all sub-regions of Sub-Saharan Africa" (ibid., p. 14).

In South Asia, wheat imports are assumed to grow at 6.4% per annum (roughly from 2 to 15 million tons), mostly for Pakistan, which combines a large increase in population with a slowdown in domestic production. The reduction in the number of undernourished children will be confined mostly to India.

The report is somewhat complacent about China, although it forecasts an increase of wheat imports from 15 to 26 million tons plus a shift to meat consumption due to large (6%) per annum growth in real per capita income and slow population growth. As indicated, a large decrease (46%) in malnourished children is assumed. The possible water bottleneck is not taken into account.

The United States is assumed to increase its cereal exports from 89 to 122 million tons in the period examined; Australia and (mainly) Canada from 9 to 20 million tons; and Western Europe from 24 to 30 million tons. The total increase of 50 million tons is impressive and perhaps optimistic.

5. Hamish McRae, *The World in 2020* (London: HarperCollins, 1995), p. 124.

6. Ibid.

7. Sandra Postel, "Conserving Water: The Untapped Alternative," *World Watch Institute* 67 (September 1985): 11.

8. Linda Starke, ed., "Facing Water Scarcity," in *State of the World 1993* (New York: World Watch Institute, 1993), pp. 31–32, and Dennis Senft, "Weather Network Helps Protect Crops, Cut Irrigation," *Agricultural Research* (April 1993): 22.

9. Fred Pierce, *The Dammed: Rivers, Dams, and the Coming World Water Crisis* (London: Bodley Head, 1992), p. 184.

10. Lester R. Brown, *Who Will Feed China?* World Watch Environmental Alert Series (New York: W. W. Norton, 1995).

11. W. W. Rostow, *The World Economy: History and Prospect* (Austin: University of Texas Press, 1978), p. 619.

12. McRae, *The World in 2020*, pp. 136–137. McRae's evaluation is as fair a summary of the present state of knowledge and ignorance as one is likely to find: "The most contentious environmental issue of our times is climatic change, and in particular global warming. There is no doubt that the accumulation of carbon dioxide and other 'greenhouse gases' in the earth's atmosphere will, in principle, cause the climate to grow warmer, but this 'greenhouse effect' (so called because of the way the gases trap the heat in the earth's atmosphere) will be offset in several ways. For example, the extra warmth will cause more water to evaporate, and create clouds which will help to cool the earth. Nobody can predict how fast the earth's temperature will rise, how far, or where the main changes in climate will take place. Some parts of the world may gain if the climate becomes warmer and wetter, because they will be able to grow more food. Other parts of the world will lose, for climate change may speed up the advance of the deserts. But the effects of global warming will be quite limited for a generation at least. Even if the earth's temperature warms by enough to start melting the polar ice caps, leading to a rise in the sea level (and scientists seem less sure than they once were that such a rise is probable), it would be a couple of generations before the rise became evident. There are good reasons for seeking to cut the amount of fossil fuels being used, the best being that it is unwise to conduct a giant experiment with the earth's weather, when we know so little about the long-term consequences of what we are doing, but the costs of stopping the build-up of carbon dioxide or other gases would be large, while global warming will not be a significant factor in the world economy in the year 2020. A more immediate problem may be the consequences of the thinning of the stratospheric ozone layer, worries about which led to one of the swiftest ever international responses to an environmental threat, the Montreal Protocol in 1987. The industrial countries now plan to stop production of CFCs, the chemicals which seem to have caused the depletion, by 1997. A more immediate threat to the economies of many of the world's poorest countries than global warming is a deterioration of local weather conditions, brought about largely by deforestation."

Chapter Five

1. Robert A. Gordon, "The Stability of the U.S. Economy," in Martin Bronfenbrenner, ed., *Is the Business Cycle Obsolete?* (New York: John Wiley, 1969), p. 105.

2. J. M. Keynes, *General Theory of Employment, Interest, and Money* (London: Macmillan, 1936), p. 318.

3. J. M. Keynes, "Some Economic Consequences of Declining Population," *Eugenics Review*, 29, no. 1 (April 1937): 13–17. Paul Samuelson returned to this problem a half century later in "The Keynes, Hansen, Samuelson Accelerator-Multiplier Model of Secular Stagnation," *Japan and the World Economy* 1 (1988): 3–19. In this article, celebrating the centennial of Alvin Hansen, Samuelson explores the impact on growth and unemployment of various versions of the multiplier-accelerator models, taking into account Franco Modigliani's lifetime-saving hypothesis. Hansen's (and Keynes's) intuition about secular stagnation fare tolerably well in this stylish review.

4. W. B. Reddaway, *The Economics of a Declining Population*, 2d ed. (London: Allen and Unwin, 1946).

5. Keynes, "Some Economic Consequences," p. 18.

Chapter Six

1. Mary Clabaugh Wright, *The Last Stand of Chinese Conservatism* (Stanford: Stanford University Press, 1957), pp. 43–44.

2. Hung preceded Malthus in publishing his thesis by five years. See Ping-Ti Ho, *Studies on the Population of China, 1368–1953* (Cambridge, Mass.: Harvard University Press, 1959).

3. Adam Smith, *Wealth of Nations*, ed. Edwin Cannan (New York: Random House, 1937), pp. 9–10.

4. Edwin Cannan, ed., *Lectures by Adam Smith* (Oxford: Clarendon Press, 1896), pp. 94–95.

5. Ibid., pp. 579–582.

6. Thomas Malthus, *Essay on Population* (London: Macmillan), pp. 226–227.

7. Ibid.

8. Piero Sraffa and M. H. Dobb, *Works and Correspondence: Ricardo* (Cambridge: Cambridge University Press), vol. 1, pp. 96–97.

9. *Manifesto of the Communist Party*, in Robert C. Tucker, ed., *The Marx-Engles Reader* (New York: W. W. Norton, 1978), p. 491.

10. *The Collected Works of Karl Marx and Frederick Engels* (New York: International Publishers, 1989), vol. 24, p. 87.

11. Isaiah Berlin, *Karl Marx: His Life and Environment* (London: Oxford University Press, 1939), p. 137.

12. William Stanley Jevons, *The Coal Question*, 2d ed. (London: Macmillan, 1866), p. vii.

13. J. M. Keynes, "Official Papers, 'Return of Estimated Value of Foreign Trade of United Kingdom at Prices of 1900,'" *Economic Journal* 22,

no. 88 (Dec. 1912): 628–632. For Keynes's evolution down to the 1920s on the terms-of-trade question, see W. W. Rostow, *The Process of Economic Growth* (Oxford: Clarendon Press, 1960), pp. 184–192.

14. D. H. Robertson, *A Study of Industrial Fluctuations* (London: P. S. King, 1915; repr. London: London School of Economics, Reprints of Scarce Works on Political Economy, no. 8, 1948), p. 169 n. 1.

15. J. M. Keynes, *The Economic Consequences of the Peace* (New York: Harcourt Brace, 1920), pp. 22, 238.

16. Ibid., p. 204.

17. J. M. Keynes, "Reply to Sir William Beveridge," *Economic Journal* (1923): 482. The post–*Economic Consequences of the Peace* controversy, which focused on Britain's overly favorable terms of trade, can be traced in this article and in William Beveridge, "Population and Unemployment," *Economic Journal* (1923): 447–475, and Beveridge, "Mr. Keynes' Evidence on Overpopulation," *Economica* (1924): 1–10.

18. D. H. Robertson, "Note on the Real Ratio of International Interchange," *Economic Journal* 34, no. 134 (June 1924): 286–291.

19. What follows is a summary of Hansen's and Schumpeter's views as described in W. W. Rostow, *Theorists of Economic Growth from David Hume to the Present: With a Perspective on the Next Century* (New York: Oxford University Press, 1990), pp. 321–325.

20. Alvin Hansen, in *American Economic Review* 29, no. 1, pt. 1 (March 1939): 15.

21. Joseph Schumpeter, *Business Cycles* (New York: McGraw-Hill, 1939), vol. 2, p. 89.

22. Ibid., p. 1026.

23. Ibid., p. 1032.

24. Ibid., pp. 1036–1038.

25. Ibid.

26. Donella Meadows, Dennis Meadows, Jørgen Randers, and William W. Behrens III, *The Limits of Growth* (New York: Universal Books, 1972), p. 23.

27. The Meadows team then ran its model on assumptions that differed from their measurement of or hypotheses about past relationships:

- If natural-resource reserves are doubled, the crisis, brought on by their estimates of pollution level, is merely delayed.
- If "unlimited resources" are assumed, due to breakthroughs in renewable energy and recycling techniques for raw materials, again pollution brings the system down.
- If successful pollution control is added to "unlimited resources," limits on arable land and the increased diversion of investment to higher-cost agriculture set limits to growth and yield a downturn — a result postponed but not avoided by population limitations brought about by an increase in the effectiveness of birth control.
- If average land yields in the 1970s are doubled under the "unlimited-resources" and pollution-control assumptions, the system can

expand to higher levels, but the scale of industrial production again brings on a pollution crisis during the next century.

• If radical improvements are simultaneously assumed in resource availabilities, pollution control, land yields, and birth control, a period of transient opulence results (at, say, U.S. 1970 income per capita levels), which gives way to decline when the scale of industrialization again depletes resources, generates excessive pollution, and forces a reduction in food production.

28. Although the five-volume Paley Commission report was completed in 1952, after the relative prices of basic commodities had peaked and begun to decline, its method made it unlikely to produce a result that merely reflected the relative rise of those prices from the mid-1930s. It viewed basic prices systematically from a perspective reaching back to 1870. Thus, the Kondratieff cycles appear as fluctuations around a longer trend. The long trend for all commodities since 1970 is for constant or slightly falling real costs and prices except for timber, with rising real costs and prices. In the case of timber, other construction materials have taken the place of wood to an important degree.

The thoughtful long-term perspective of the Paley Commission report (and subsequently Resources for the Future) is perhaps best reflected in Harold J. Barnett and Chandler Morse, *Scarcity and Growth: The Economics and Natural Resource Availability* (Baltimore: Johns Hopkins University Press, 1962). Barnett and Morse first summarize various views of resource shortage starting with those of Malthus, Ricardo, and Mill and ending with the conservation movement, historical and contemporary. They present formal models of these views then show how technical change and substitution has permitted vast expansion of output with, excepting timber, constant or slightly falling real costs. They conclude with temperate optimism as follows: "That man will face a series of particular scarcities as the result of growth is a foregone conclusion; that these will impose general scarcity—increasing cost—is not a legitimate corollary. The twentieth century's discovery of the uniformity of energy and matter has increased the possibilities of substitution to an unimaginable degree, and placed at man's disposal an indefinitely large number of alternatives from which to choose. To suppose that these alternatives must eventually become so restricted, relative to man's wants, that increasing cost will be inescapable, is not justified by the evidence. An absolute limit to the possibilities of escape may exist, but it cannot be defined or specified. The finite limits of the globe, so real in their unqueried simplicity, lose definition under examination. . . . Population growth may or may not become a problem in societies already industrialized, but it is a current threat to growth and welfare in many of the nonindustrial regions of the world. . . . What we are saying is exceedingly simple: our debt to future generations will be discharged to the extent that we maintain a high rate of quantitative and qualitative progress, to the extent that we alter—in a direction favorable to human welfare generally—the conditions that determine the choices open to men when they are free to choose" (pp. 244, 245, 250).

It is worth noting that the debate about resource constraints was opened for the fifth time in the past two centuries before the publication of *The Limits to Growth* (1972) and before the price revolution of 1972–1977. In October 1970, the U.S. Congress passed the National Materials Policy Act. Its primary underlying concern at the time was not pressure on supplies of food, energy, or raw materials but the pressure of the American economy on the environment. A National Commission on Materials Policy was created in the wake of this legislation. It reported shortly before the explosive rise in the oil price (June 1973). The title of its report reflects its focus: "Material Needs and the Environment." This perspective began to suffuse public and intellectual life in the OECD world during the 1960s and early 1970s. And, of course, clean air and water, as well as land preserved for recreation and against corrosive use, are resources as real as food, energy, and raw materials and are, in fact, more finite.

Chapter Seven

1. E. V. Rostow, *Toward Managed Peace* (New Haven: Yale University Press, 1983), pp. 152–170, captures remarkably the transition from the transatlantic diplomacy of the first half of the 19th century to that of the Civil War, and then the period from the Emancipation Proclamation to World War I.

2. Ibid., 169.

3. General George C. Marshall, *The Winning of the War in Europe and the Pacific* (New York: Simon and Schuster, 1945), p. 118.

4. I have contributed to this "mountainous literature" four substantial works: *The United States in the World Arena* (New York: W. W. Norton, 1960); *The Diffusion of Power* (New York: Macmillan, 1972); *The United States and the Regional Organization of Asia and the Pacific* (Austin: University of Texas Press, 1985); and a lengthy review of Robert McNamara's *In Retrospect* (New York: Random House, 1995) in the *Times Literary Supplement*, June 9, 1995. In a more reflective mood, Chapter 7 ("The Politics of the Search for Quality") in my *Politics and the Stages of Growth* (Cambridge: Cambridge University Press, 1971) surveys the dissatisfactions of the affluent young in the 1960s in Washington, Paris, and Tokyo. In the United States, of course, this endemic mood of unrest and confrontation was much exacerbated by the divisions over the war in Southeast Asia.

5. Jean Monnet, *Memoirs* (Garden City, N.Y.: Doubleday, 1978), pp. 309–311.

6. Ibid., p. 324.

7. *Economist*, July 13, 1996, p. 29.

8. Dean Acheson, *Fragments of My Fleece* (New York: W. W. Norton, 1971), pp. 25–26. In the context of this chapter and its conclusions, the full context of this bon mot is worth quoting: "To do these jobs and conduct our own affairs with passable restraint and judgment—the type of judgment, as Justice Brandeis used to say, which leads a man not to stand in front of a locomotive—will be an achievement. Moreover, it will be an achievement which

will profoundly modify many situations which now concern us, including—and I am now guessing—our relations with the Soviet Union. Problems which are difficult against a background of confusion, hesitation, and disintegration may well become quite possible of solution as national and international institutions and activities become healthy and confident and vigorous in a large part of the world. Certainly our troubles would not increase.

But it is a long and tough job and one for which we as a people are not particularly suited. We believe that any problem can be solved with a little ingenuity and without inconvenience to the folks at large. We have trouble shooters to do this. And our name for problems is significant. We call them headaches. You take a powder and they are gone. These pains about which we have been talking are not like that. They are like the pain of earning a living. They will stay with us until death. We have got to understand that all our lives the danger, the uncertainty, the need for alertness, for effort, for discipline will be upon us. This is new to us. It will be hard for us. But we are in for it and the only real question is whether we shall know it soon enough."

Chapter Eight

1. The occasion was a meeting in Washington, sponsored by Secretary Henry Cisneros of the Department of Housing and Urban Development, on September 21, 1995.

2. Center for Demographic and Socioeconomic Research and Education Department of Rural Sociology, *Texas Challenged: The Implications of Population Change for Public Service Demand in Texas*, summary report prepared and published for the Texas Legislative Council (Texas A&M University, 1996). This is an analytic summary of a three-volume research report prepared by the state demographer and staff at Texas A&M.

3. For the United States as a whole, the nearest equivalent of the figures in the text are for total population, and they stop at 2020 rather than 2030. They nevertheless indicate roughly the degree to which Texas is exceptional, notably with respect to the future proportion of Hispanics. Frank D. Bean, Robert G. Cushing, and Charles W. Hayes, "The Changing Demography of U.S. Immigration Flows: Patterns, Projections, and Contexts," in Klaus J. Bade and Myron Weiner, eds., *Migration Past, Migration Future: Germany and the United States* (Oxford: Berghahn Books, 1997), table 3.

U.S. Population by Race/Ancestry, 2000–2020

Anglos		Black		Hispanic		Other	
1000	2020	2000	2020	2000	2020	2000	2020
70.6%	62.5%	12.8%	13.9%	11.3%	15.7%	4.4% (0.9)*	7.0% (0.9)*

*The figures in parentheses indicate the proportion of American Indians. The figure for "Other" therefore indicates the proportion of Asians in the population.

4. Ibid., pp. 59–60.

5. Simon Head, "The Mean, Ruthless Economy," *New York Review of Books*, February 29, 1996, pp. 47–52.

6. Martin H. Gerry, "Estimated Annual Public Expenditures for Children's Services in the United States during the Period, 1990–1992," unpublished paper for the Danforth Foundation, Austin, July 1993.

7. Let me cite as an example of fragmentation and little synthesis a volume containing a series of admirable essays: James B. Steinberg, David W. Lyon, and Mary C. Vaiana, eds., *Urban America: Policy Choices for Los Angeles and the Nation* (Santa Monica: Rand, 1992).

8. These were the terms used by the mayor of Austin, the county judge of Travis County, and the president of the Austin Independent School Board in announcing the beginning of The Austin Project on May 6, 1992.

9. The anonymous White House briefing on May 10, 1994, was even more explicit: "No applicant will be eligible for a single dollar of federal enterprise support unless it submits a comprehensive strategic plan that brings together the community, the private sector and local government and demonstrates how the community will reform the delivery of government services. The challenge-grant process is designed to empower local communities to be as innovative as possible."

10. W. W. Rostow, *The Stages of Economic Growth* (Cambridge: Cambridge University Press, 1990), pp. xxxiii–xxxiv.

11. See, notably, the account in Jean Monnet, *Memoirs* (Garden City, N.Y.: Doubleday, 1978), pp. 309–311. Also, Gordon Craig and Francis Loewenheim, *The Diplomats, 1939–1979* (Princeton: Princeton University Press, 1994), pp. 260–261.

12. Jean Monnet, *Memoirs*, p. 111.

Chapter Nine

1. Walt Whitman *Leaves of Grass* (Philadelphia: Ferguson Bros., 1889), p. 425.

Appendix A

1. This period is dealt with in more detail in Chapter 14 of my *The World Economy: History and Prospect* (Macmillan: New York, 1972).

Appendix B

As background to Chinese population through the 1990 census (and, in some cases, to 1995), I am indebted to the International Programs Center of the Bureau of the Census and to Professor Dudley L. Poston Jr. of Texas A&M. He put me on to the magisterial survey, *The Population of Modern China*, edited by Professor Poston and David Yaukey (New York: Plenum, 1992).

I was also aided in this evaluation of the current mainland Chinese population status by my colleagues at the University of Texas, Ping Chen and

Frank Bean. Ping Chen not only translated Rui-Chuan Zha's article but also gave me his own impresson of the course of Chinese population. Frank Bean, head of the Population Center at the university, took time to look into the matter. Neither is, of course, responsible for the views in this Appendix.

The articles consulted are Cheng-Rui Li, "A Census of One Billion People," *Economic Information Agency*, Hong Kong (1987); Daniel M. Goodkind, "Creating New Traditions in Modern Chinese Populations: Aiming for Birth in the Year of Dragon," *Population and Development Review* 17, no. 4 (1991): 663–685; Griffith Feeney and Jian-Hua Yuan, "Below Replacement Fertility in China?: A Close Look at Recent Evidence," *Population Studies* 48 (1994): 381–394; Rui-Chuan Zha, "Some Issues in Age Structure of China's Population," *Population and Economy* (in Chinese), no. 2 (1996); "New Challenges to Social Safe Guard System," *People's Daily*, April 10, 1997, p. 17, translated and published in English by Li Jianxing in *Inside China Mainland* 19, no. 7, issue no. 223, pp. 72–74. Finally, I wish to take this occasion to thank Professor Ni Shixiong. He attended the workshop at the Harvard Faculty Club that reviewed a draft of this book, urged me to look into the population of the People's Republic of China, and forwarded Rui-Chuan Zha's article.

1. Feeney and Yuan, "Below Replacement Fertility in China?," pp. 393–394. The degree to which Chinese family planning policy is in flux is well captured in a long article in the *New York Times*, August 17, 1997, pp. 1, 6. The article makes four main points: (1) The fines for having more than one child vary greatly in the various districts of China roughly in proportion to the degree of development: from loss of job and three years salary for each parent in Shanghai and Peking; $1,500 in Guangzhou, a major city; $1,000 in medium-sized cities such as Dongguan; to zero on the island of Hainan. (2) In general, local communist officials have shifted from detailed direct and overbearing control over people's lives in carrying out population policy to fines used in local government and popular among officials. (3) The large floating population of about 100 million imparts a degree of uncertainty to Chinese population figures which official stand at 1.22 billion as of the 1990 census. (4) There is a growing conviction among Chinese officials that "only economic development is going to control population growth." The Bureau of the Census, Department of Commerce, International Programs Center projects a declining rate of increase for the Chinese mainland population until 2027 when the overall population turns down, falling from 1.4 billion in 2027 to 1.3 billion in 2050. The International Programs Center emphasizes the approximate nature of these projections and the arbitrary nature of the assumptions that necessarily underlie them.

2. Jianxing, "New Challenges," pp. 72–73.

3. Poston and Yaukey, *"Population of Modern China*, pp. 706–707.

4. Judith Banister, "Implications of the Aging of China's Population," in Poston and Yaukey, *Population of Modern China*, pp. 463–490.

Index

Acheson, Dean, 155, 216–17n.8
Adams, John Quincy, 140
Adenauer, Konrad, 144, 178, 179
aerospace industry, 58, 60, 63
Africa, 5, 6, 7, 36, 181, 182
  economic development, 33, 34–36
  food issues, 94, 210–11n.4
  population projections, 27, 29, 31, 33
  Sub-Saharan, 31, 33–36, 210–11n.4
  See also specific countries
Agcaoili-Sombilla, Mercedita, 210–11n.4
aging population
  in industrialized nations, 36, 37
  pension funds, 38, 39–40
  social services for, 6, 184, 206–8n.17
  in Taiwan, 30
agriculture
  genetically engineered, 50, 73, 75
  irrigation, 92–93, 182
  population growth and, 87
  price cycles, 82–83
  projected outlook, 183, 210–11n.4
  See also foodstuffs

AIDS, 7, 27
aircraft, 60, 63, 76
Algeria, 31, 205n.7
American Philosophical Society, 11
APEC. *See* Asia-Pacific Economic Cooperation
Argentina, 99, 150
arms control, 148, 149, 151–52
ASEAN. *See* Association of Southeast Asian Nations
Ashton, T. S., 98
Asia, 6, 29, 79, 150–52
  Cold War era, 145, 146
  economic development, 35–36, 90, 181
  malnourishment in, 210–11n.4
  See also specific countries
Asia-Pacific Economic Cooperation, 146, 148, 150–51, 152, 181
assembly line, 58
Association of Southeast Asian Nations, 145, 146, 151, 152
Austin Project, The, 171–74, 218n.8
Australia, 210–11n.4
Austria, 176, 184

221

automobiles, 58–60, 76, 86, 105
avarice, 7–8

Babbage, Charles, 68–69
Bacon, Francis, 53
balance of payments, 108–9
Bangladesh, 152
Barnett, Harold J., 215–16n.28
Belgium, 51, 55, 109
Bell Laboratories, 58
Benelux countries. *See* Belgium;
    Netherlands
Beveridge, William, 128
biotechnology. *See* genetic engineering
birth control. *See* family-planning policy
birth rates
    in developing nations, 6
    economic growth and, 121, 123, 124
    in Europe, 17–20, 23
    gross national product and, 16, 33
    income as factor, 5, 20–22
    in industrialized nations, 20, 23, 38
    post–World War II, 23–26
Bismarck, Otto von, 82, 141, 205n.4
Black, Joseph, 58
Blum, Léon, 105
Brahe, Tycho, 54
Brazil, 150
Brown, Lester R., 11, 73, 93–94, 134
business and industry. *See* economic
    development; industrialization;
    specific industries
business cycles. *See* cycles

Calhoun, John C., 140
Cambodia, 151
Canada, 36, 99, 152, 210–11n.4
capital, 9, 77–78, 115
capitalism, 124, 131, 132–33
carbon dioxide, 96, 212n.12
Carson, Rachel, 133
censuses, inception of, 16
CFCs production, 212n.12
chemicals, 58, 60, 61
Cheng, Jessie, 30–31
Chen Kuan-jeng, 30
Chien Tai-lang, 30
China, 17, 53, 79, 209n.6
    dynastic cycle, 120–21
    economic development, 27, 35,
        90, 181

food issues, 94, 210–11n.4
    industrialization, 6, 53
    population growth, 29, 45
    post–Cold War status, 151, 152, 155
    See also Taiwan
civil wars, 17, 27, 82, 140–41
Clark, J. M., 64
Clifford, Clark, 143
climatic change, 10, 212n.12
Clinton, Bill, 175
Cold War, 7, 110–12, 143–45, 146,
    148–49
Coleman, Ken, 66, 67
Coleridge, Samuel Taylor, 139, 143
Columbus, Christopher, 53
commercial revolution, 53, 54
commodity prices, 80–82, 91
communism, 124, 125
computers, 64, 66, 67–73, 209n.14
construction sector, 48, 110, 111, 112
consumer demand, 124, 129–33
consumer price index, 106, 107
Copernicus, 53, 54
cotton textiles, 50–52, 54, 55, 82, 99
Crick, Francis, 73
Crocker, Chester, 205n.9
Cuban missile crisis, 145
currency rates, 87
cycles, 97–117
    Chinese dynastic, 120–21
    Kondratieff, 80–91, 126–29, 132, 136
Czech Republic, 91

Danube River, 92
death rates, 17–20, 24, 25–26
defense
    post–Cold War, 7, 146–49, 151–55
    research and development, 77
    See also arms control; Cold War
demographic transition, 20–21,
    25–26, 123
demography, 15–26, 158–62, 217n.3
    agriculture and, 87
    economic development and, 40–41,
        45, 77–78, 121, 130, 134, 137
    first censuses, 16
    growth deceleration and, 46, 115–17
    historical patterns, 3–5, 9, 17–26,
        204n.1
    medical advances and, 24–26
    projections, 10–11, 26–27, 182, 205n.6

term inception, 17
theoretical assertions, 5–7
Deng Xiaoping, 90
dependency rates, 206–8n.17
depression (1930s). *See* Great
   Depression
desalination, 93, 94
Descartes, René, 48
developing nations
   agricultural needs, 50, 75
   population growth, 5, 6, 29, 87
   projected population patterns,
      26–27
   water resources, 93
drug abuse, 167
Du Pont, Pierre, 58
durable goods, 86, 105, 106

Economic Commission for Europe,
   148
economic development, 6–7, 147
   in Africa, 33, 34–36
   limits to, 119–37
   population factor, 5, 8–9, 77–78
   projected outlook, 27–31
   takeoff stage, 42
   technological advances and,
      47–78
   See also industrialization
education, 23, 122, 160–64, 167, 174
Egypt, 31
elderly people. *See* aging population
electricity production, 58, 60, 62, 183
employment. *See* unemployment;
   workforce
empowerment/enterprise zones, 175,
   218n.9
energy resources
   fusion power, 76, 93, 95, 183
   projected outlook, 94–95
   U.S. consumption, 90
   See also specific types
England. *See* Great Britain
ENIAC computer, 69
environmental concerns, 6, 10, 79, 90
   projected outlook, 95–96, 182,
      212n.12
   supply-side theory and, 133–37,
      214–16nn.27,28
Ethiopia, 34, 205n.7
Euphrates River, 92

Europe
   African aid, 35
   aging population, 206–8n.17
   birth rates, 17–20
   business cycles, 98–105, 106, 109,
      112–13
   chemicals production, 61
   Cold War, 144, 145, 146, 148–49
   death rates, 17–20
   electricity production, 62
   employment levels, 23–24, 84–85,
      112
   grain exports, 210–11n.4
   immigration, 39, 182
   industrialization, 50–55, 58, 60
   price cycles, 82, 84–86
   regional unity, 178–79
   See also specific countries
European Coal and Steel
   Community, 144, 178
European Community, 144, 149
European Union, 148

faith, personal, 11–12
family, 161, 164, 168
family-planning policy, 29, 30–31
   Chinese, 94
   pronatalist, 6, 40, 117, 182, 184,
      206n.13
FAO, 210–11n.4
farming. *See* agriculture
Federal Reserve, 183–84
fertility rates, 21, 37, 38, 116–17, 205n.7
fiscal policy, 176
Fisher, William L., 11–12
Food and Agriculture Organization,
   210–11n.4
foodstuffs
   prices, 6, 79, 82–83, 86, 100
   production and consumption,
      92–94, 183, 210–11n.4
Ford, Henry, 58
foreign aid, 87, 109, 182
foreign policy, 9, 12–13, 139, 140–55,
   216–17n.8 (*see also* Cold War;
   defense)
foreign trade, 86–87, 143
   balance of payments, 108–9
   balance shifts, 111, 112
   business cycles and, 100, 108
   terms of trade, 127–29

Forrester, Jay, 134
France, 53, 105, 140–41, 144, 178
  agriculture, 82
  average age projections, 36
  business cycles, 98, 100–104, 106,
    109
  commodity prices index, 80
  industrialization, 51, 55, 57
  inflation rates, 106
  population growth, 205n.4
  unemployment rates, 85
Franklin, Benjamin, 17
French Academy, 57
Freud, Sigmund, 73
fusion power, 76, 93, 95, 183

Gabcikovo Dam, 92
Galileo, 54
Gandhi, Indira, 29
Gates, Robert, 204n.1
GATT, 143
Gaunt, John, 16
Genentech, 73
General Agreement in Tariffs and
  Trade, 143
General Motors, 58
genetic engineering, 50, 66, 73–76,
  183
Genome Project, 75
Germany, 36, 45, 141, 142, 205n.4
  business cycles, 99, 100–105, 109
  industrialization, 51, 55
  post–World War II, 144, 148, 178,
    184
  price cycles, 85, 210n.2
  technological development, 53
  unemployment rates, 84, 91, 176
Gerry, Martin, 169
Gilbert, William, 54
Gillispie, Charles, 57
global warming, 10, 212n.12
GNP. See gross national product
Godwin, William, 125–26
gold, 99
Gorbachev, Mikhail, 110, 111
Gordon, Robert A., 106
Gordon, Robert J., 67, 69, 209nn.13,14
grain. See wheat
Great Britain, 36, 117, 140–41, 143, 182
  agriculture, 82, 100
  business cycles, 98–104, 109

Industrial Revolution, 50–53, 55,
  100
  price cycles, 80, 82, 84, 126–29
  technological development, 48,
    49, 69
  unemployment rates, 84, 85, 91
Great Depression, 7, 21, 24, 84–85,
  97, 104, 105, 113
Greece, 140, 143
greenhouse effect, 10, 212n.12
Green Revolution, 73, 75
gross national product, 16, 27–29, 33,
  105–6
growth, limits to, 119–37
Gulf War, 146, 147, 148, 155

Halley, Edmond, 54
Hansen, Alvin, 213n.3
Hansen-Schumpeter debate, 116,
  129–33
Hashimoto, Ryutaso, 206n.13
HDI, 33, 34
Head, Simon, 161
Head Start, 168, 169, 172
health and medicine
  cost increases, 90
  death rate declines, 20
  genetic engineering, 75
  medical advances and, 24–26
  nutrition and, 210–11n.4
  as population growth factor, 7
Helsinki Accords, 148
Henry VII, king of England, 53
Henry the Navigator, prince of
  Portugal, 53
Hicks, J. R., 77, 124
Hitler, Adolf, 85, 113, 148
Holland. See Netherlands
Hong Kong, 151
housing, 48, 98, 104
Human Development Index, 33, 34
human rights, 147, 148, 154
Hume, David, 15, 73
Hungary, 91
Hung Liang-chi, 121, 137
Huygens, Christian, 48

IMF, 33, 142
immigration, 6, 39, 182
  United States, 17, 23, 38, 41, 43–44,
    158, 163, 183

Immigration Act, U.S., 23
IMPACT model, 210–11n.4
income
    birth rates and, 5, 20–22
    distribution gap, 112
    economic development and, 27–29
    inflation and, 88, 108, 109, 176
    policy development, 105, 114, 177,
        183–84
    technology and, 162
India, 79, 152, 155
    economic development, 27, 35
    food supply, 94, 210–11n.4
    industrialization, 6, 53
    population growth, 29, 45, 116–17
industrialization, 5, 6, 40–41, 45,
    47–78, 100
industrial materials, 66, 76, 210n.28
industrial nations
    genetic engineering, 73, 75
    inflation and, 87, 88, 106, 107
    net reproduction rates, 23
    population patterns, 26–27, 36–40,
        206–8n.17
    post-World War II boom, 86
    price cycles, 91
    social services, 6, 113
    See also specific countries
Industrial Revolution, 50–66, 90,
    100, 112, 122, 209n.14
inflation, 6–7, 87, 88, 106–8, 114, 176
information superhighway, 71–72
infrastructure investment, 111, 112
internal-combustion engine, 60, 63
International Monetary Fund, 33, 142
Internet, 71, 72
inventories, 48, 97–98, 106
Iranian Revolution, 63, 81, 88, 109
Iraq, 146
Ireland, 116
iron production, 50–52
irrigation, 92–93, 182
Israel, 92, 116
Italy, 36, 51, 53, 86, 109, 206–8n.17
Ivan III, tsar of Russia, 54

Japan, 35, 45, 142, 147, 184
    aging population, 36, 206–8n.17
    business cycles, 105, 106, 109, 113
    family-planning policy, 206n.13
    foreign policy, 151, 152, 154, 155

foreign trade, 111
    immigration, 39, 182
    industrialization, 52, 55, 100
    population growth decline, 206n.13
    price cycles, 85, 86, 91
    unemployment rates, 85, 176
Jevons, W. S., 126, 134
Jones, R. V., 54
Jordan, Barbara, 172

Kahn, Herman, 66–67
Kennan, George, 143
Kennedy, John F., 145
Kenya, 205n.7
Kepler, Johannes, 54
Kettering, Charles, 58
Keynes, John Maynard, 5, 7–8, 73,
    114–16, 117, 119, 126–29, 142
King, Gregory, 15–16
Kondratieff, N. D., 80
Kondratieff cycles, 80–91, 126–29,
    132, 136
Korea. See South Korea
Kuwait, 146

lasers, 66, 76, 77
Latin America, 6, 29, 79, 99
    Cold War era, 145, 146
    economic development, 35, 181
    Monroe Doctrine and, 140, 145
    post–Cold War status, 149–50, 151
    See also specific countries
leading sectors, 50, 64, 113–14
League of Nations, 142, 143, 146–48
Lebanon, 149
Leblanc, Nicolas, 57
Lend-Lease Act (U.S.), 142
Lewis, W. Arthur, 45
Liberia, 34
Libya, 31
life expectancy, 30, 36, 206–8n.17
literacy, 36
Louis XI, king of France, 53

macroeconomics, 208n.1
Mahan, Alfred T., 141
Malthus, Thomas, 7, 16, 116, 121,
    122–23, 125–26, 137
Manchuria, 147
Mao Tse-tung, 90
Marshall, Alfred, 126, 129, 157

Marshall, George, 143
Marshall Plan, 144
Marx, Karl, 69, 123–24, 125
McRae, Hamish, 13, 15, 38, 41, 66, 71, 73, 92, 185, 212n.12
Meadows, Dennis, 133, 134–35, 214–15n.27
Medicaid, 206–8n.17
Medicare, 169, 206–8n.17
medicine. See health and medicine
mercantilism, 54
Mexico, 35, 44, 160, 162–63
    foreign policy, 142, 145, 150, 152
    wheat strains development, 50, 75
Middle East, 6, 149 (see also specific countries)
military spending. See defense
Mill, John Stuart, 7, 69, 77–78, 123–25, 204n.2
Minkin, Barry, 66
Modigliani, Franco, 213n.3
Moldova, 36
monetary policy, 87, 114, 142–43, 176
Monnet, Jean, 144, 178, 179
Monroe Doctrine, 140–41, 142, 145
Montreal Protocol, 212n.12
morality. See religious and moral beliefs
Morgenstern, Oskar, 209n.13
Morocco, 31
Morse, Chandler, 215–16n.28
mortality rates. See death rates
Mulhall, Michael, 55
multiracialism, 13, 154, 162
Mussolini, Benito, 85
Myrdal, Gunnar, 21

NAFTA, 150
Namier, Lewis, 139
Napoleon I, emperor of France, 82
National Advisory Committee for Aeronautics, 58
National Bureau of Economic Research, 100–104
National Committee on Materials Policy, 215–16n.28
national-incomes policy, 105, 114, 177, 183–84
National Recovery Administration, 105
nation-states, 53–54

NATO. See North Atlantic Treaty Organization
natural gas, 11, 90
natural law, 54–55
Negroponte, Nicholas, 71
Netherlands, 55, 98, 109
net reproduction rate, 21, 23, 24, 27, 44, 137
Newton, Isaac, 54, 68
Nigeria, 27, 34, 205n.7
Nile River, 92
nonresidential investment, 48
North American Free Trade Agreement, 150
North Atlantic Treaty Organization, 144, 145, 146, 147, 148, 149
North Korea, 151, 152
nutrition, 210–11n.4

OAS, 146, 148, 150, 181
OCED, 39, 108, 146, 181
oil prices/consumption, 63, 81, 86–90, 95, 108–10
OPEC, 81, 86–90, 108–9
optimum rate of population, 21
Organization for Economic and Cooperative Development, 39, 108, 146, 181
Organization of American States, 146, 148, 150, 181
Organization of Petroleum Exporting Countries, 81, 86–90, 108–9
outsourcing, 161, 162
ozone layer, 10, 96, 212n.12

Pakistan, 152, 210–11n.4
Palestine, 149
Paley, William S., 136
Papert, Seymour, 71
patents, 52
Pecora, W. T., 11
pensions, 38, 39–40, 206–8n.17
Perez, Nicostrato D., 210–11n.4
Petty, William, 15
Philippines, 50, 75
Plato, 73
Plaza Agreement, 112
Poland, 36, 91, 116
pollution. See environmental concerns
population factors. See demography

Portugal, 53
President's Materials Policy
    Commission, 136, 215–16n.28
prices, relative, 6, 79–96, 100, 108,
    136, 181, 210–16nn.4,12,28
pronatalist policies, 6, 40, 117, 182,
    184, 206n.13

R&D. *See* research and development
racism, 162
railroads, 55–57, 58, 99, 123
raw materials, 6, 79, 80–81, 84, 86, 100
recession, economic, 108–10, 112
Reddaway, W. B., 116
religious and moral beliefs, 7–8,
    11–12, 54–55, 147–48
Renshaw, Edward, 63, 64
research and development, 6, 58, 75,
    77, 78, 183, 184
residential investment, 48
Resources for the Future, 136
Ricardo, David, 122, 123
rice, 50, 75
Robertson, Dennis, 126–29
Roosevelt, Franklin, 143, 144
Rosegrant, Mark W., 210–11n.4
Rostow, E. V., 141
Rusk, Dean, 153
Russia, 20, 45, 50, 54, 142
    foreign policy, 140, 151, 152, 155
    industrialization, 52, 55, 100
    population growth decline, 36, 117
    See also Soviet Union

Sachs, Jeffrey, 34–35
Samuelson, Paul, 213n.3
Sato, Seizaburo, 154
Saudi Arabia, 95
Sauvy, Alfred, 16
Scandinavia, 84, 85, 100 (*see also*
    Sweden)
Schuman Plan, 178
Schumpeter, Joseph, 80, 116, 129–33
science and technology, 5, 6, 160, 182
    as economic growth factor, 7, 131,
        132, 136
    industrialization and, 47–78, 208n.1
scientific revolution, 53, 57
Sea of Galilee, 92
self-sufficiency policy, 35
Shinohara, Miyosei, 86

shipping freight rates, 83
silver, 99
Slovakia, 92
Smith, Adam, 15, 47, 50, 67, 119, 121–22
socialism, 124
social policy, 167–68
Social Security, 206–8n.17
social services, 5
    for the elderly, 6, 184, 206–8n.17
    expansion effects, 109
    policies and programs, 168–71
    spending cutbacks, 91, 113
    welfare, 164, 167, 170, 171, 175
soda manufacture method, 57
South Africa, 31, 36
South Asian Regional Cooperation,
    151
South Korea, 33, 146, 147, 205n.7
Soviet Union, 36, 90, 116, 148
    Gorbachev era, 110, 111
    technological development, 49–50
    See also Cold War; Russia
Spain, 51, 53, 86
Sri Lanka, 152
stagflation, 108–10
Stalin, Joseph, 80, 143
state leadership policy, 35
steam engines, 51, 55, 58
steel industry, 55, 57, 58, 60
Stoll, Clifford, 71–72
Sub-Saharan Africa, 31, 33–36,
    210–11n.4
Sung dynasty, 53
supply-side economics, 133–37,
    214–16nn.27,28
Sweden, 21, 38, 40
Switzerland, 51, 176, 184
Syria, 92, 149

Taiwan, 30–31, 32, 151
technology. *See* science and
    technology
Teller, Edward, 69
textile manufacture. *See* cotton
    textiles
Tigris River, 92
total fertility rate, 21
trade. *See* foreign trade
trade unions, 105, 210n.2
Treaty of Westphalia, 149
trend periods, 97

Truman, Harry, 143, 144
Truman Doctrine, 143
Tunisia, 31
Turkey, 92, 143
Turks (people), 53, 140

Ukraine, 96
unemployment
    business cycles and, 105, 106, 108, 116
    European, 23–24, 84–85, 91
    Great Depression, 7, 84–85
    immigrants and, 39
    inflation and, 88
    1990s, 90–91
    post–World War II, 86
    urban problems and, 163–66, 173,
        176
United Kingdom. See Great Britain
United Nations, 75, 143, 144–48, 153
United States
    African aid, 35
    age of population, 36–38,
        206–8n.17
    agriculture, 82, 92–93, 210–11n.4
    business cycles, 99–106, 108–13
    chemicals production, 61
    computer purchases, 68–70
    consumer price indexes, 107
    "critical margin" role, 45–46,
        146–55, 185
    demographic trends, 20–26,
        158–60, 162, 217n.3
    dependency rates, 206–8n.17
    electricity production, 62, 183
    energy consumption, 90
    foreign policy, 9, 12–13, 139–55,
        216–17n.8
    foreign trade, 87, 108–12, 129
    immigration, 17, 23, 38, 41, 43–44,
        158, 163, 182, 183
    industrialization, 51, 52, 55, 58, 60,
        65, 100
    inflation rates, 106
    life expectancy, 206–8n.17
    monetary policy, 87, 142–43, 176,
        183–84
    multiracialism, 13, 154, 162
    price cycles, 80–91, 107, 136,
        215–16n.28
    social welfare, 164, 167, 170–71,
        175, 206–8n.17

stagflation, 108–10
    unemployment rates, 7, 84, 85,
        90–91, 106, 163–66
    urban problems, 9–10, 13, 154,
        157–79, 185
UNIVAC computer, 69
urbanization, 17, 20, 29
urban problems, U.S., 9–10, 13, 154,
    157–79, 185, 218n.9

Vichinsky, Andrei, 153
Vietnam, 145, 151, 152

wages. See income
Waggoner, Paul, 12, 160
Walker, Francis, 17
war, 7, 82, 84, 85
Warner, Andrew, 34–35
Water Carrier (Israel), 92
water resources, 92–93, 94, 182
Watson, James, 73
Watt, James, 50–51, 58
welfare policy, 164, 167, 170–71, 175
welfare state, 21
wheat, 50, 75, 82, 83, 210–11n.4
Wheeler, John, 66
Whitman, Walt, 185
Wiener, Norbert, 209n.13
Wilhelm II, emperor of Germany, 141
Wilson, Woodrow, 142, 144, 145
workforce
    in aging societies, 38–40
    education and, 160–62, 163–64, 173
    expansion of, 183–84
    full-level maintenance, 5, 6–7,
        112–14, 182
    as inflation factor, 106–8, 109
    political policy and, 105
    technology and, 78, 91, 160, 161
    See also income; unemployment
World Bank, 33, 44, 73, 143
World War I, 84, 104, 141, 142
World War II, 85, 104, 105, 113, 142,
    144
World Watch Institute, 11
Wright, Mary, 120

Young, John E., 73
Yugoslavia, 146, 147, 148, 155

Zaire, 205n.7